CHAPTER 43

Belldandy's Tempestuous Heart

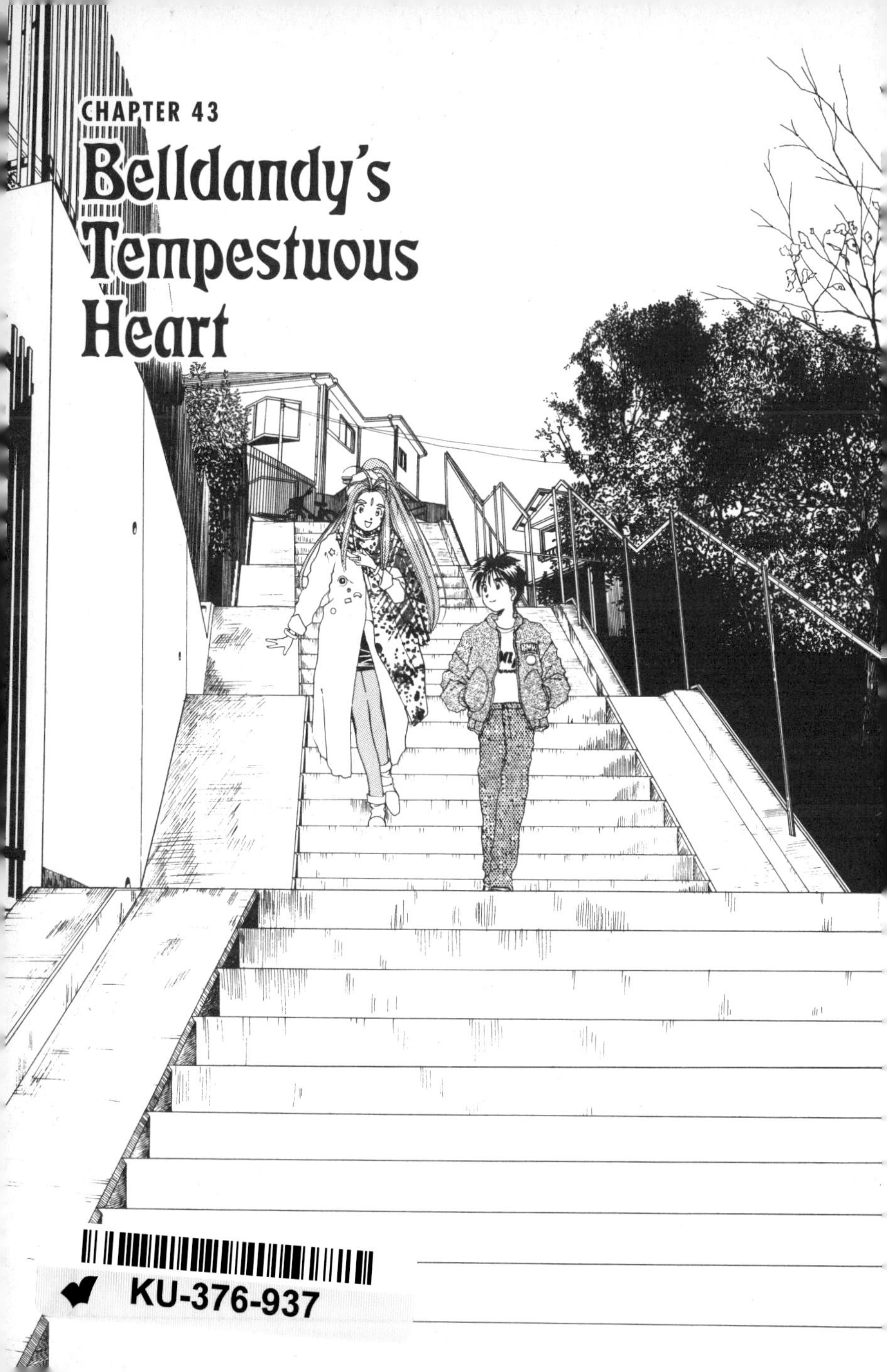

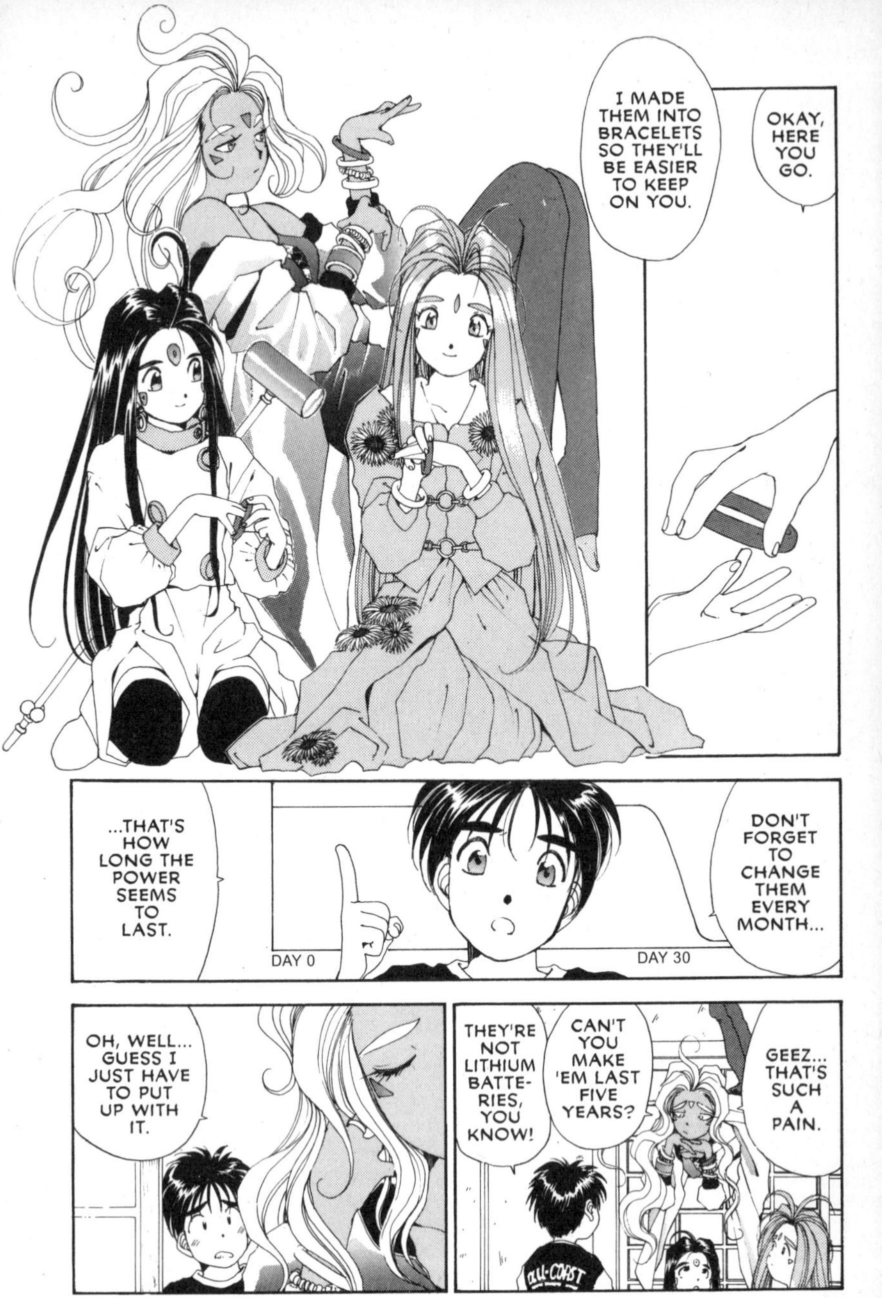
OKAY, HERE YOU GO.
I MADE THEM INTO BRACELETS SO THEY'LL BE EASIER TO KEEP ON YOU.
DON'T FORGET TO CHANGE THEM EVERY MONTH...
DAY 30
DAY 0
...THAT'S HOW LONG THE POWER SEEMS TO LAST.
GEEZ... THAT'S SUCH A PAIN.
CAN'T YOU MAKE 'EM LAST FIVE YEARS?
THEY'RE NOT LITHIUM BATTERIES, YOU KNOW!
OH, WELL... GUESS I JUST HAVE TO PUT UP WITH IT.

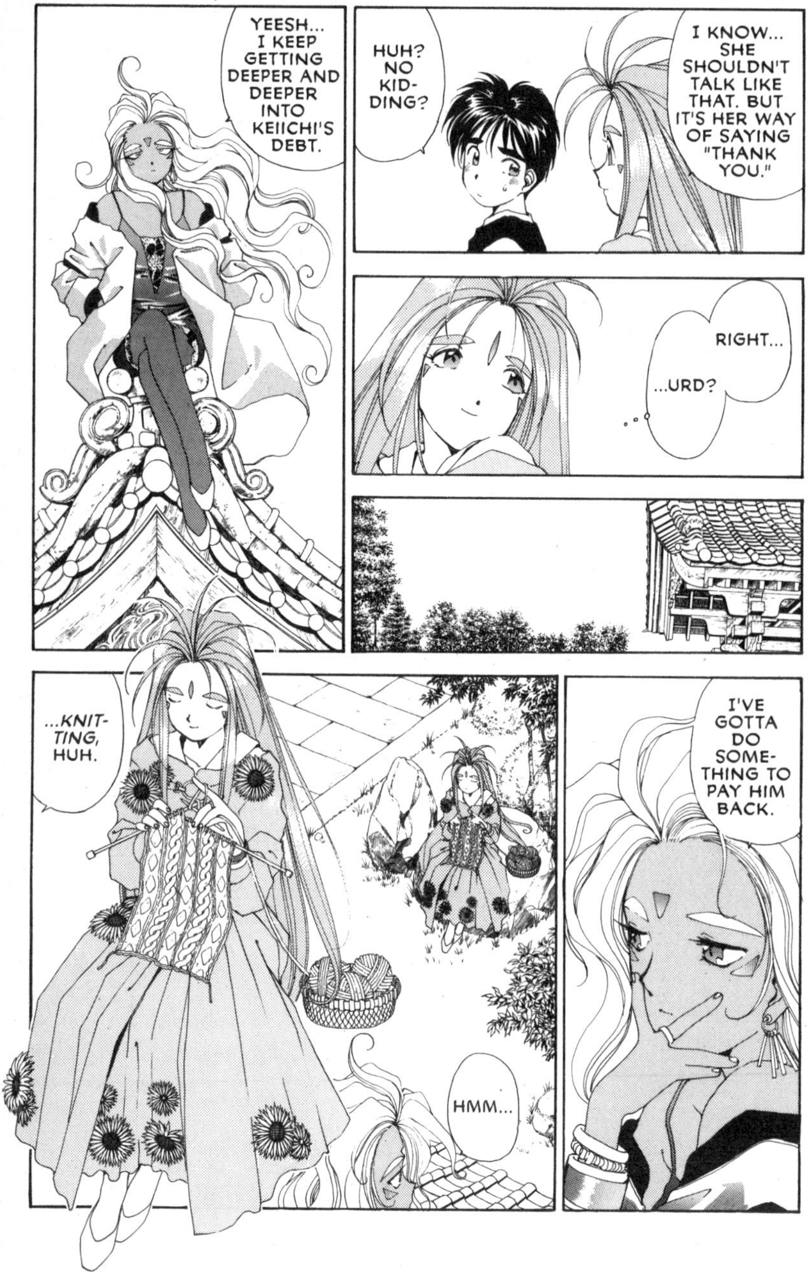
YEESH... I KEEP GETTING DEEPER AND DEEPER INTO KEIICHI'S DEBT.
HUH? NO KID-DING?
I KNOW... SHE SHOULDN'T TALK LIKE THAT. BUT IT'S HER WAY OF SAYING "THANK YOU."
RIGHT...
...URD?
...KNIT-TING, HUH.
HMM...
I'VE GOTTA DO SOME-THING TO PAY HIM BACK.

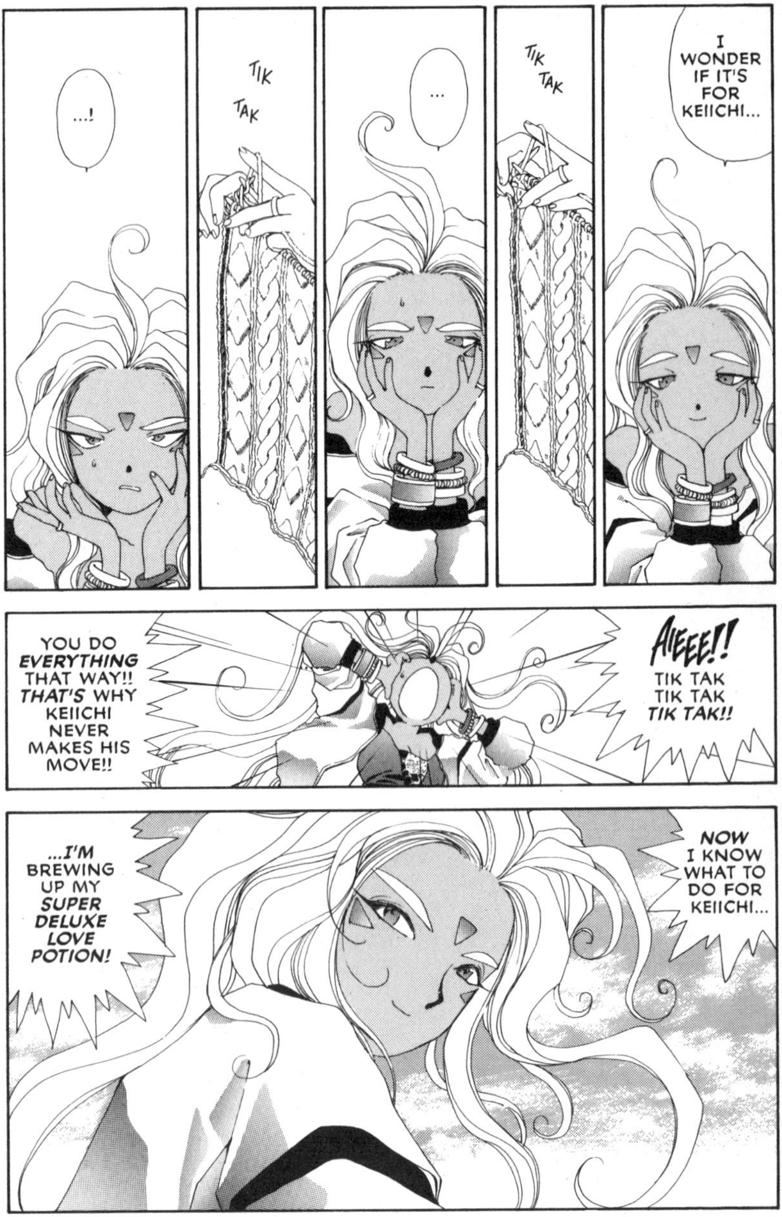
I WONDER IF IT'S FOR KEIICHI...
TIK TAK
...
TIK TAK
...!
AIEEE!!
TIK TAK TIK TAK TIK TAK!!
YOU DO EVERYTHING THAT WAY!! THAT'S WHY KEIICHI NEVER MAKES HIS MOVE!!
NOW I KNOW WHAT TO DO FOR KEIICHI...
...I'M BREWING UP MY SUPER DELUXE LOVE POTION!

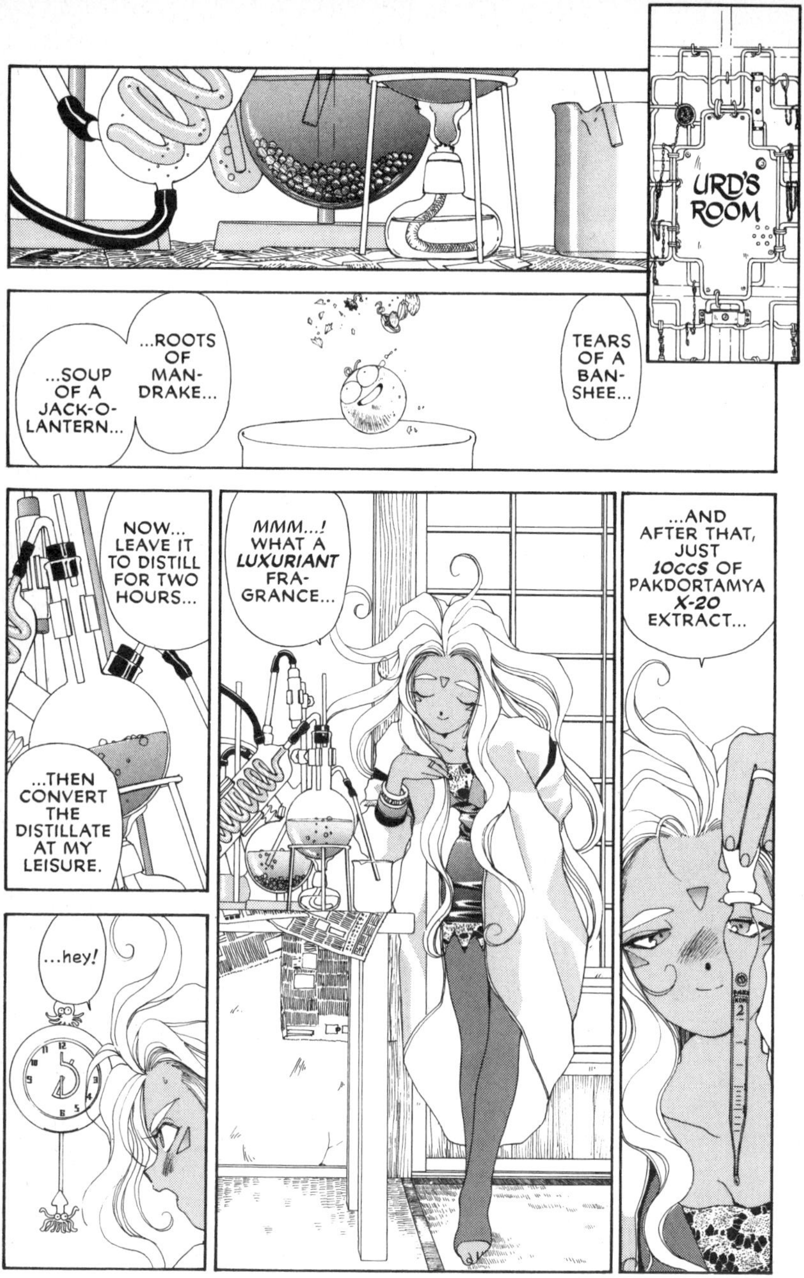
URD'S ROOM
TEARS OF A BAN-SHEE...
...ROOTS OF MAN-DRAKE...
...SOUP OF A JACK-O-LANTERN...
...AND AFTER THAT, JUST 10ccs OF PAKDORTAMYA X-20 EXTRACT...
MMM...! WHAT A LUXURIANT FRA-GRANCE...
NOW... LEAVE IT TO DISTILL FOR TWO HOURS...
...THEN CONVERT THE DISTILLATE AT MY LEISURE.
...hey!

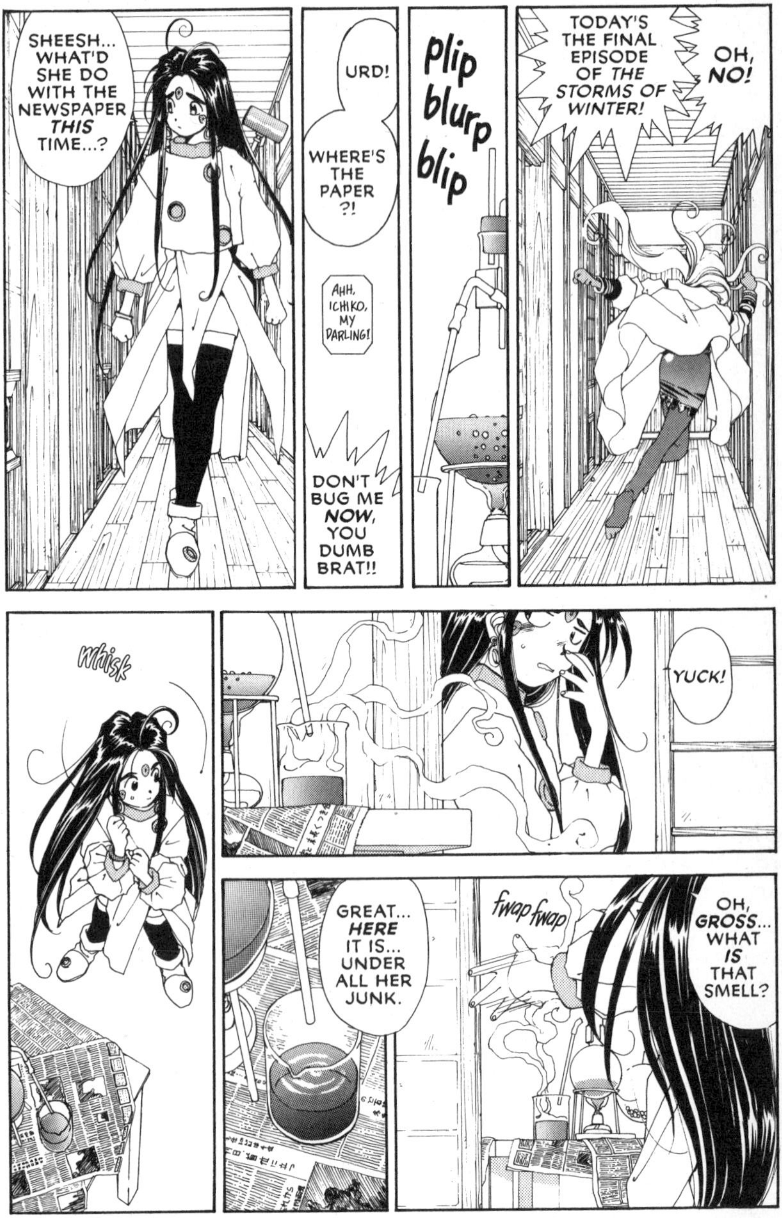
SHEESH... WHAT'D SHE DO WITH THE NEWSPAPER THIS TIME...?
URD!
WHERE'S THE PAPER ?!
AHH, ICHIKO, MY DARLING!
DON'T BUG ME NOW, YOU DUMB BRAT!!
plip blurp blip
TODAY'S THE FINAL EPISODE OF THE STORMS OF WINTER!
OH, NO!
whisk
YUCK!
GREAT... HERE IT IS... UNDER ALL HER JUNK.
fwap fwap
OH, GROSS... WHAT IS THAT SMELL?

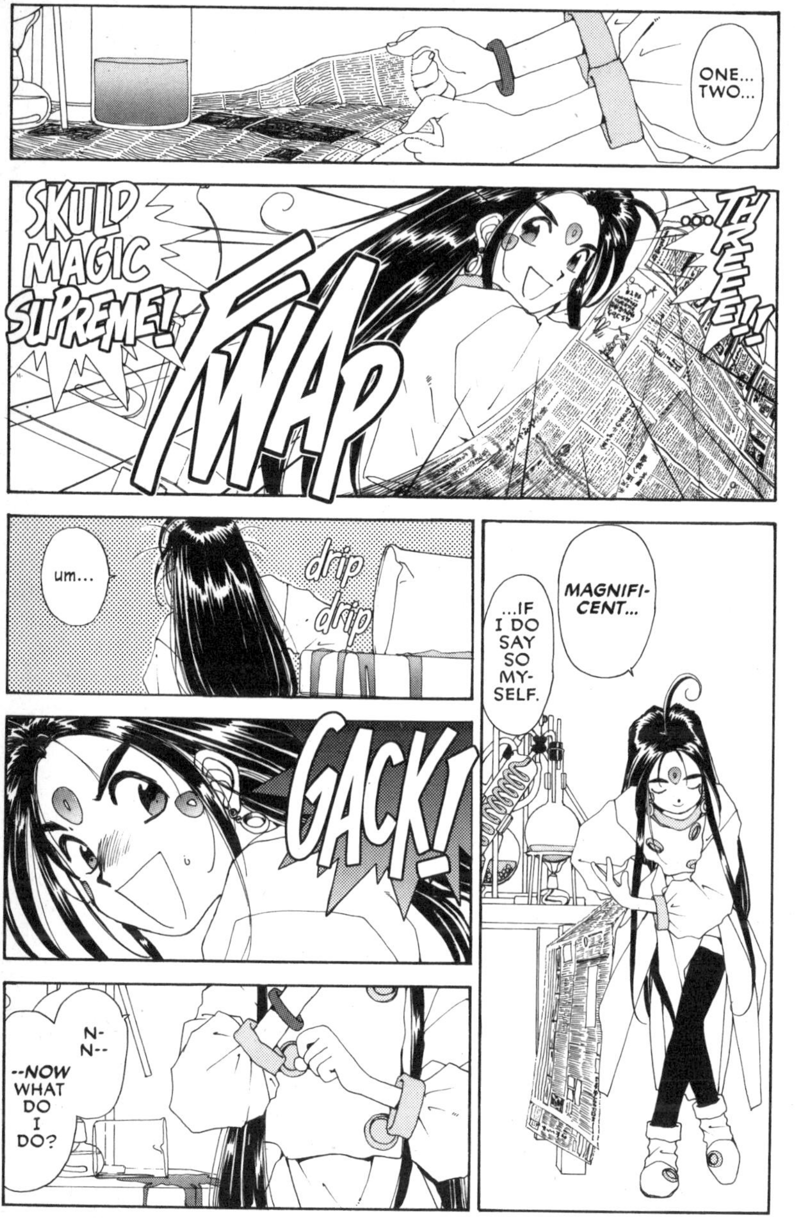
ONE... TWO...
...THREE!!
SKULD MAGIC SUPREME!
FWAP
MAGNIFICENT...
...IF I DO SAY SO MYSELF.
um...
drip drip
GACK!
N-N--
--NOW WHAT DO I DO?

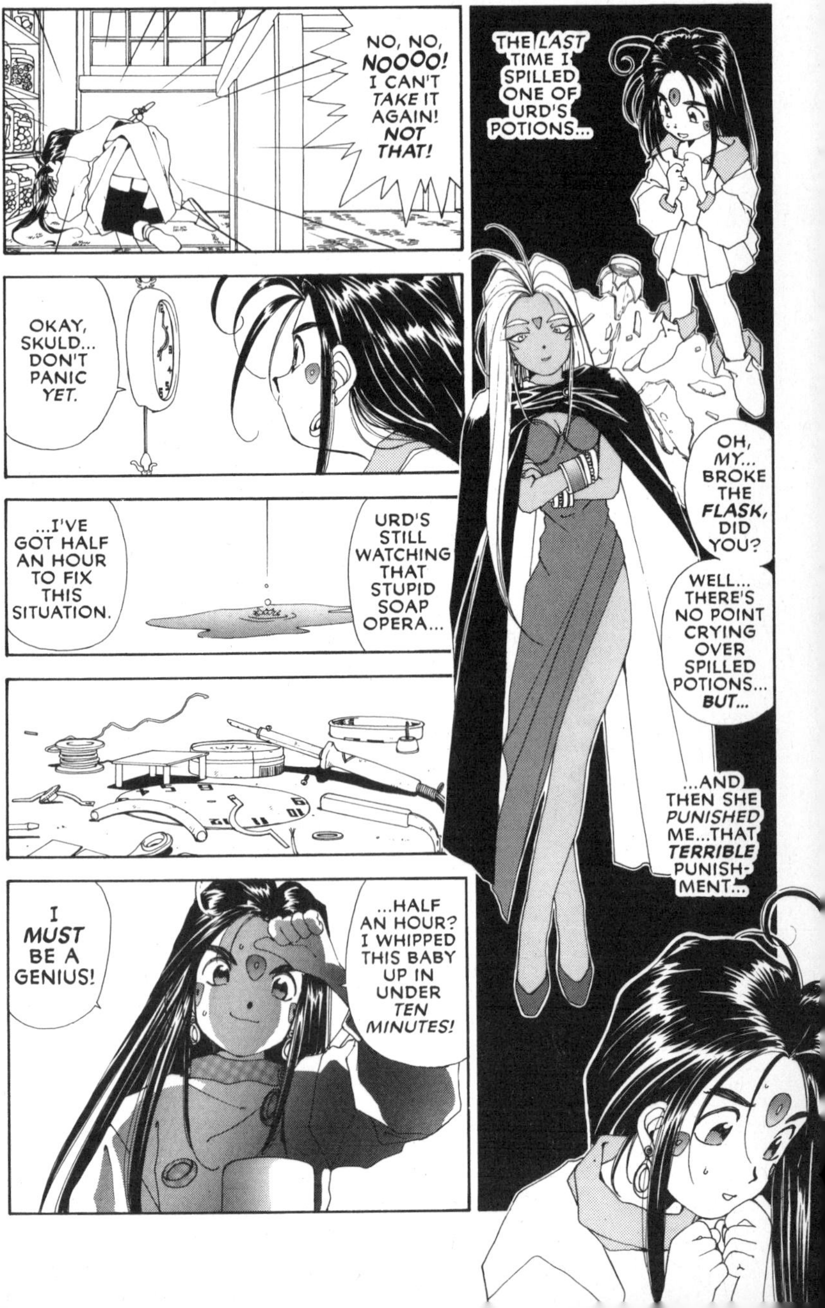
NO, NO, NOOOO! I CAN'T TAKE IT AGAIN! NOT THAT!
THE LAST TIME I SPILLED ONE OF URD'S POTIONS...
OH, MY... BROKE THE FLASK, DID YOU?
WELL... THERE'S NO POINT CRYING OVER SPILLED POTIONS... BUT...
...AND THEN SHE PUNISHED ME...THAT TERRIBLE PUNISH-MENT...
OKAY, SKULD... DON'T PANIC YET.
URD'S STILL WATCHING THAT STUPID SOAP OPERA...
...I'VE GOT HALF AN HOUR TO FIX THIS SITUATION.
...HALF AN HOUR? I WHIPPED THIS BABY UP IN UNDER TEN MINUTES!
I MUST BE A GENIUS!

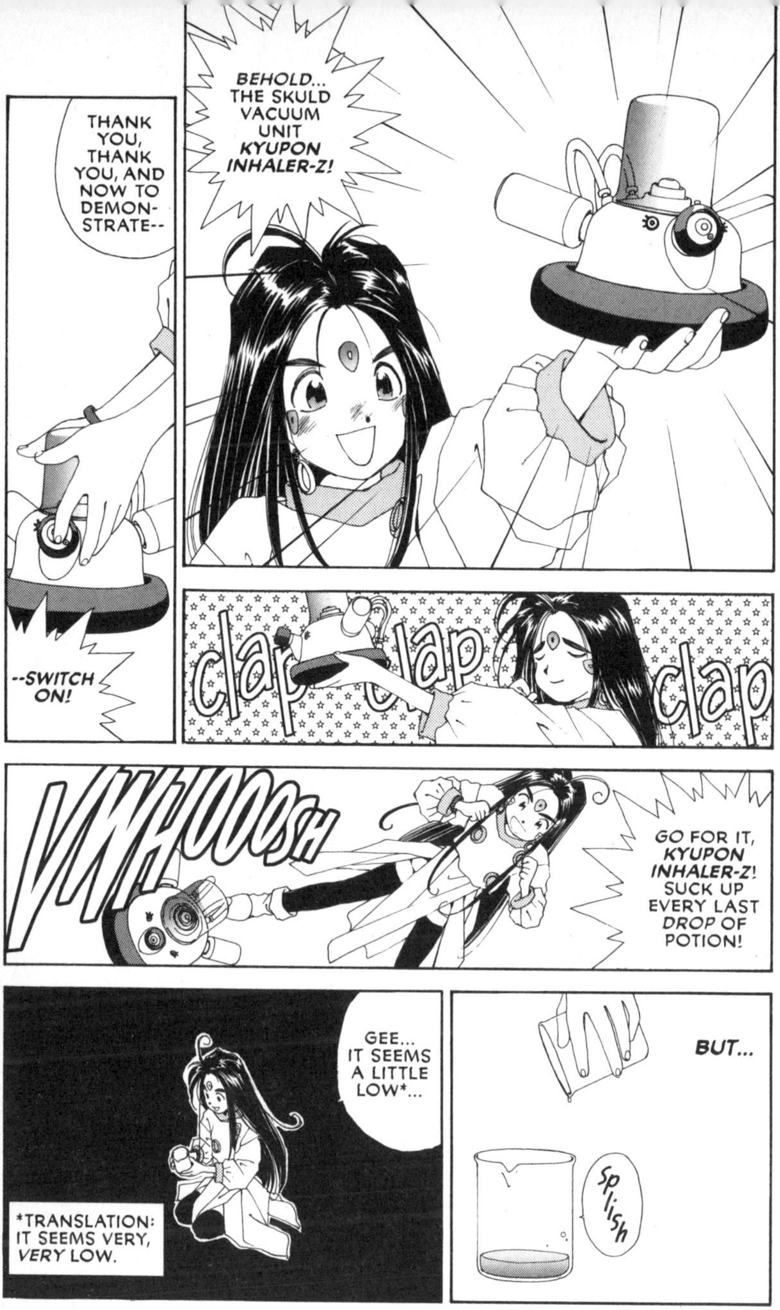
THANK YOU, THANK YOU, AND NOW TO DEMON-STRATE--
BEHOLD... THE SKULD VACUUM UNIT *KYUPON INHALER-Z!*
--SWITCH ON!
clap clap clap
VWHOOOSH
GO FOR IT, *KYUPON INHALER-Z*! SUCK UP EVERY LAST *DROP* OF POTION!
BUT...
Splish
GEE... IT SEEMS A LITTLE LOW*...
*TRANSLATION: IT SEEMS VERY, *VERY* LOW.

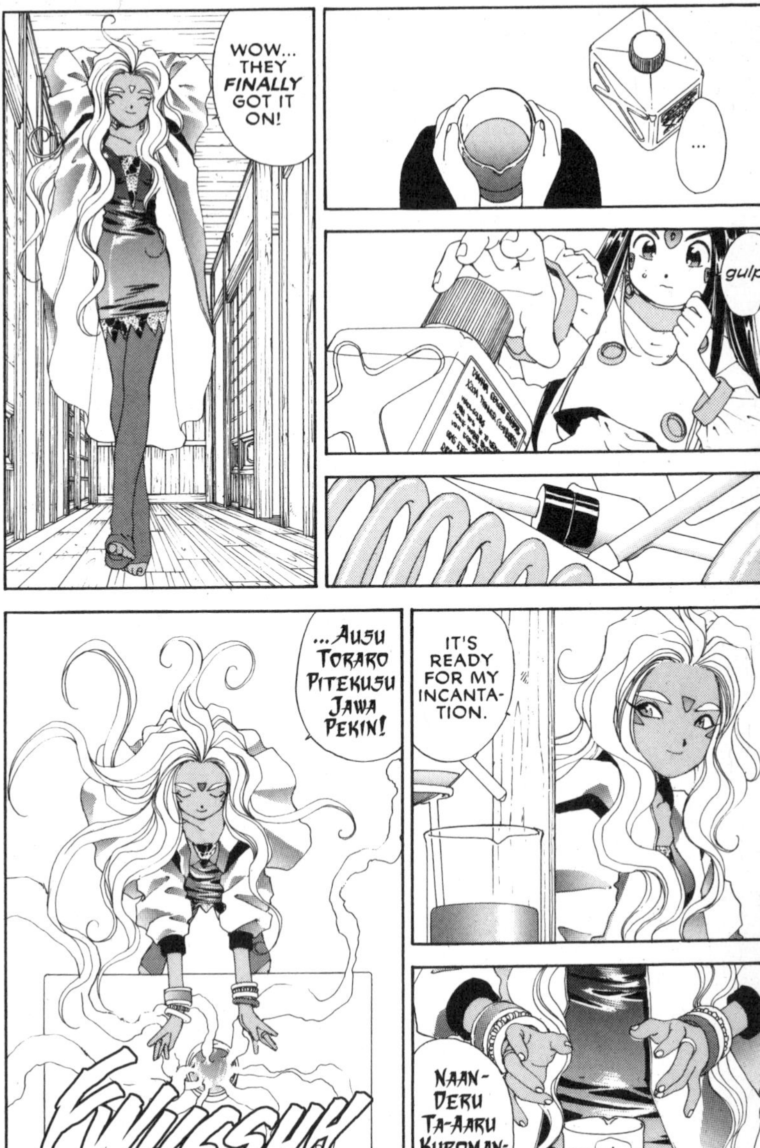
...
gulp
WOW... THEY FINALLY GOT IT ON!
IT'S READY FOR MY INCANTATION.
...AUSU TORARO PITEKUSU JAWA PEKIN!
NAAN-DERU TA-AARU KUROMAN-YOHN...
FWHSSHH

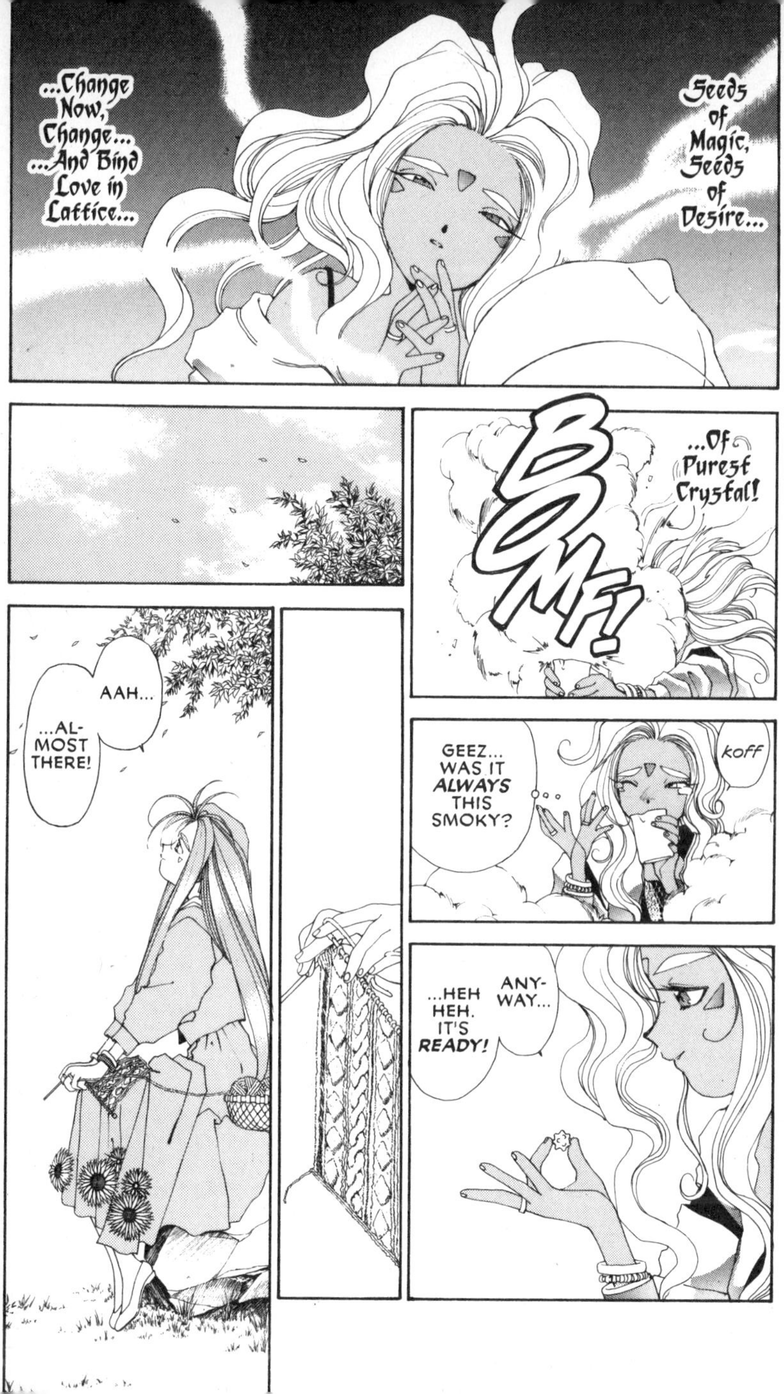
Seeds of Magic, Seeds of Desire...
...Change Now, Change... ...And Bind Love in Lattice...
...Of Purest Crystal!
BOMF!
koff
GEEZ... WAS IT ALWAYS THIS SMOKY?
ANY-WAY...
...HEH HEH. IT'S READY!
AAH...
...AL-MOST THERE!

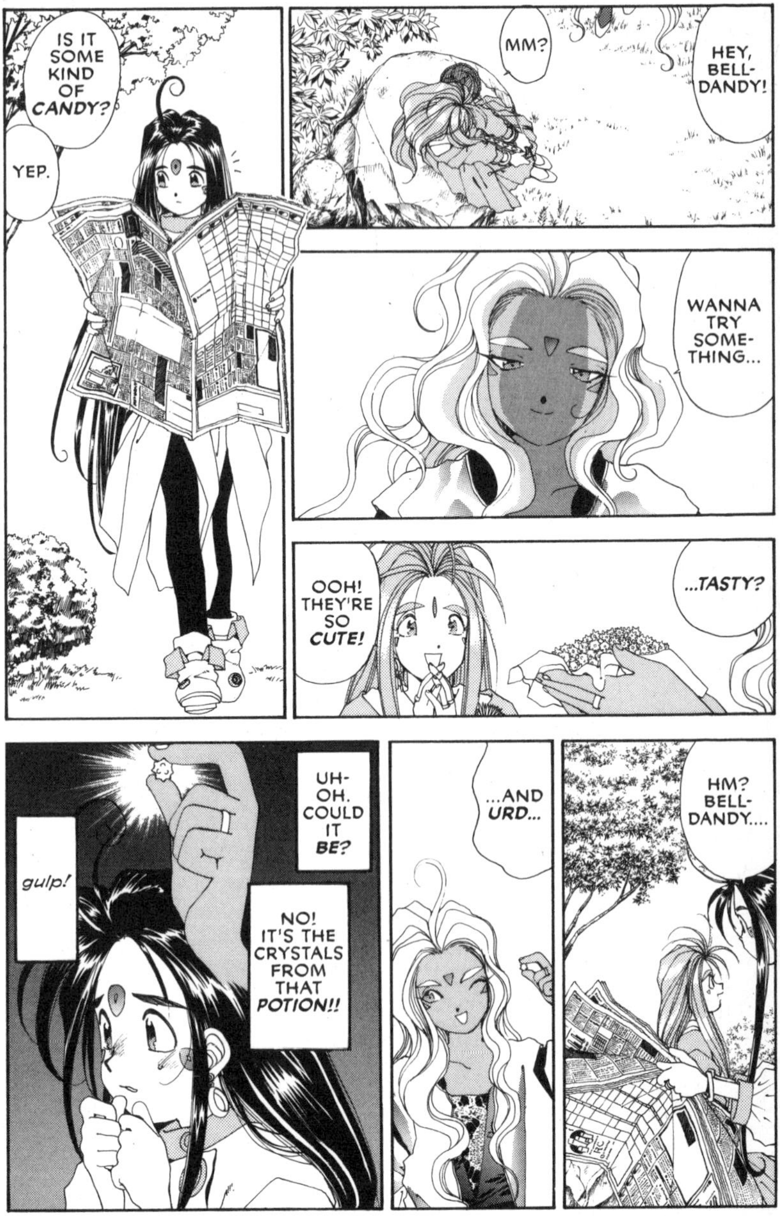
HEY, BELL-DANDY!
MM?
WANNA TRY SOME-THING...
...TASTY?
OOH! THEY'RE SO CUTE!
IS IT SOME KIND OF CANDY?
YEP.
HM? BELL-DANDY....
...AND URD...
UH-OH. COULD IT BE?
NO! IT'S THE CRYSTALS FROM THAT POTION!!
gulp!

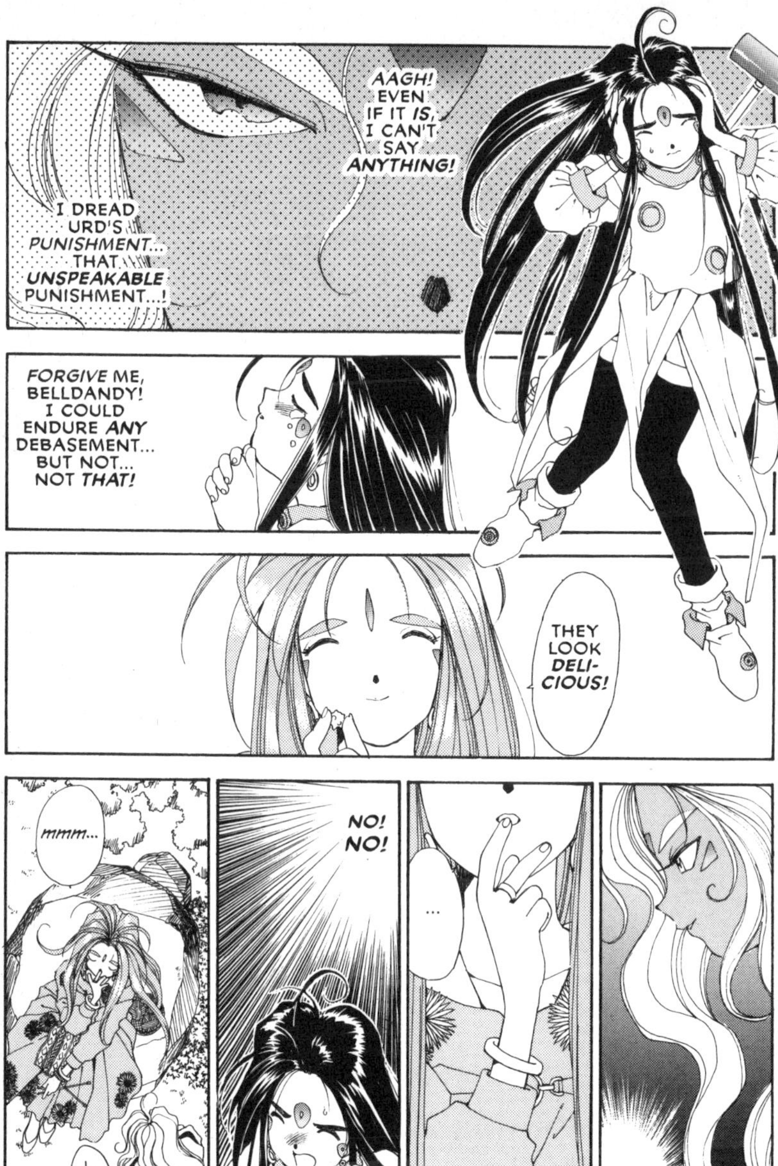
AAGH! EVEN IF IT IS, I CAN'T SAY ANYTHING!
I DREAD URD'S PUNISHMENT... THAT UNSPEAKABLE PUNISHMENT...!
FORGIVE ME, BELLDANDY! I COULD ENDURE ANY DEBASEMENT... BUT NOT... NOT THAT!
THEY LOOK DELICIOUS!
mmm...
do it! do it!
NO! NO!
...
COME ON ...!

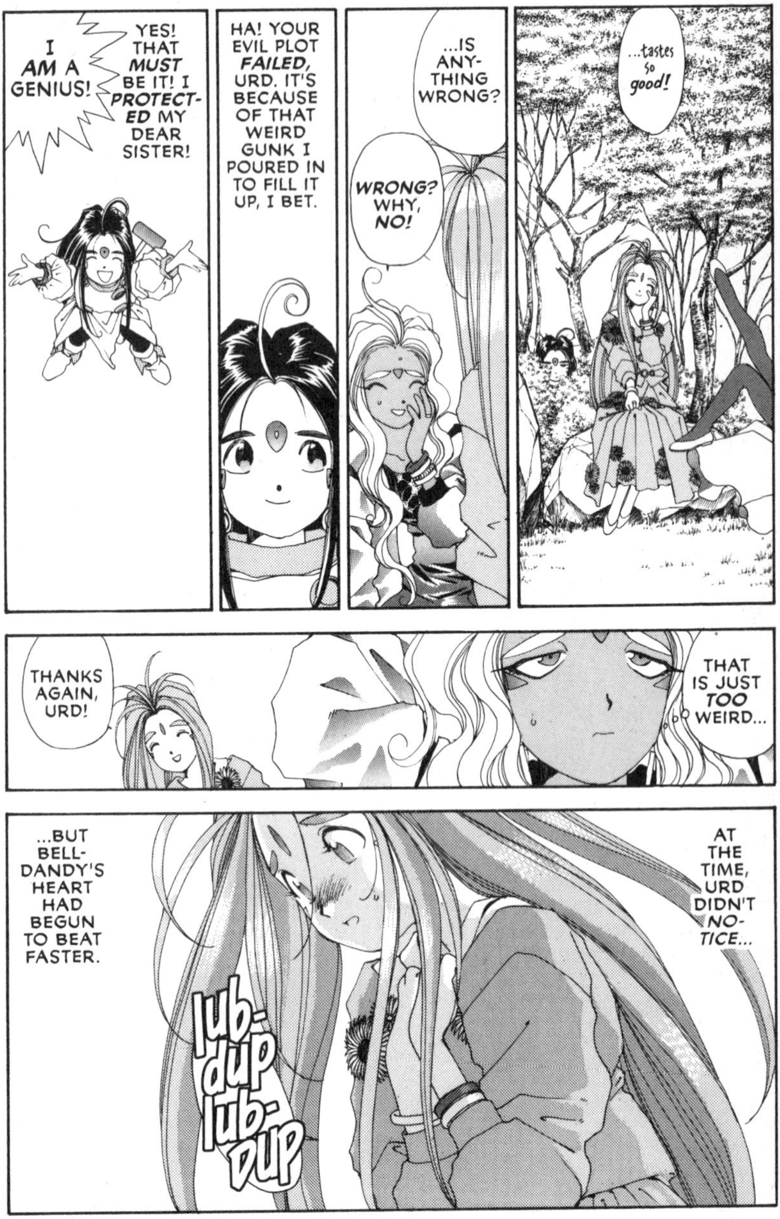
...tastes so good!
...IS ANY-THING WRONG?
WRONG? WHY, NO!
HA! YOUR EVIL PLOT FAILED, URD. IT'S BECAUSE OF THAT WEIRD GUNK I POURED IN TO FILL IT UP, I BET.
YES! THAT MUST BE IT! I PROTECT-ED MY DEAR SISTER!
I AM A GENIUS!
THAT IS JUST TOO WEIRD...
THANKS AGAIN, URD!
AT THE TIME, URD DIDN'T NO-TICE...
...BUT BELL-DANDY'S HEART HAD BEGUN TO BEAT FASTER.
lub-dup lub-DUP

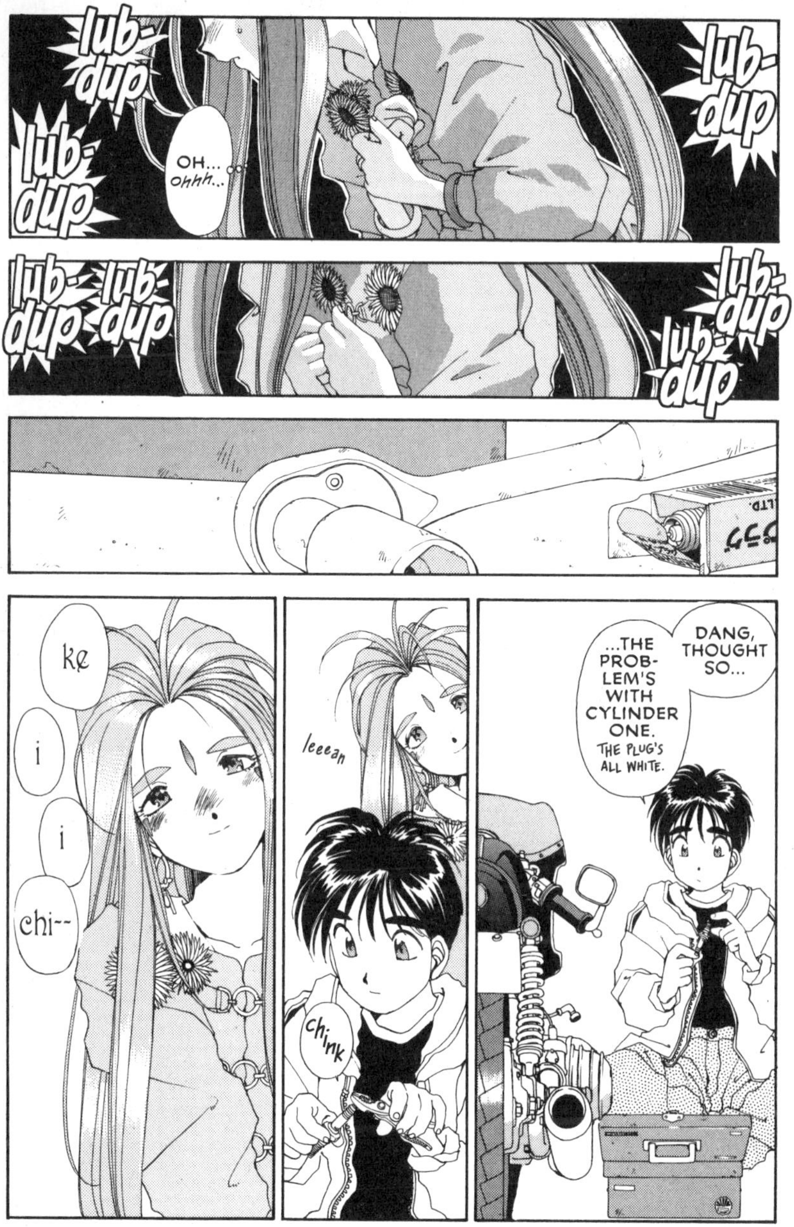
lub-dup
lub-dup
OH... ohhh...
lub-dup
lub-dup
lub-dup
lub-dup
lub-dup
LTD.
DANG, THOUGHT SO...
...THE PROB-LEM'S WITH CYLINDER ONE. THE PLUG'S ALL WHITE.
leeean
chink
ke
i
i
chi--

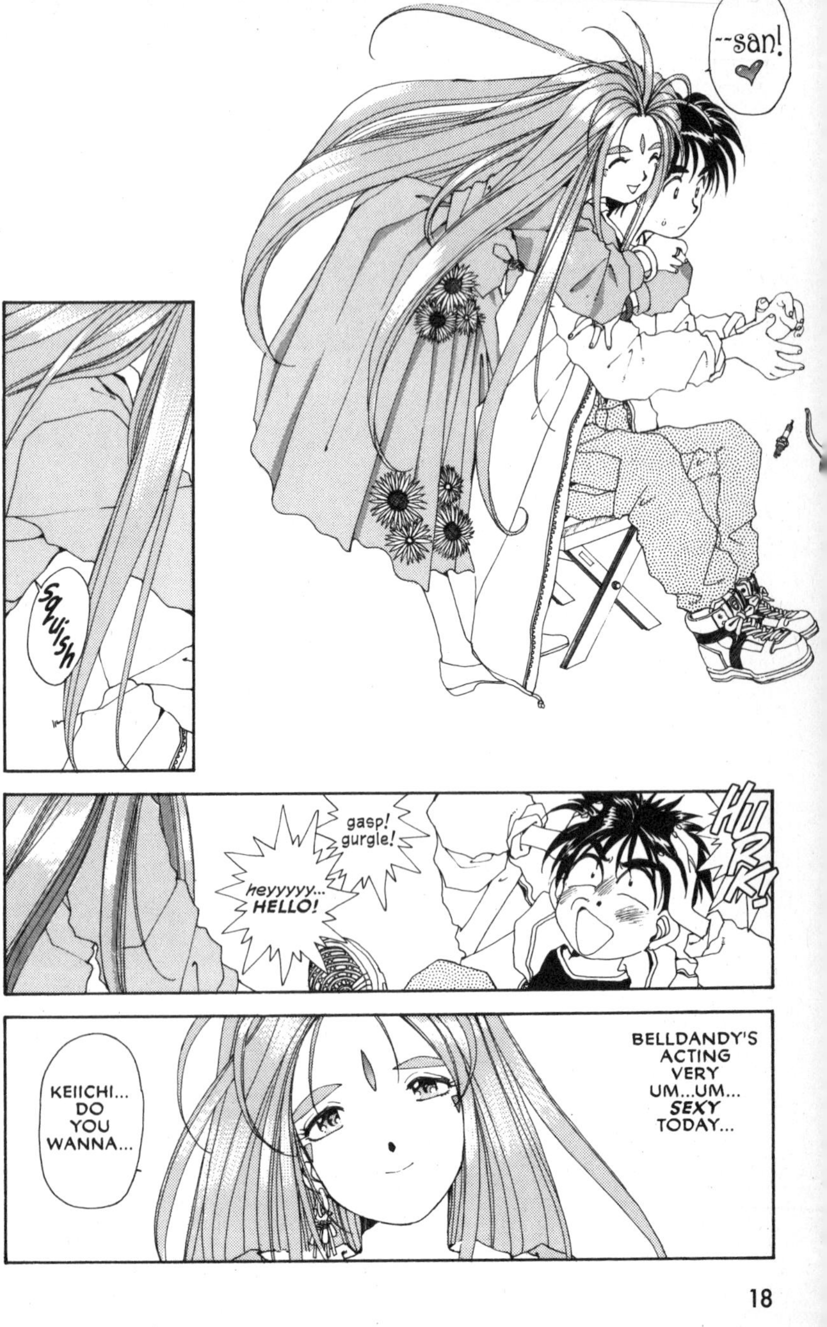
--san! ♥
squish
HURK!
gasp! gurgle!
heyyyyy... HELLO!
BELLDANDY'S ACTING VERY UM...UM... SEXY TODAY...
KEIICHI... DO YOU WANNA...

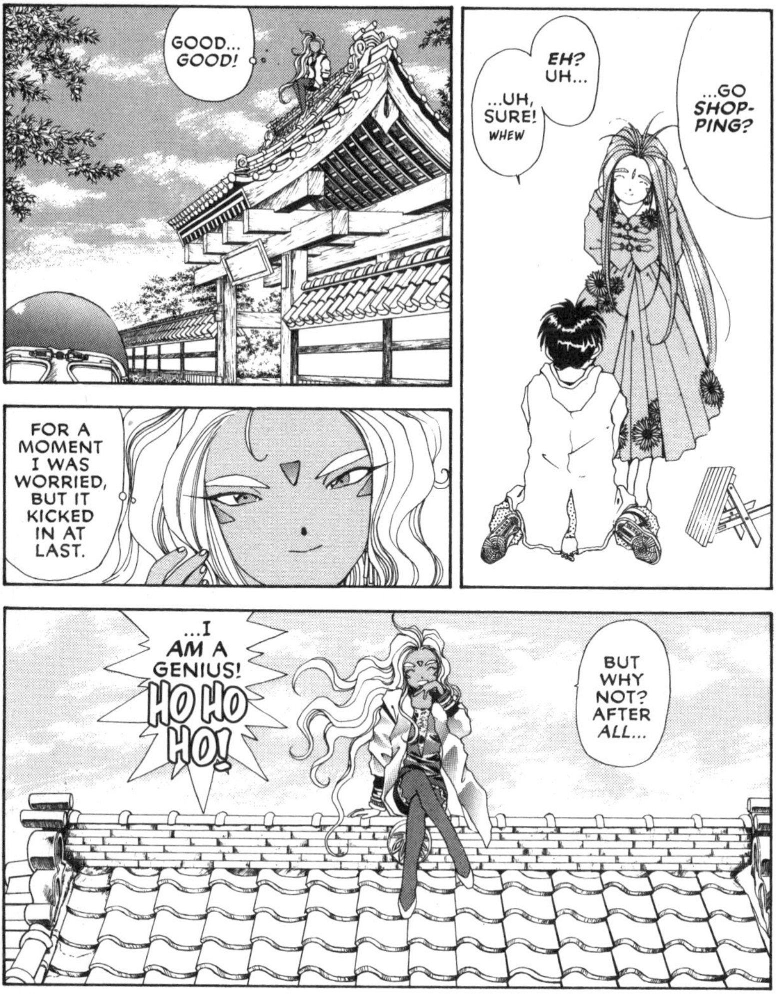
...GO SHOPPING?
EH? UH...
...UH, SURE! WHEW
GOOD... GOOD!
FOR A MOMENT I WAS WORRIED, BUT IT KICKED IN AT LAST.
...I AM A GENIUS! HO HO HO!
BUT WHY NOT? AFTER ALL...

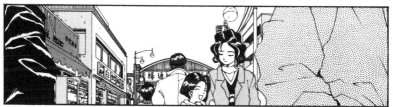

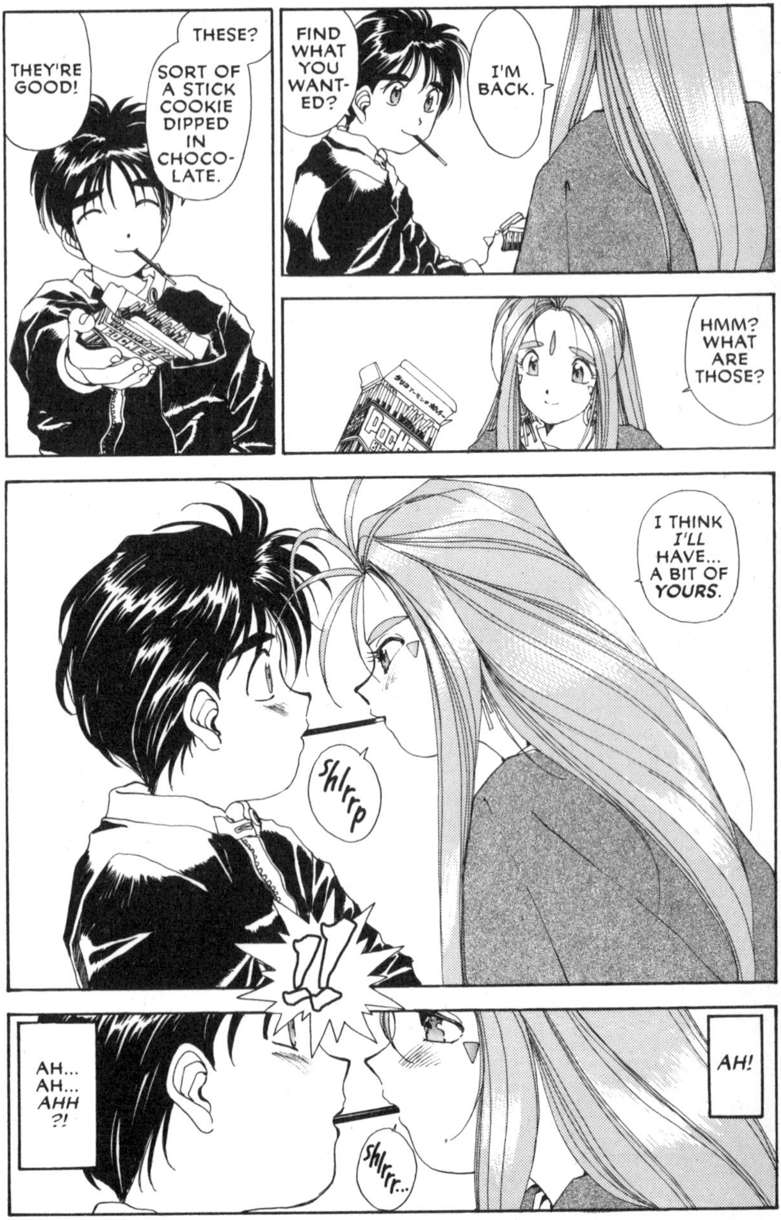
I'M BACK.
FIND WHAT YOU WANTED?
HMM? WHAT ARE THOSE?
THESE?
SORT OF A STICK COOKIE DIPPED IN CHOCOLATE.
THEY'RE GOOD!
I THINK *I'LL* HAVE... A BIT OF *YOURS*.
Shlrrp
!!
AH!
AH... AH... *AHH* ?!
shlrrr...

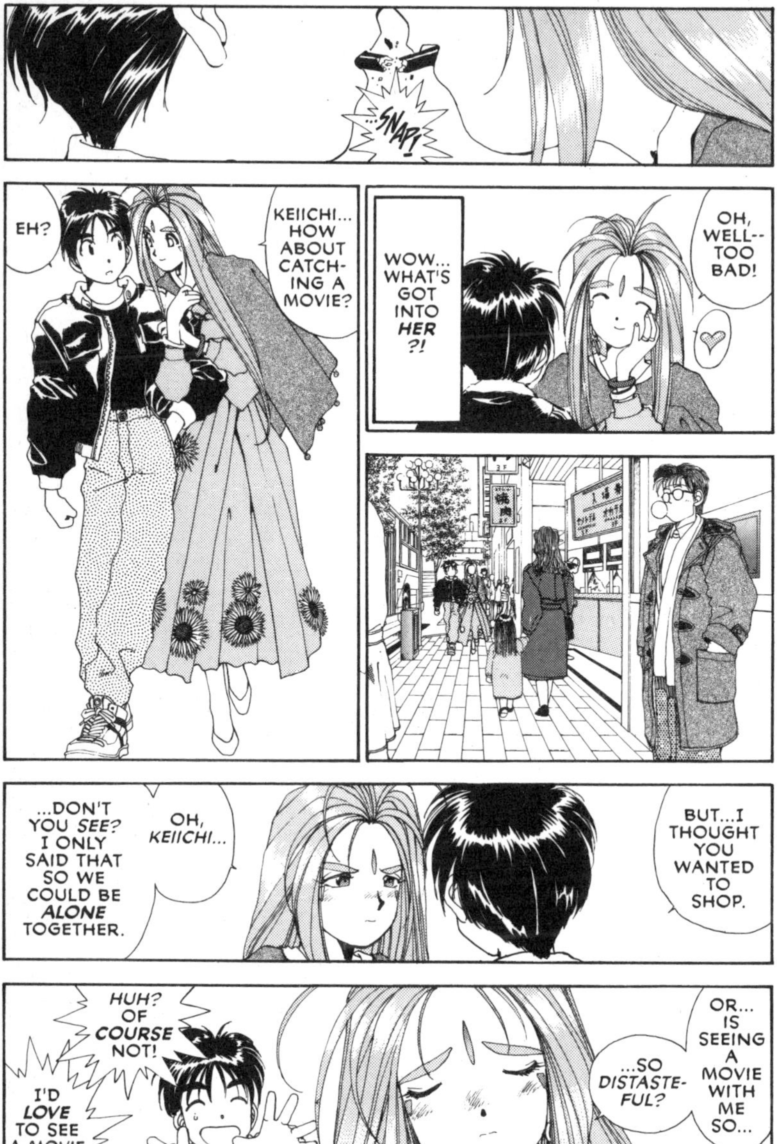

...SNAP!
EH?
KEIICHI... HOW ABOUT CATCHING A MOVIE?
WOW... WHAT'S GOT INTO *HER* ?!
OH, WELL-- TOO BAD!
BUT...I THOUGHT YOU WANTED TO SHOP.
OH, *KEIICHI*...
...DON'T YOU *SEE?* I ONLY SAID THAT SO WE COULD BE ***ALONE*** TOGETHER.
OR... IS SEEING A MOVIE WITH ME SO...
...SO *DISTASTEFUL?*
HUH? OF ***COURSE*** NOT!
I'D ***LOVE*** TO SEE A MOVIE WITH YOU!

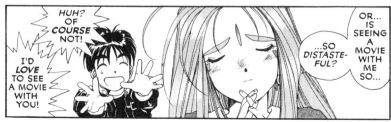

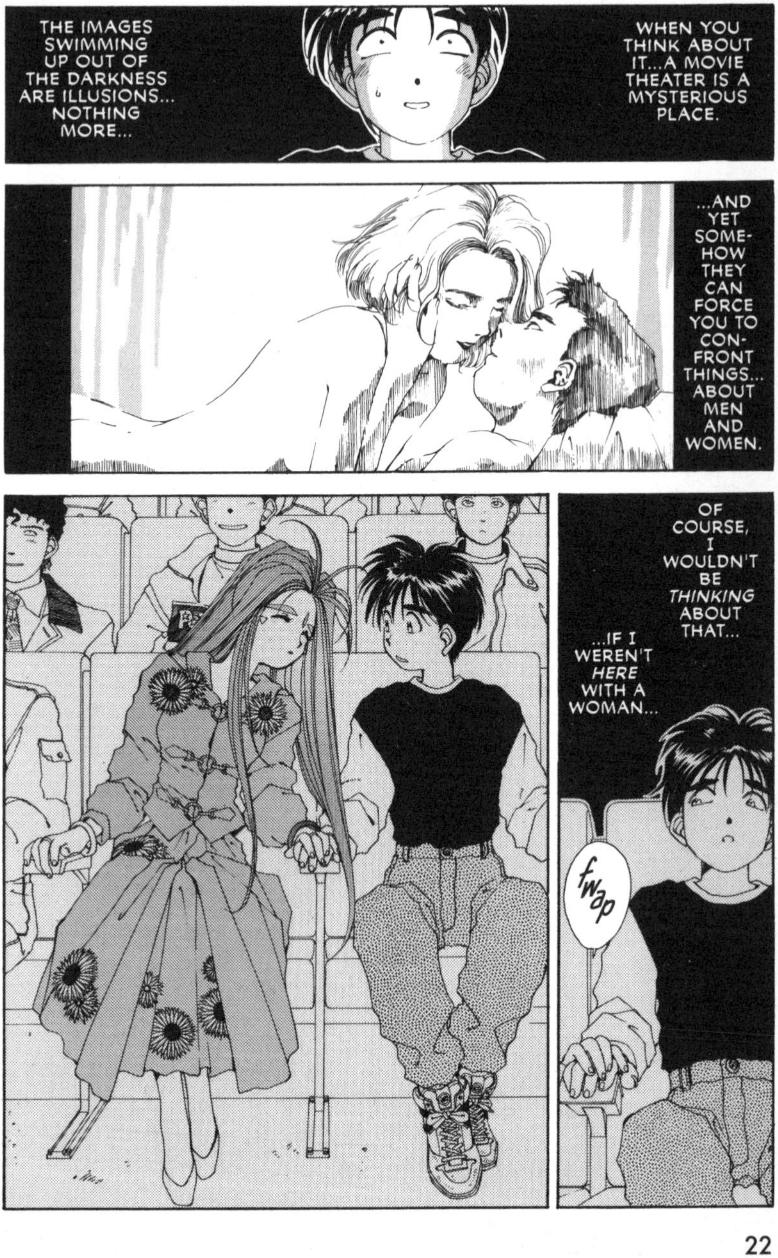
WHEN YOU THINK ABOUT IT...A MOVIE THEATER IS A MYSTERIOUS PLACE.
THE IMAGES SWIMMING UP OUT OF THE DARKNESS ARE ILLUSIONS... NOTHING MORE...
...AND YET SOME-HOW THEY CAN FORCE YOU TO CON-FRONT THINGS... ABOUT MEN AND WOMEN.
OF COURSE, I WOULDN'T BE *THINKING* ABOUT THAT...
...IF I WEREN'T *HERE* WITH A WOMAN...
fwap

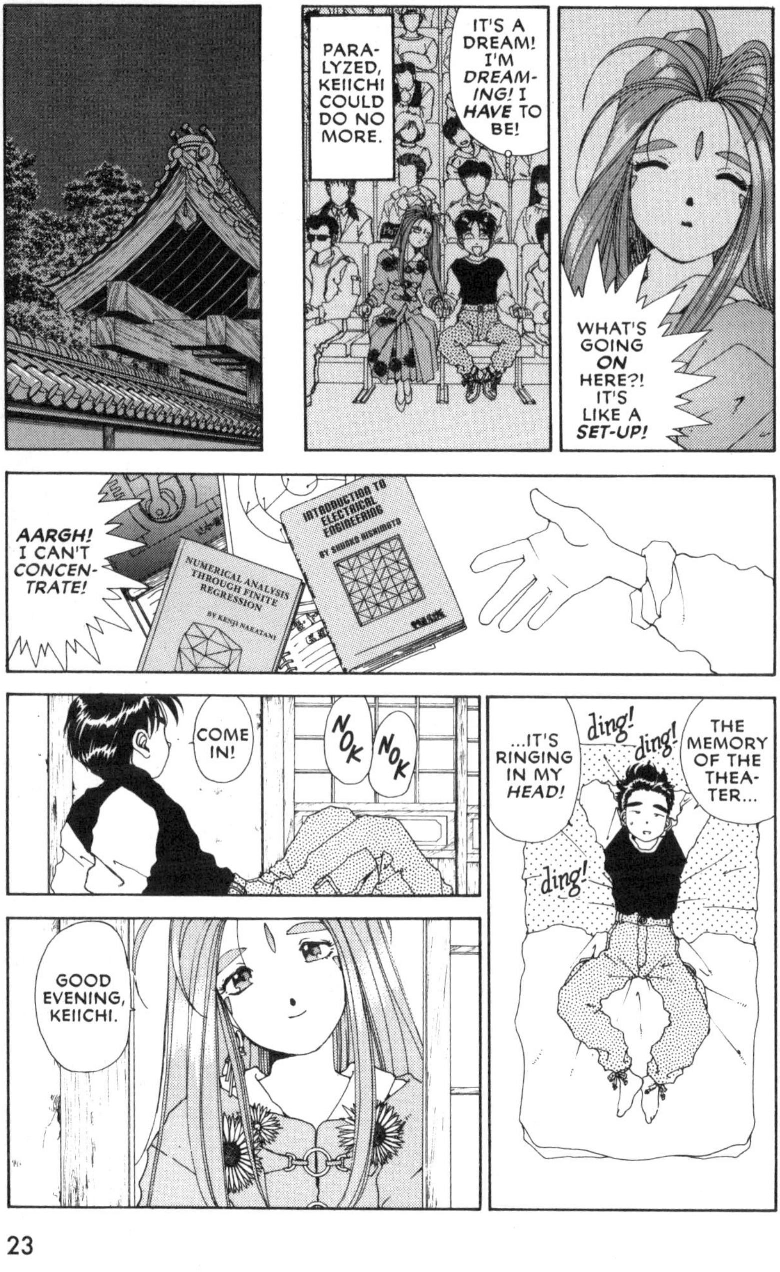
PARA-LYZED, KEIICHI COULD DO NO MORE.
IT'S A DREAM! I'M *DREAM-ING!* I *HAVE* TO BE!
WHAT'S GOING *ON* HERE?! IT'S LIKE A *SET-UP!*
AARGH! I CAN'T *CONCEN-TRATE!*
INTRODUCTION TO ELECTRICAL ENGINEERING
NUMERICAL ANALYSIS THROUGH FINITE REGRESSION
BY KENJI NAKATANI
THE MEMORY OF THE THEA-TER...
ding!
ding!
...IT'S RINGING IN MY *HEAD!*
ding!
NOK
NOK
COME IN!
GOOD EVENING, KEIICHI.

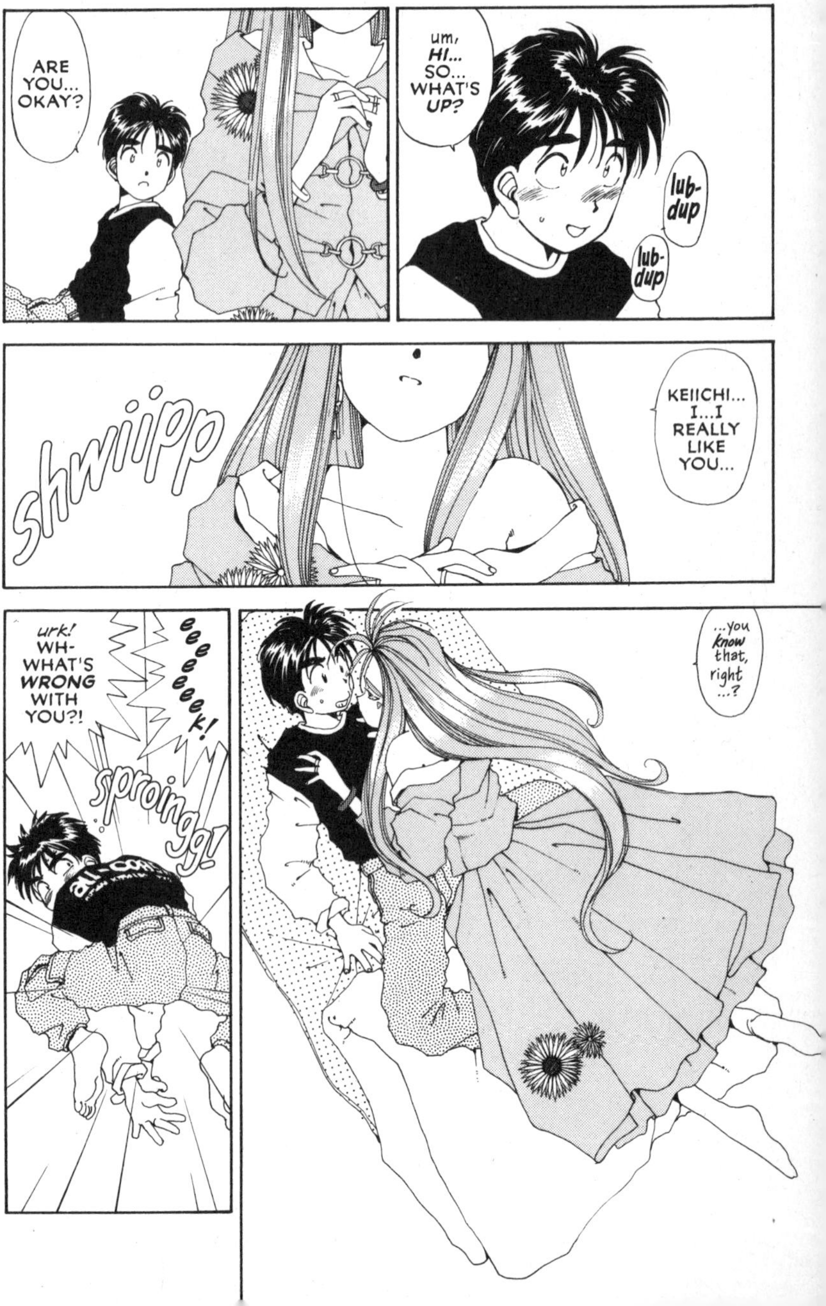
um, HI... SO... WHAT'S UP?
lub-dup
lub-dup
ARE YOU... OKAY?
KEIICHI... I...I REALLY LIKE YOU...
shwiipp
...you know that, right ...?
eeeeeeek!
urk! WH-WHAT'S WRONG WITH YOU?!
sproingg!

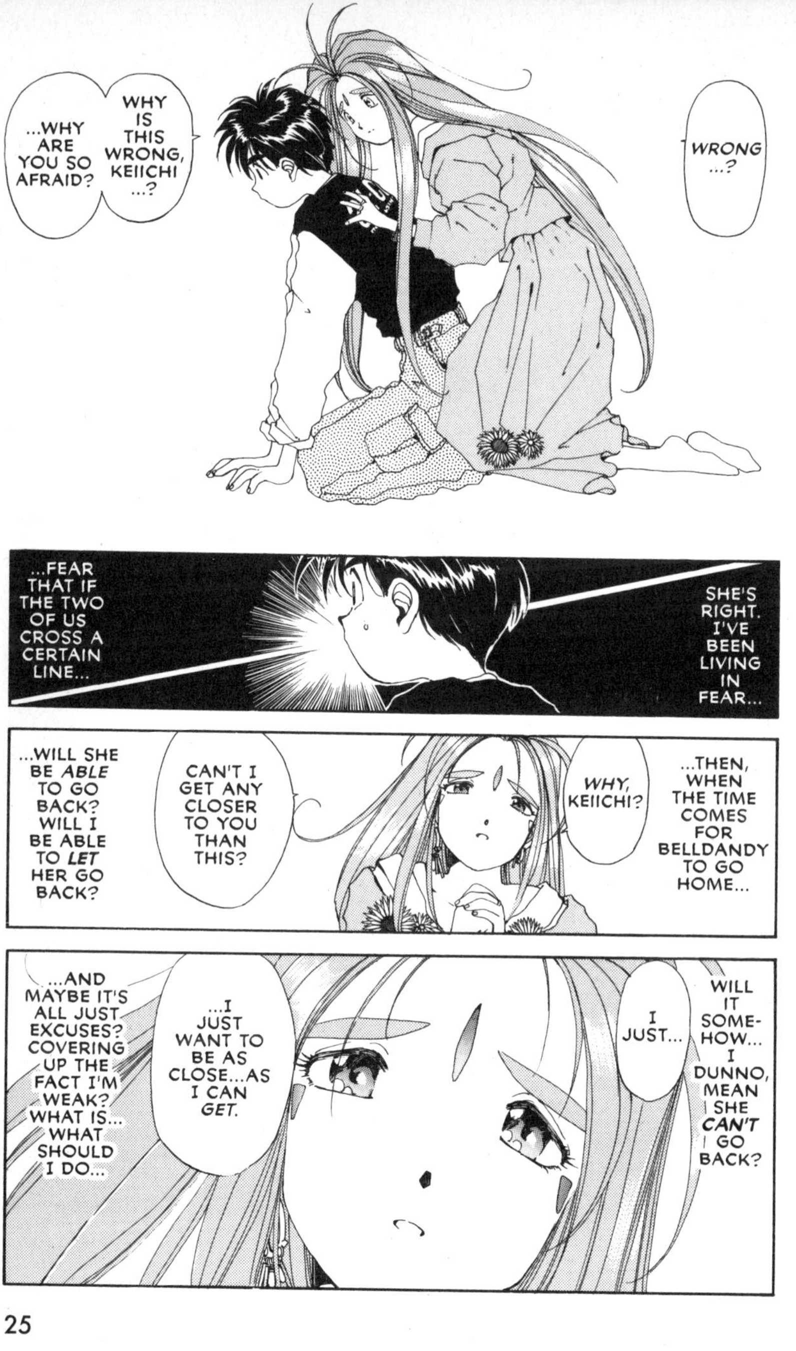
WRONG ...?
WHY IS THIS WRONG, KEIICHI ...?
...WHY ARE YOU SO AFRAID?
SHE'S RIGHT. I'VE BEEN LIVING IN FEAR...
...FEAR THAT IF THE TWO OF US CROSS A CERTAIN LINE...
...THEN, WHEN THE TIME COMES FOR BELLDANDY TO GO HOME...
WHY, KEIICHI?
CAN'T I GET ANY CLOSER TO YOU THAN THIS?
...WILL SHE BE *ABLE* TO GO BACK? WILL I BE ABLE TO *LET* HER GO BACK?
WILL IT SOME-HOW... I DUNNO, MEAN SHE ***CAN'T*** GO BACK?
I JUST...
...I JUST WANT TO BE AS CLOSE...AS I CAN *GET*.
...AND MAYBE IT'S ALL JUST EXCUSES? COVERING UP THE FACT I'M WEAK? WHAT IS... WHAT SHOULD I DO...

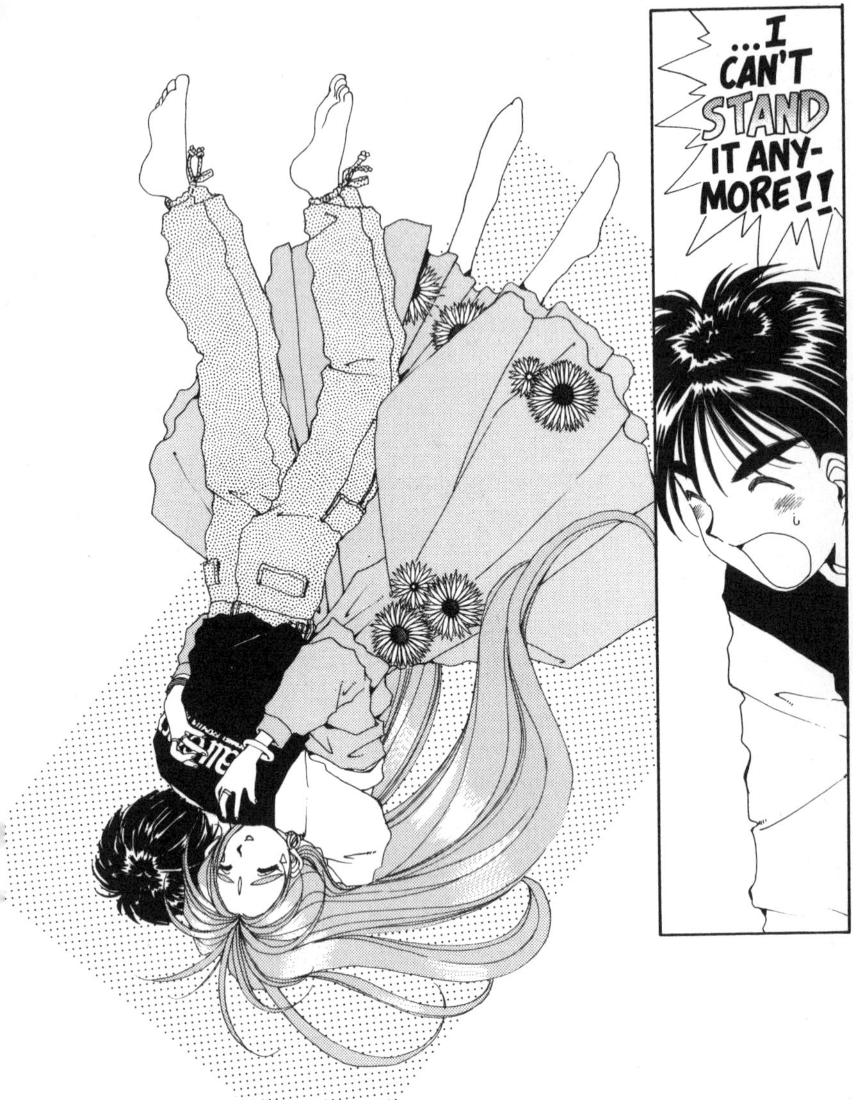
...I CAN'T STAND IT ANY-MORE!!

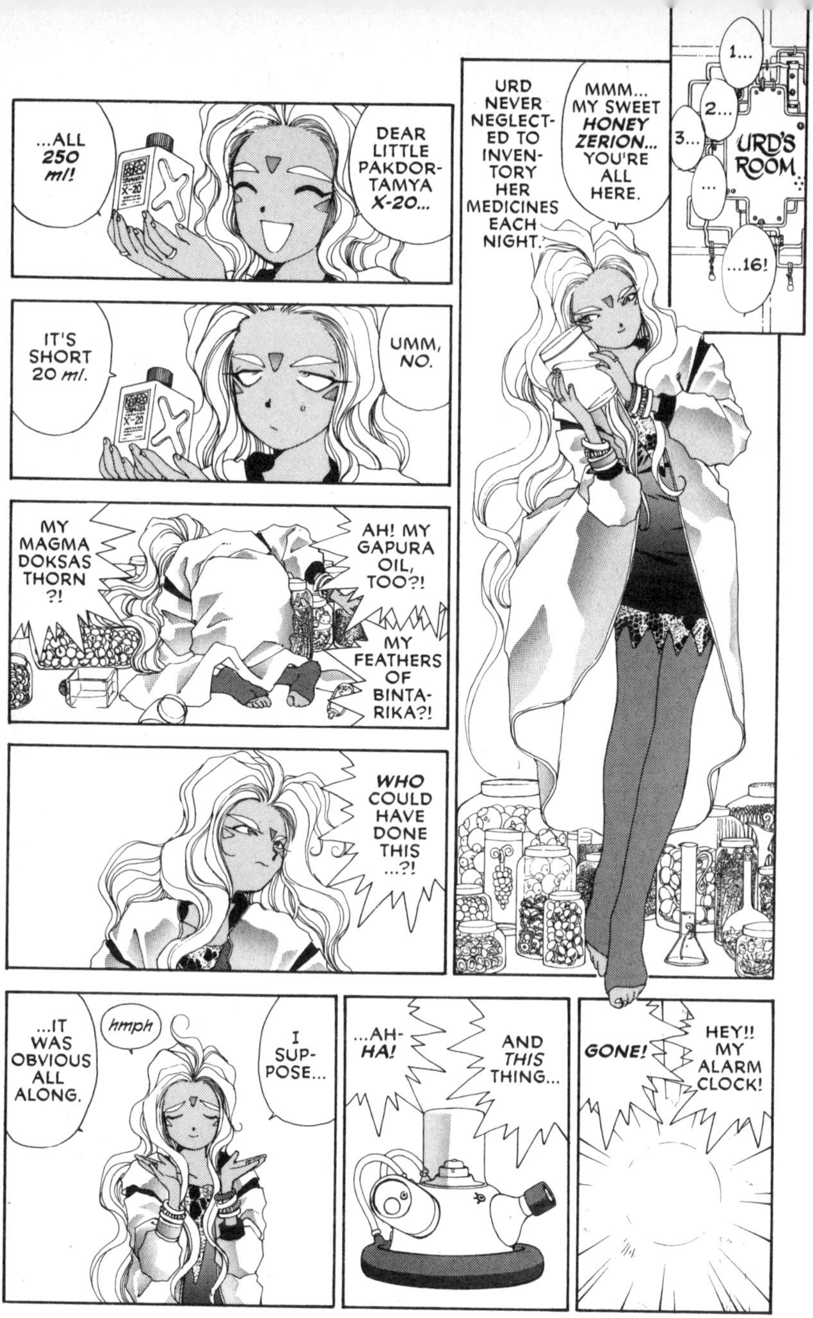
1...
2...
3...
...
...16!
URD'S ROOM
MMM... MY SWEET HONEY ZERION... YOU'RE ALL HERE.
URD NEVER NEGLECTED TO INVENTORY HER MEDICINES EACH NIGHT.
DEAR LITTLE PAKDORTAMYA X-20...
...ALL 250 ml!
UMM, NO.
IT'S SHORT 20 ml.
AH! MY GAPURA OIL, TOO?!
MY MAGMA DOKSAS THORN ?!
MY FEATHERS OF BINTARIKA?!
WHO COULD HAVE DONE THIS ...?!
HEY!! MY ALARM CLOCK!
GONE!
AND THIS THING...
...AH-HA!
I SUPPOSE...
hmph
...IT WAS OBVIOUS ALL ALONG.

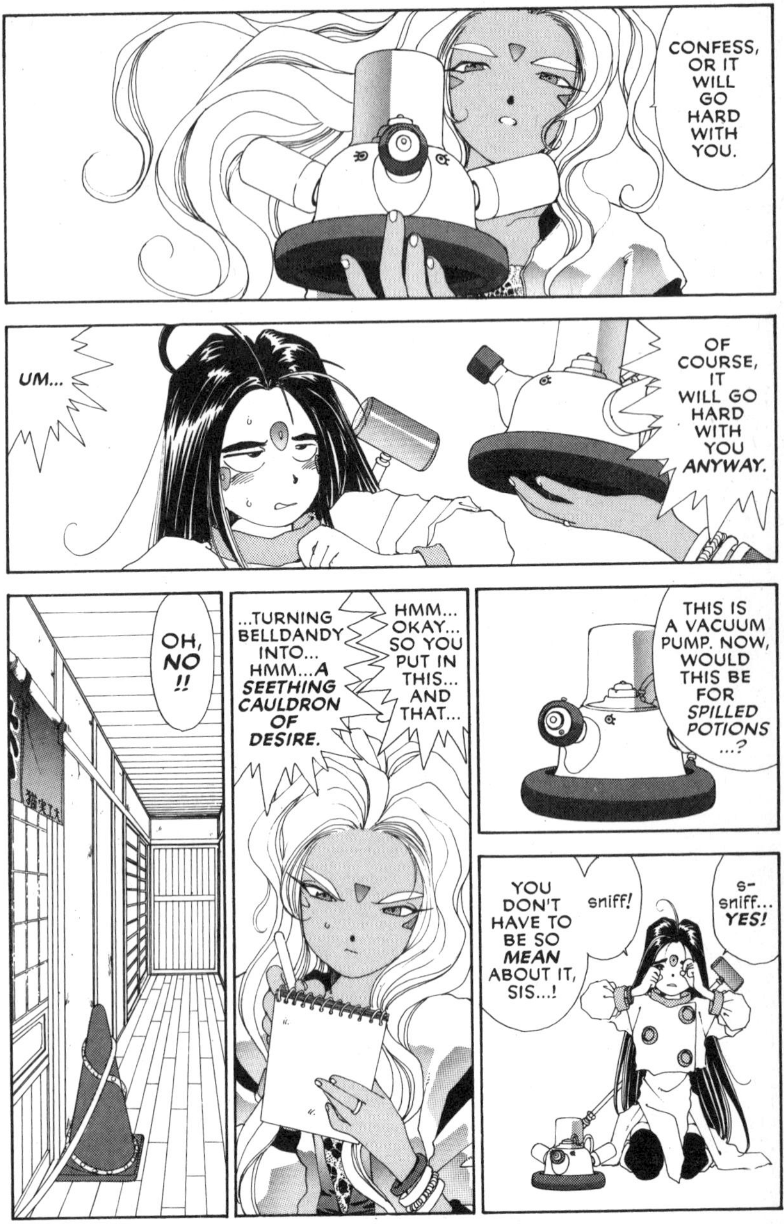
CONFESS, OR IT WILL GO HARD WITH YOU.
OF COURSE, IT WILL GO HARD WITH YOU *ANYWAY.*
UM...
THIS IS A VACUUM PUMP. NOW, WOULD THIS BE FOR *SPILLED POTIONS* ...?
s-sniff... *YES!*
sniff!
YOU DON'T HAVE TO BE SO *MEAN* ABOUT IT, SIS...!
HMM... OKAY... SO YOU PUT IN THIS... AND THAT...
...TURNING BELLDANDY INTO... HMM...*A SEETHING CAULDRON OF DESIRE.*
OH, *NO !!*

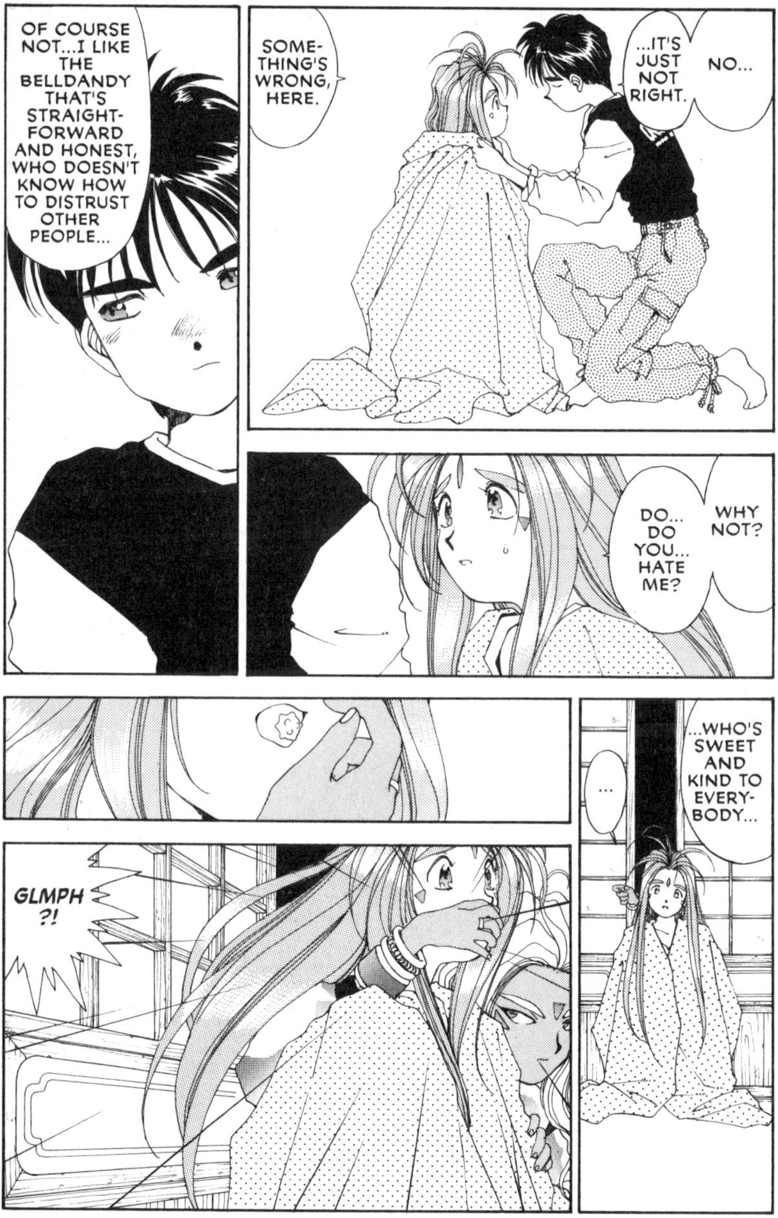
SOME-THING'S WRONG, HERE.
...IT'S JUST NOT RIGHT.
NO...
WHY NOT?
DO... DO YOU... HATE ME?
OF COURSE NOT...I LIKE THE BELLDANDY THAT'S STRAIGHT-FORWARD AND HONEST, WHO DOESN'T KNOW HOW TO DISTRUST OTHER PEOPLE...
...WHO'S SWEET AND KIND TO EVERY-BODY...
...
GLMPH ?!

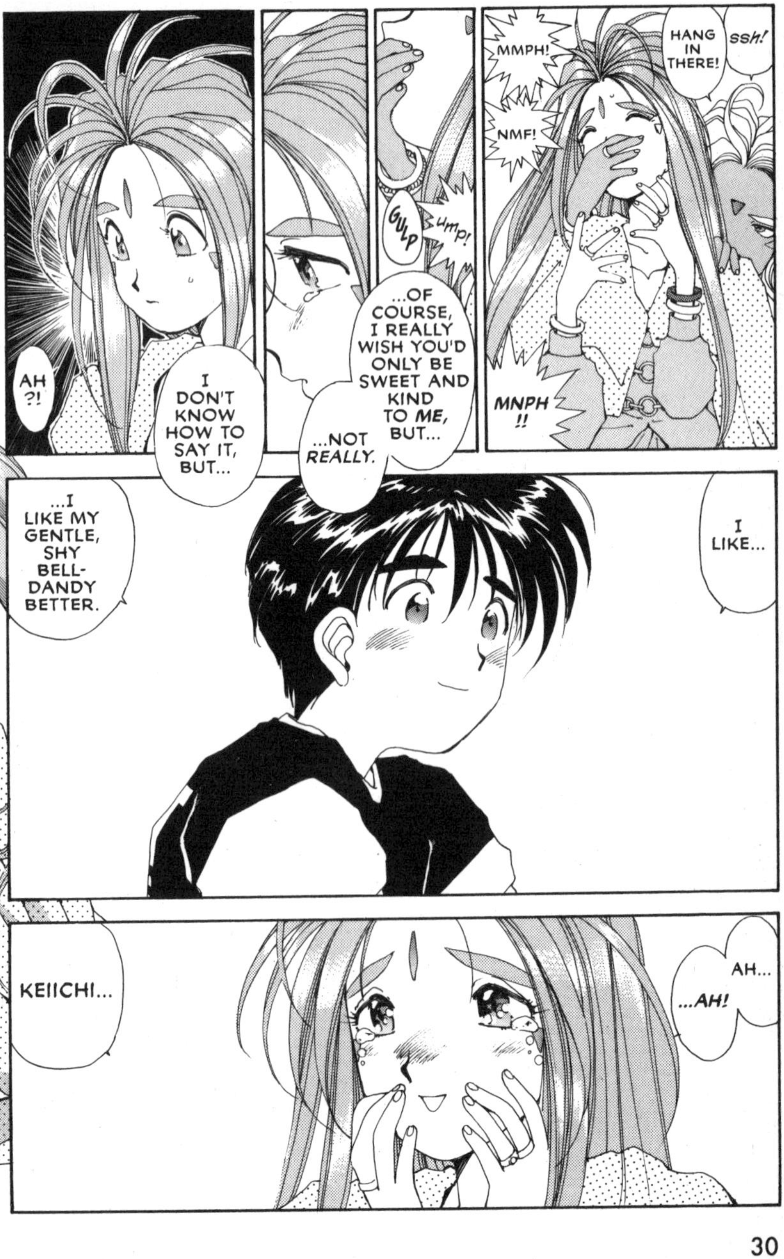
HANG IN THERE!
ssh!
MMPH!
NMF!
MNPH !!
GULP
ump!
...OF COURSE, I REALLY WISH YOU'D ONLY BE SWEET AND KIND TO *ME,* BUT...
...NOT *REALLY.*
I DON'T KNOW HOW TO SAY IT, BUT...
AH ?!
I LIKE...
...I LIKE MY GENTLE, SHY BELL-DANDY BETTER.
AH...
...*AH!*
KEIICHI...

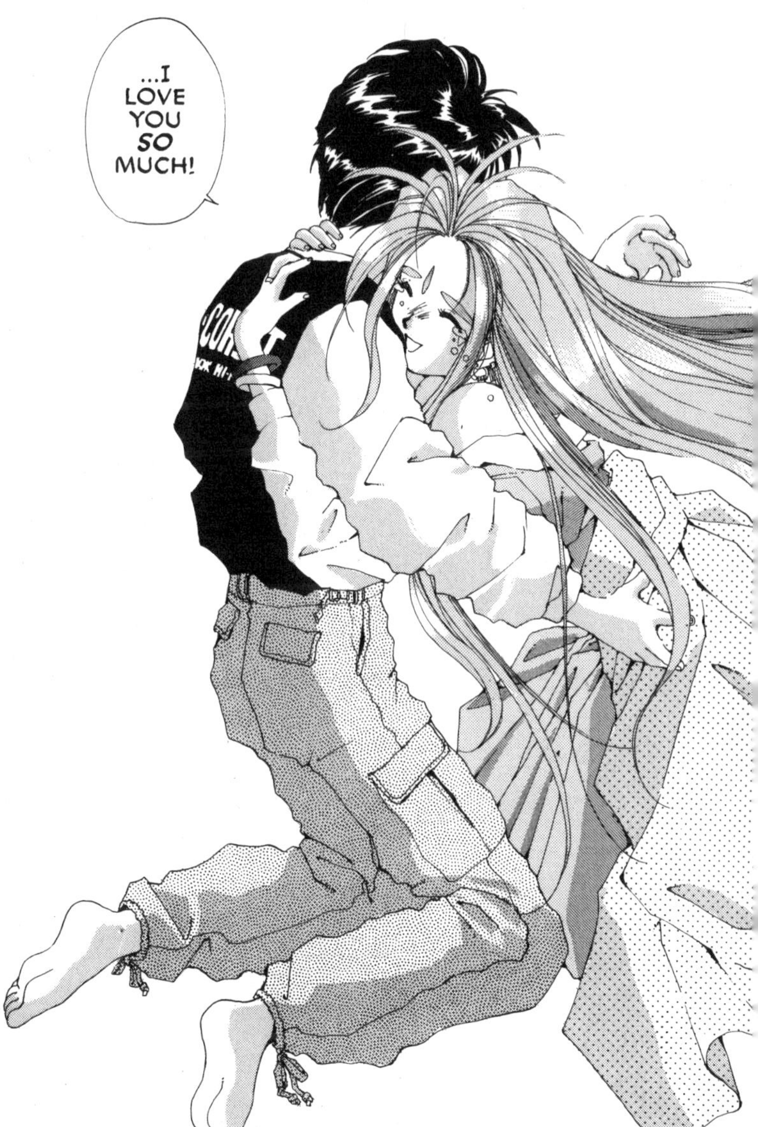
...I LOVE YOU SO MUCH!

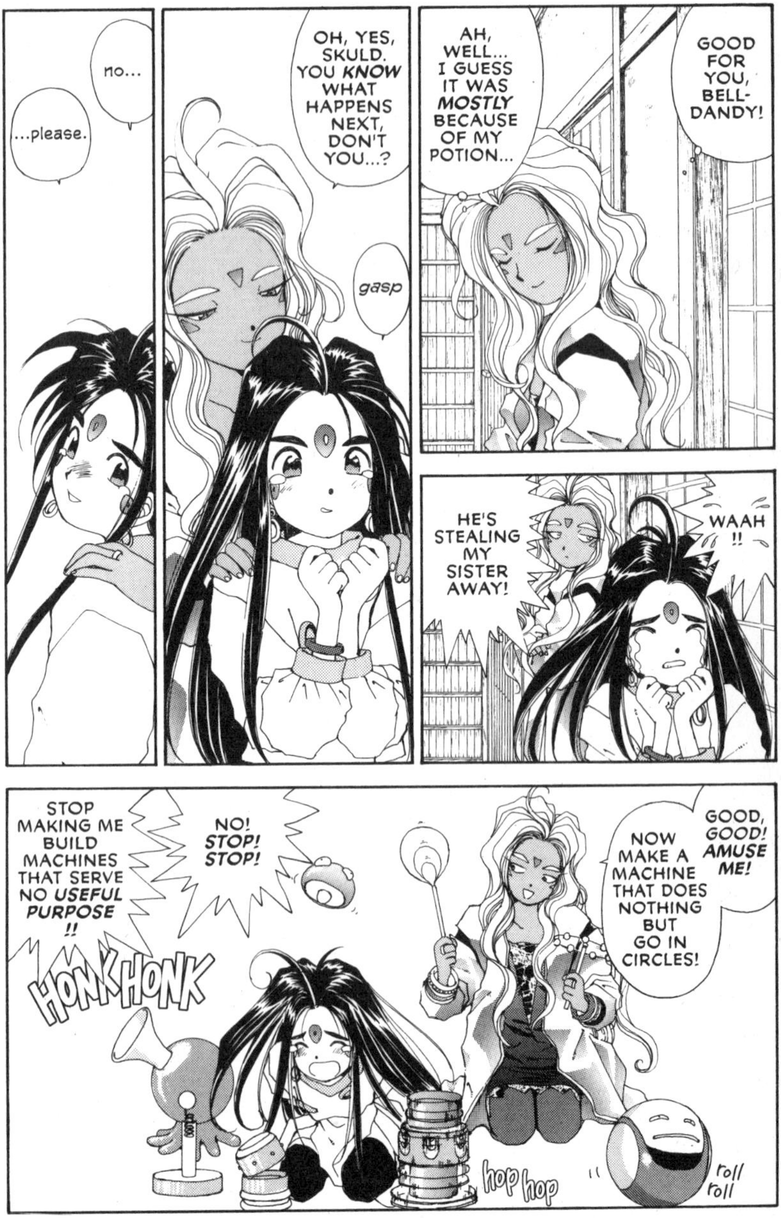
GOOD FOR YOU, BELL-DANDY!
AH, WELL... I GUESS IT WAS *MOSTLY* BECAUSE OF MY POTION...
HE'S STEALING MY SISTER AWAY!
WAAH !!
OH, YES, SKULD. YOU *KNOW* WHAT HAPPENS NEXT, DON'T YOU...?
gasp
no...
...please.
GOOD, *GOOD! AMUSE ME!*
NOW MAKE A MACHINE THAT DOES NOTHING BUT GO IN CIRCLES!
NO! *STOP! STOP!*
STOP MAKING ME BUILD MACHINES THAT SERVE NO *USEFUL PURPOSE !!*
HONK HONK
hop hop
roll roll

THE ADVENTURES OF MINI-URD

In the handy PETITE SIZE!

A COOL BREEZE IN SUMMER

CATCHING RAYS

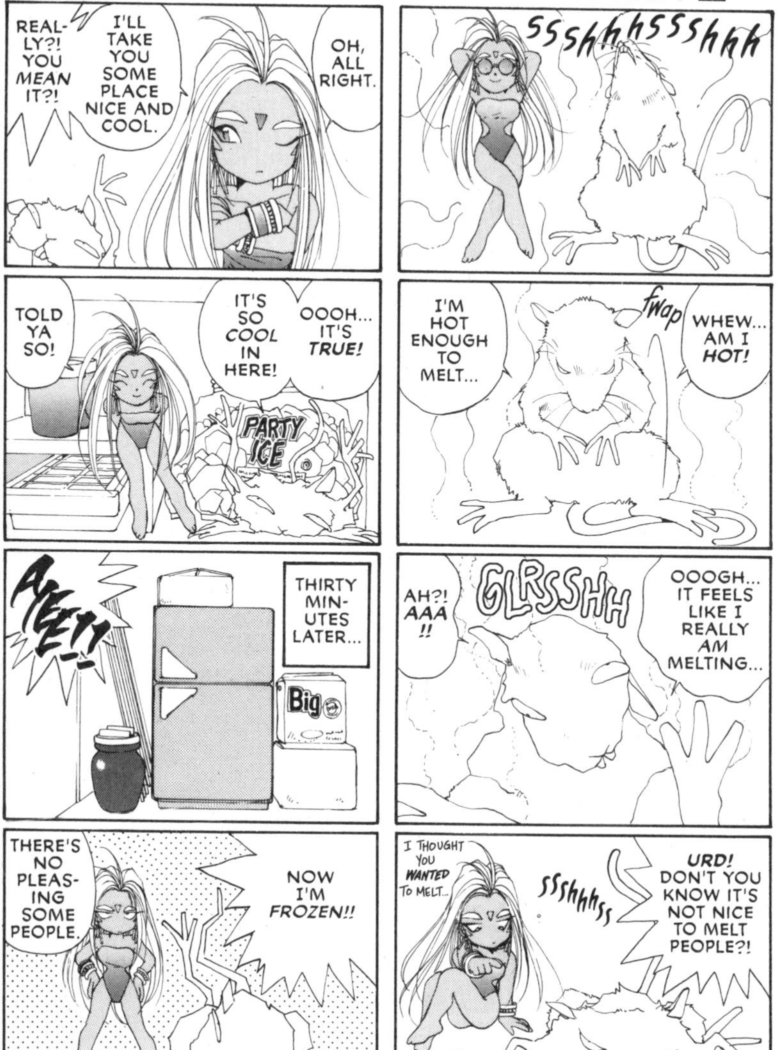
REAL-LY?! YOU MEAN IT?!
I'LL TAKE YOU SOME PLACE NICE AND COOL.
OH, ALL RIGHT.
TOLD YA SO!
IT'S SO COOL IN HERE!
OOOH... IT'S TRUE!
PARTY ICE
AIEEE!!
THIRTY MIN-UTES LATER...
Big
THERE'S NO PLEAS-ING SOME PEOPLE.
NOW I'M FROZEN!!
SSShhhSSShhh
I'M HOT ENOUGH TO MELT...
fwap
WHEW... AM I HOT!
AH?! AAA!!
GLRSSHH
OOOGH... IT FEELS LIKE I REALLY AM MELTING...
I THOUGHT YOU WANTED TO MELT...
SSShhhss
URD! DON'T YOU KNOW IT'S NOT NICE TO MELT PEOPLE?!

◆ GOLDEN GOURMAND ◆

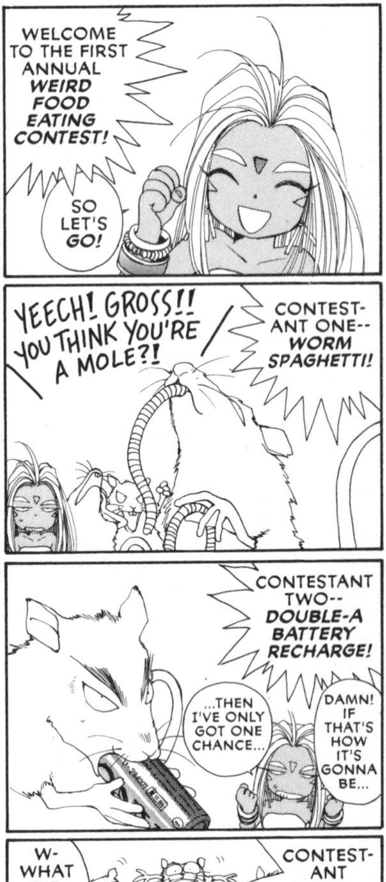
WELCOME TO THE FIRST ANNUAL *WEIRD FOOD EATING CONTEST!*
SO LET'S *GO!*
CONTESTANT ONE-- *WORM SPAGHETTI!!*
YEECH! GROSS!! YOU THINK YOU'RE A MOLE?!
CONTESTANT TWO-- *DOUBLE-A BATTERY RECHARGE!*
DAMN! IF THAT'S HOW IT'S GONNA BE...
...THEN I'VE ONLY GOT ONE CHANCE...
CONTESTANT THREE-- *BBQ RAT ON A STICK!*
W-WHAT DID YOU SAY ...?!

AMAZING! THE ALL-YOU-CAN-EAT CONTEST! ◆

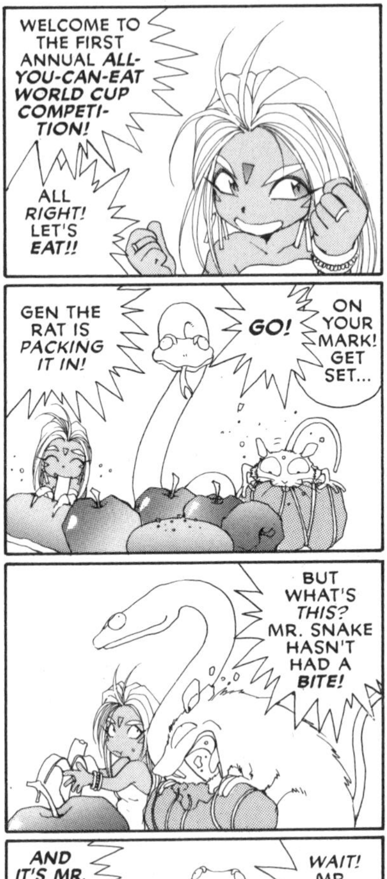
WELCOME TO THE FIRST ANNUAL *ALL-YOU-CAN-EAT WORLD CUP COMPETITION!*
ALL *RIGHT!* LET'S *EAT!!*
ON YOUR MARK! GET SET...
GO!
GEN THE RAT IS *PACKING IT IN!*
BUT WHAT'S *THIS?* MR. SNAKE HASN'T HAD A *BITE!*
WAIT! MR. SNAKE JUST ATE GEN THE RAT!!
AND IT'S MR. SNAKE BY A MILE!!
GEEZ, IT WAS JUST ANOTHER "WEIRD FOOD EATING CONTEST" AFTER ALL...

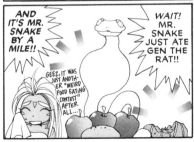

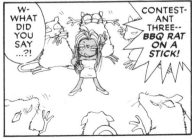

CHAPTER 44

The Queen of Vengeance

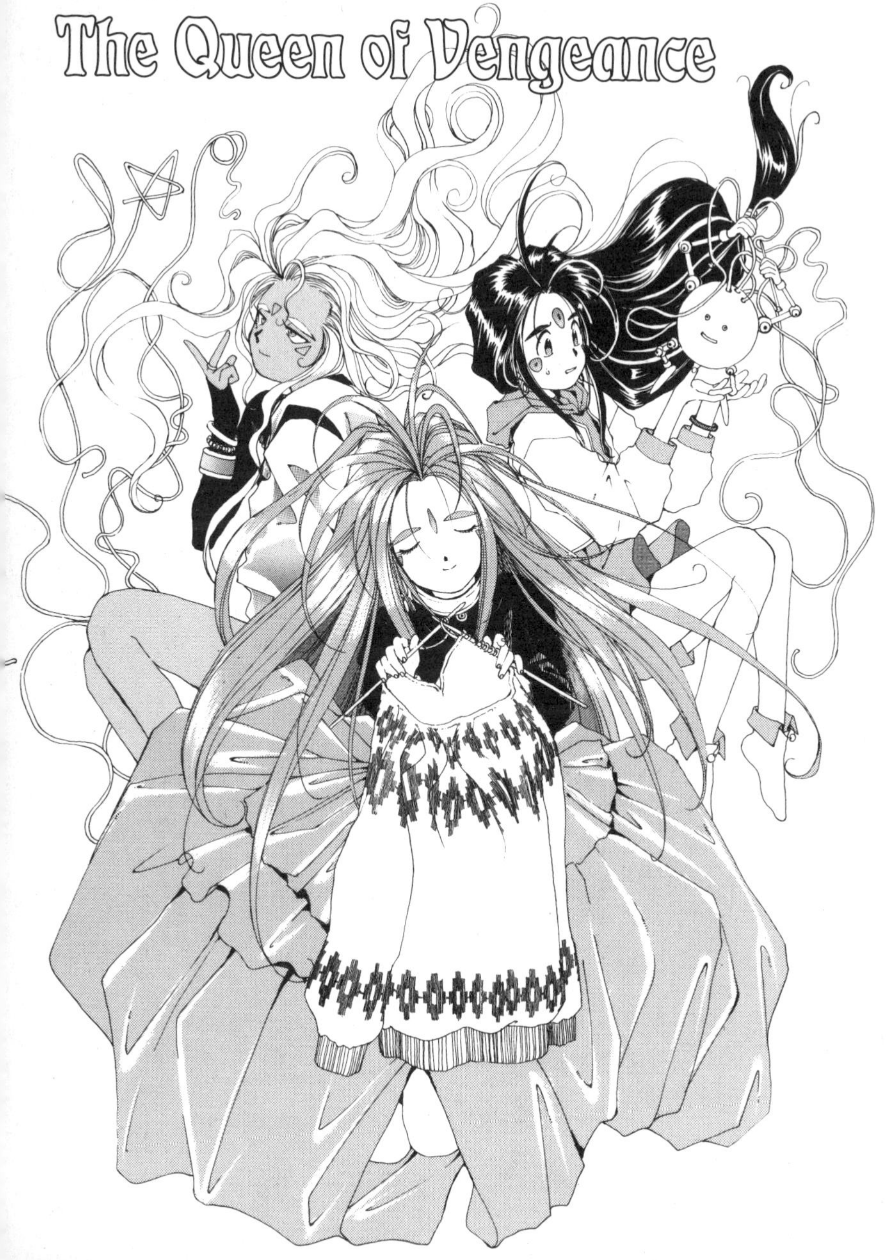

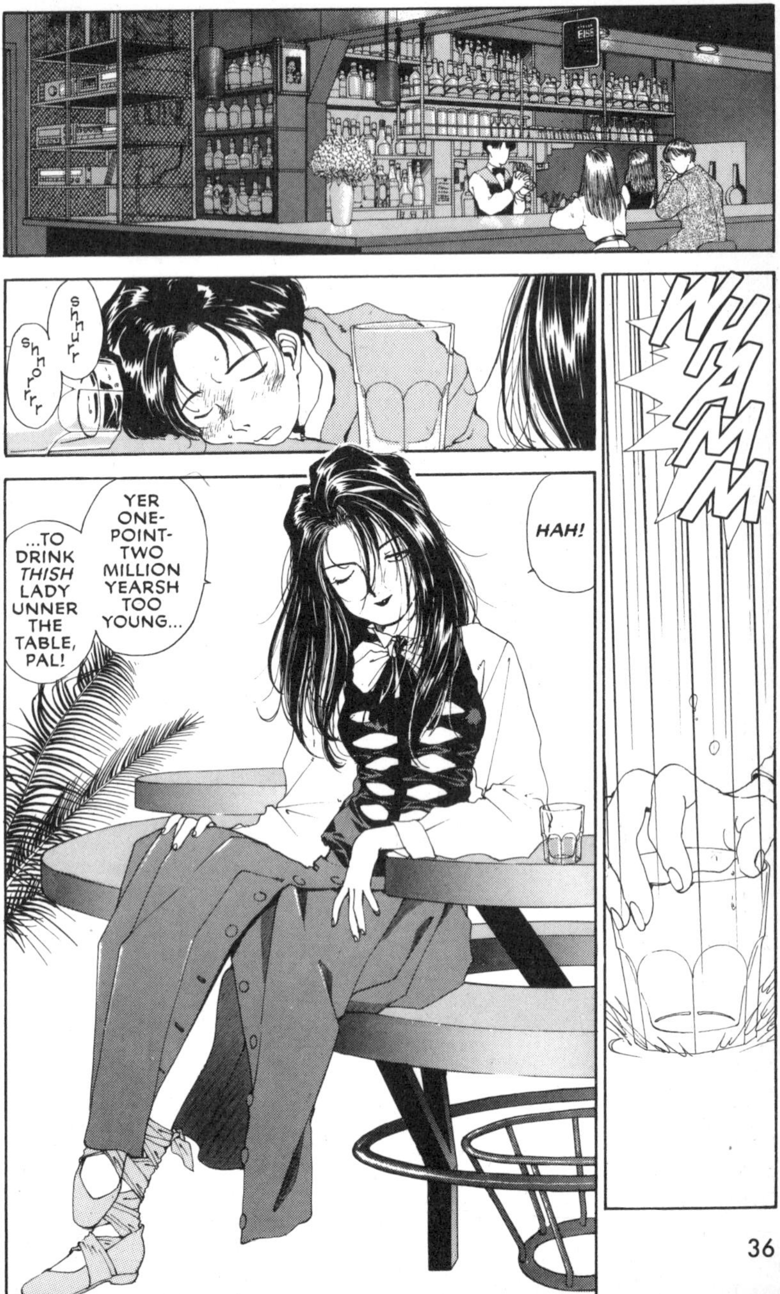
WHAMM
shnurr
shnorrrr
HAH!
YER ONE-POINT-TWO MILLION YEARSH TOO YOUNG...
...TO DRINK THISH LADY UNNER THE TABLE, PAL!

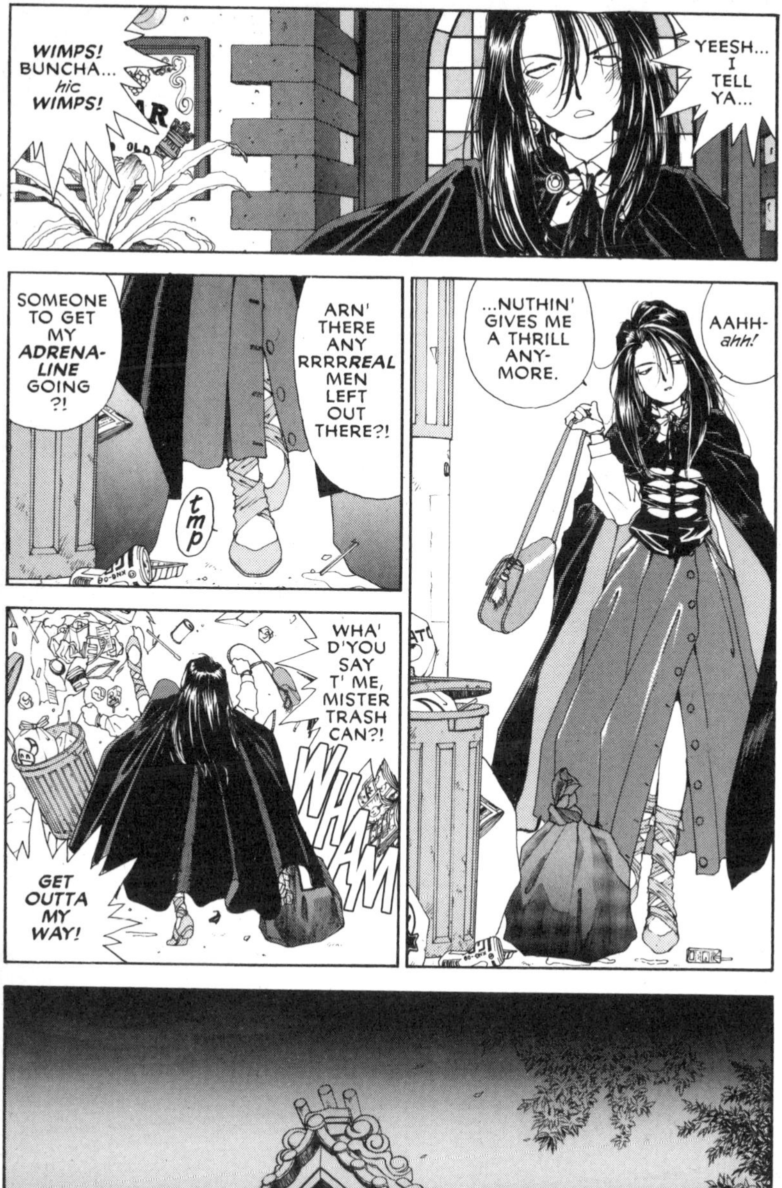
YEESH... I TELL YA...
WIMPS! BUNCHA... hic WIMPS!
AAHH-ahh!
...NUTHIN' GIVES ME A THRILL ANYMORE.
ARN' THERE ANY RRRRREAL MEN LEFT OUT THERE?!
SOMEONE TO GET MY ADRENALINE GOING?!
tmp
WHA' D'YOU SAY T' ME, MISTER TRASH CAN?!
WHAM
GET OUTTA MY WAY!

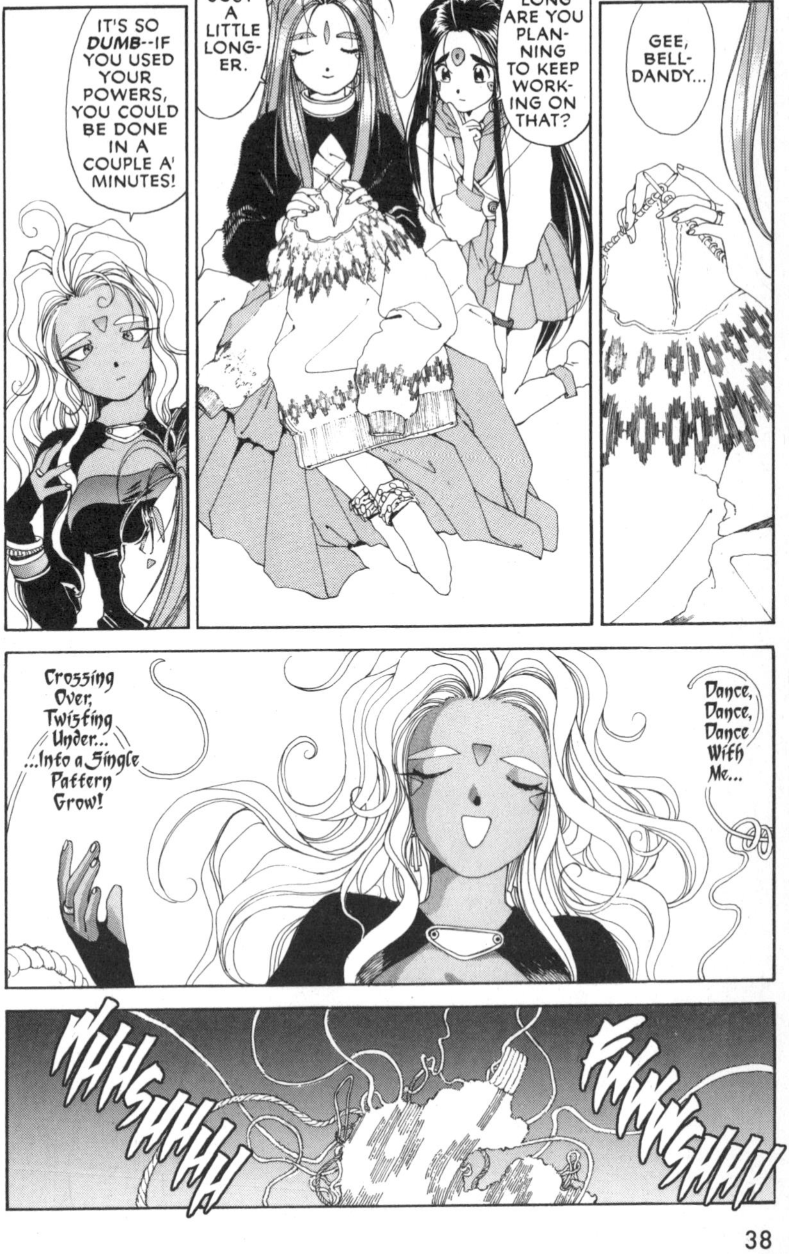
IT'S SO DUMB--IF YOU USED YOUR POWERS, YOU COULD BE DONE IN A COUPLE A' MINUTES!
...HOW LONG ARE YOU PLANNING TO KEEP WORKING ON THAT?
JUST A LITTLE LONGER.
GEE, BELLDANDY...
Crossing Over, Twisting Under... ...Into a Single Pattern Grow!
Dance, Dance, Dance With Me...

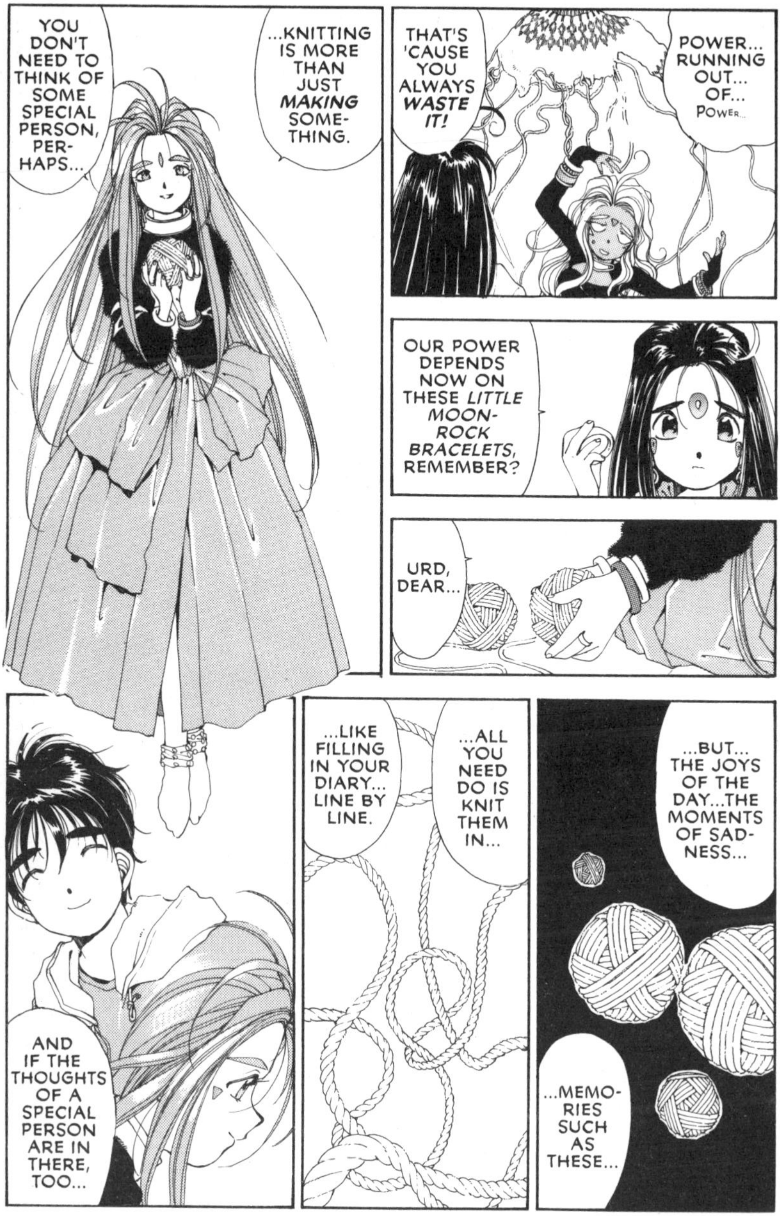
YOU DON'T NEED TO THINK OF SOME SPECIAL PERSON, PER-HAPS...
...KNITTING IS MORE THAN JUST *MAKING* SOME-THING.
THAT'S 'CAUSE YOU ALWAYS *WASTE IT!*
POWER... RUNNING OUT... OF... POWER...
OUR POWER DEPENDS NOW ON THESE *LITTLE MOON-ROCK BRACELETS,* REMEMBER?
URD, DEAR...
AND IF THE THOUGHTS OF A SPECIAL PERSON ARE IN THERE, TOO...
...LIKE FILLING IN YOUR DIARY... LINE BY LINE.
...ALL YOU NEED DO IS KNIT THEM IN...
...BUT... THE JOYS OF THE DAY...THE MOMENTS OF SAD-NESS...
...MEMO-RIES SUCH AS THESE...

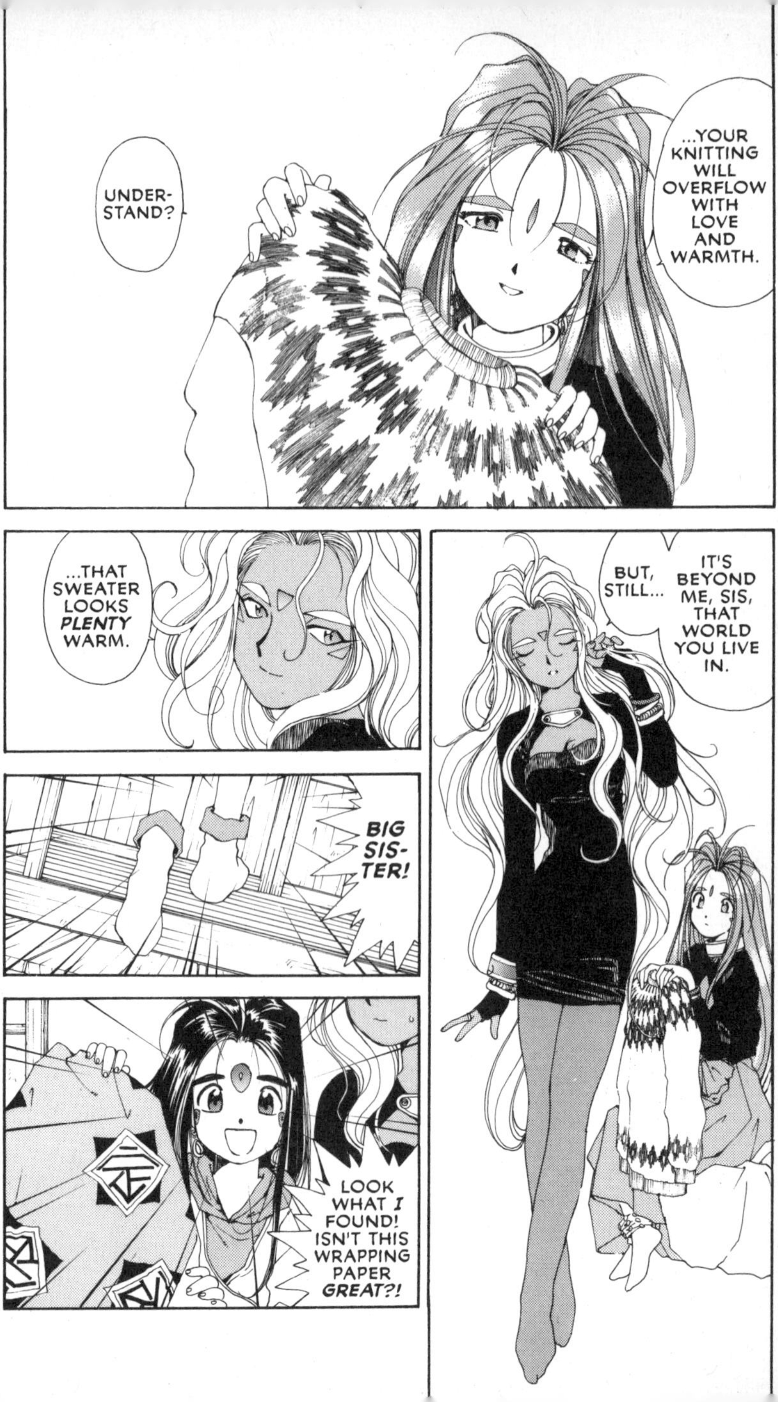
...YOUR KNITTING WILL OVERFLOW WITH LOVE AND WARMTH.
UNDER-STAND?
IT'S BEYOND ME, SIS, THAT WORLD YOU LIVE IN.
BUT, STILL...
...THAT SWEATER LOOKS PLENTY WARM.
BIG SIS-TER!
LOOK WHAT I FOUND! ISN'T THIS WRAPPING PAPER GREAT?!

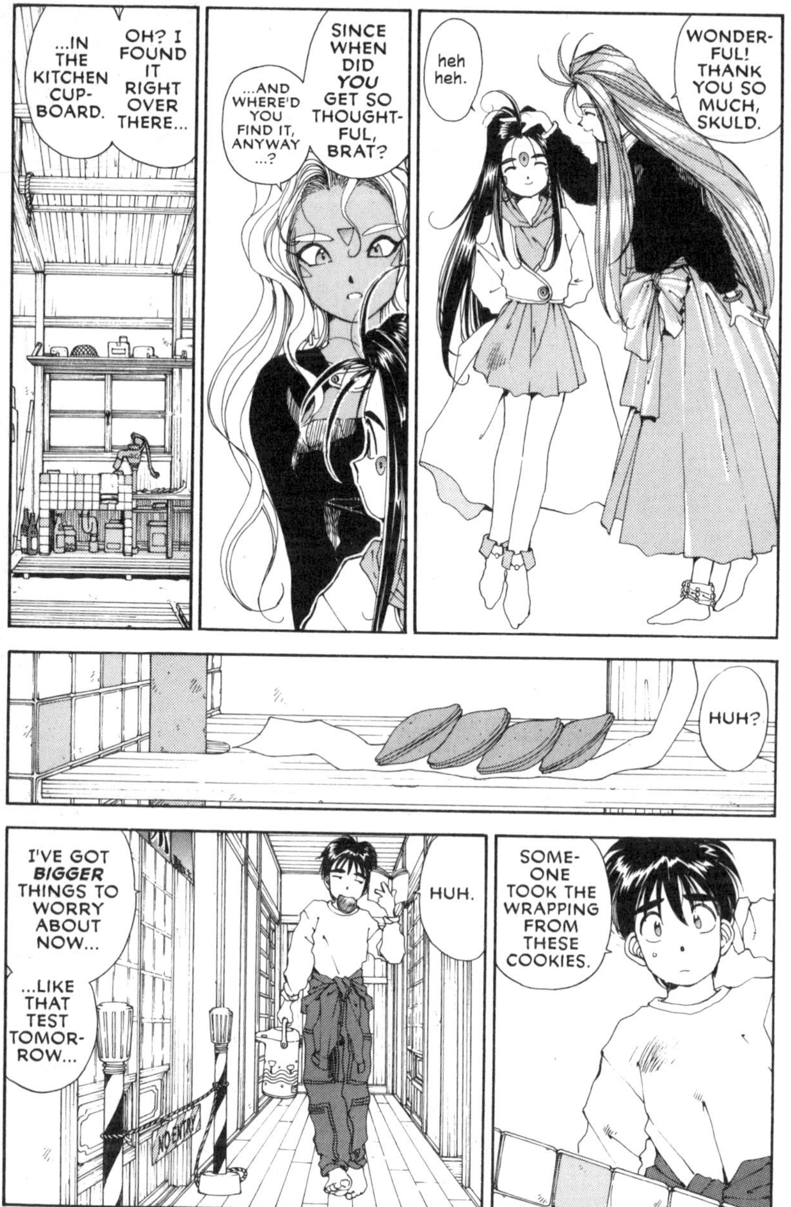
WONDERFUL! THANK YOU SO MUCH, SKULD.
heh heh.
SINCE WHEN DID YOU GET SO THOUGHTFUL, BRAT?
...AND WHERE'D YOU FIND IT, ANYWAY ...?
OH? I FOUND IT RIGHT OVER THERE...
...IN THE KITCHEN CUPBOARD.
HUH?
SOMEONE TOOK THE WRAPPING FROM THESE COOKIES.
HUH.
I'VE GOT BIGGER THINGS TO WORRY ABOUT NOW...
...LIKE THAT TEST TOMORROW...
NO ENTRY

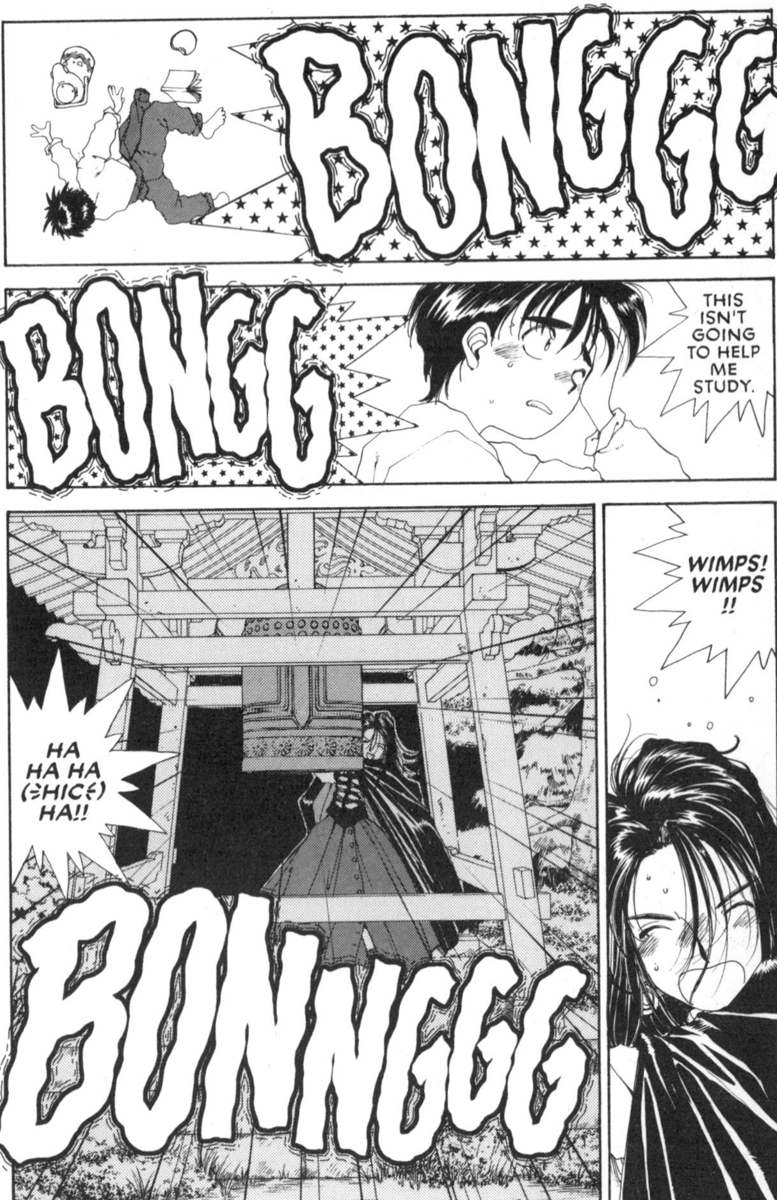
BONGGG
BONGG
THIS ISN'T GOING TO HELP ME STUDY.
WIMPS! WIMPS !!
HA HA HA (HIC) HA!!
BONNGGG

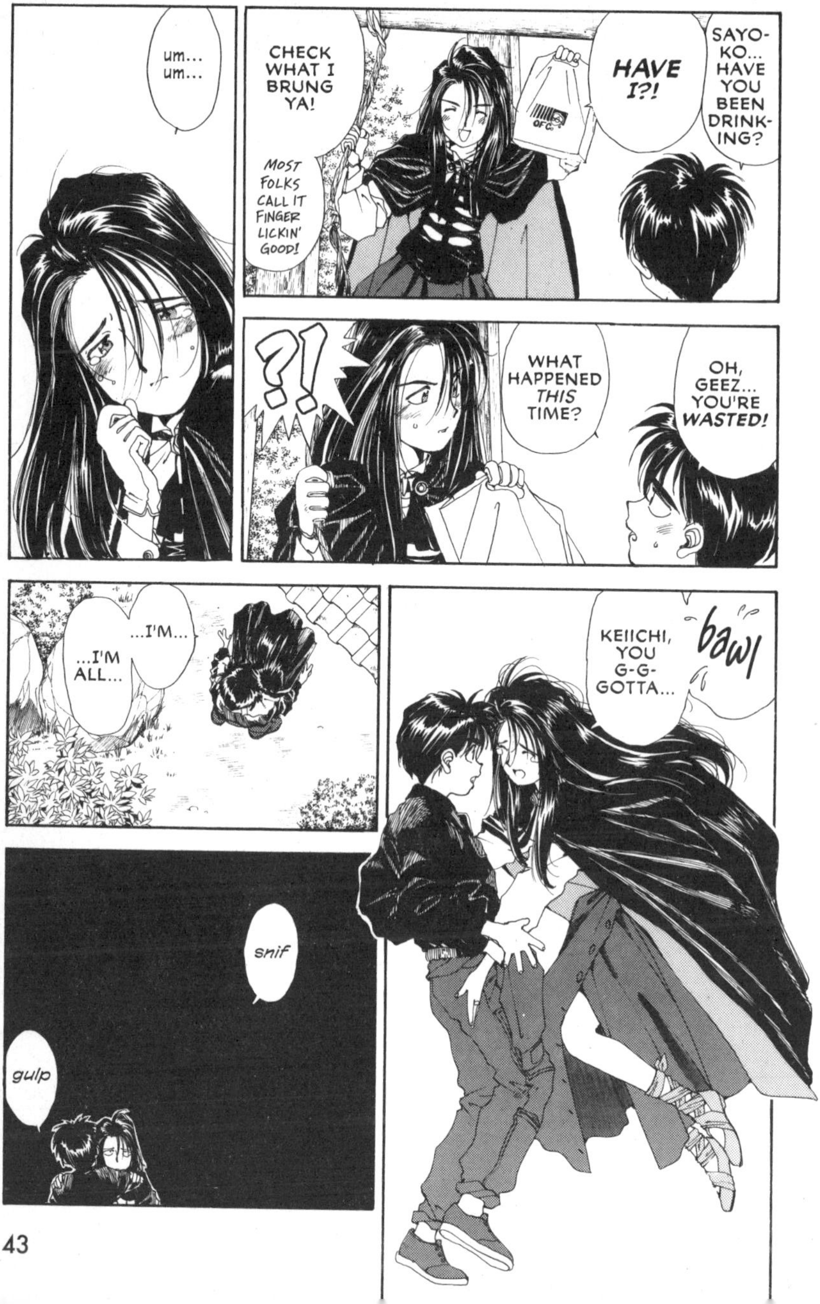

SAYO-KO... HAVE YOU BEEN DRINK-ING?
HAVE I?!
CHECK WHAT I BRUNG YA!
MOST FOLKS CALL IT FINGER LICKIN' GOOD!
OH, GEEZ... YOU'RE WASTED!
WHAT HAPPENED THIS TIME?
?!
um... um...
...I'M...
...I'M ALL...
KEIICHI, YOU G-G-GOTTA...
bawl
snif
gulp

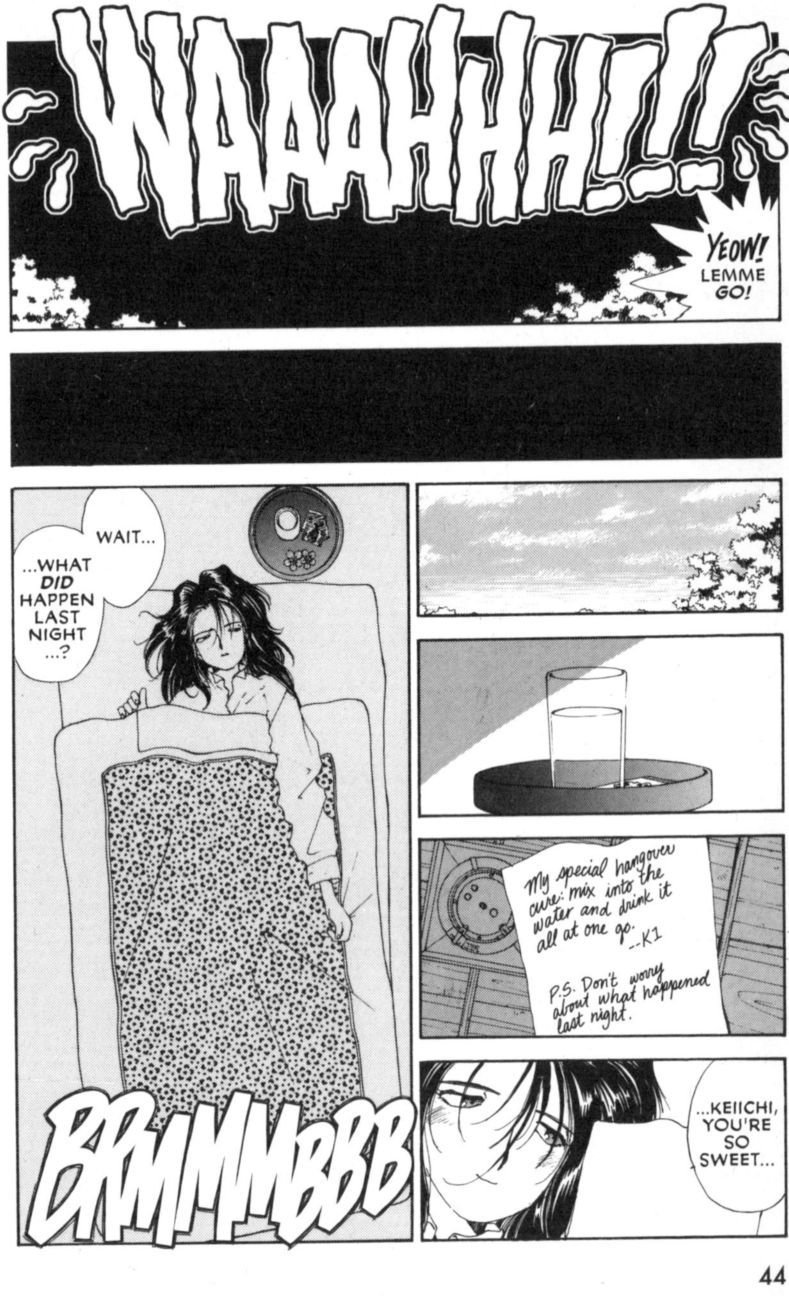
WAAAHHH!!!
YEOW! LEMME GO!
WAIT...
...WHAT DID HAPPEN LAST NIGHT ...?
My special hangover cure: mix into the water and drink it all at one go. --K1
P.S. Don't worry about what happened last night.
BRMMMBBB
...KEIICHI, YOU'RE SO SWEET...

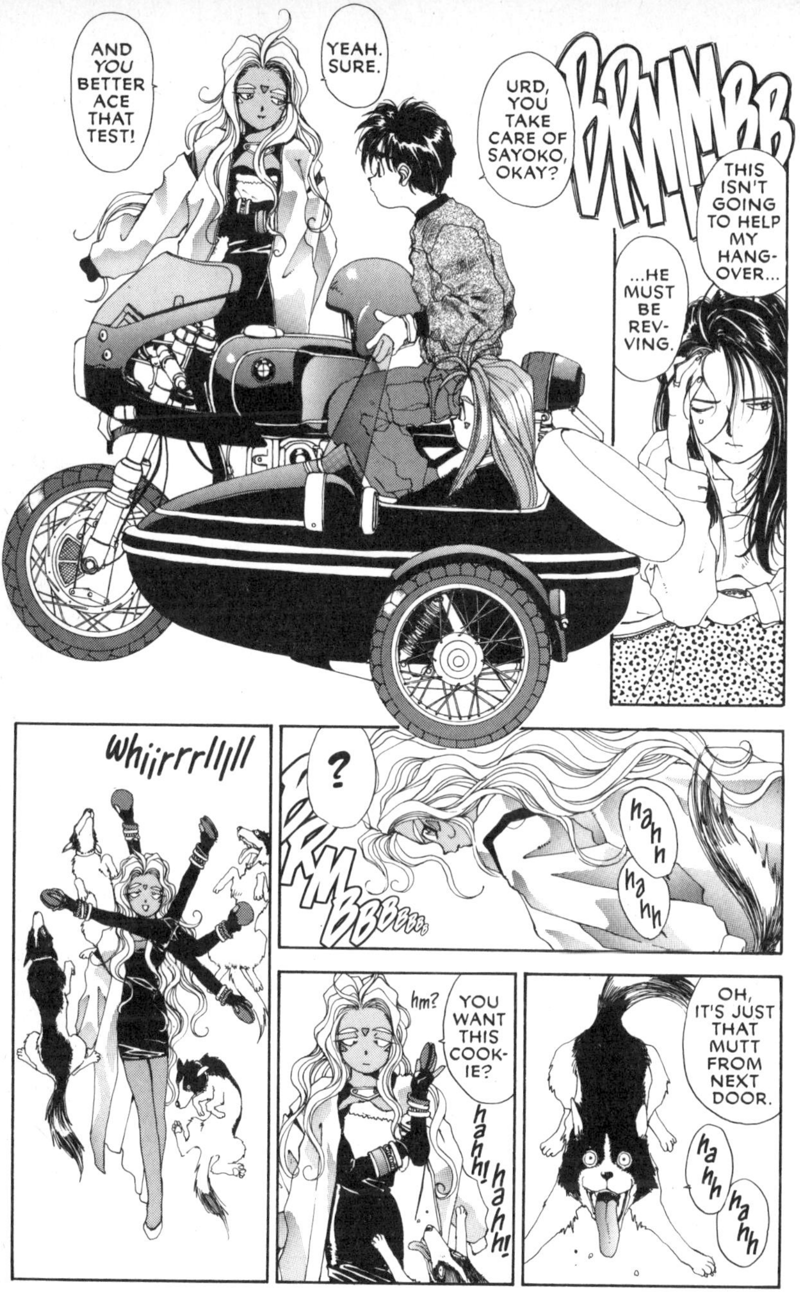
AND YOU BETTER ACE THAT TEST!
YEAH. SURE.
URD, YOU TAKE CARE OF SAYOKO, OKAY?
BRMMBB
THIS ISN'T GOING TO HELP MY HANG-OVER...
...HE MUST BE REV-VING.
Whiirrrllll
?
BRMMBBBBBB
hahh hahh
hm?
YOU WANT THIS COOK-IE?
hahh! hahh! hahh!
OH, IT'S JUST THAT MUTT FROM NEXT DOOR.
hahh hahh

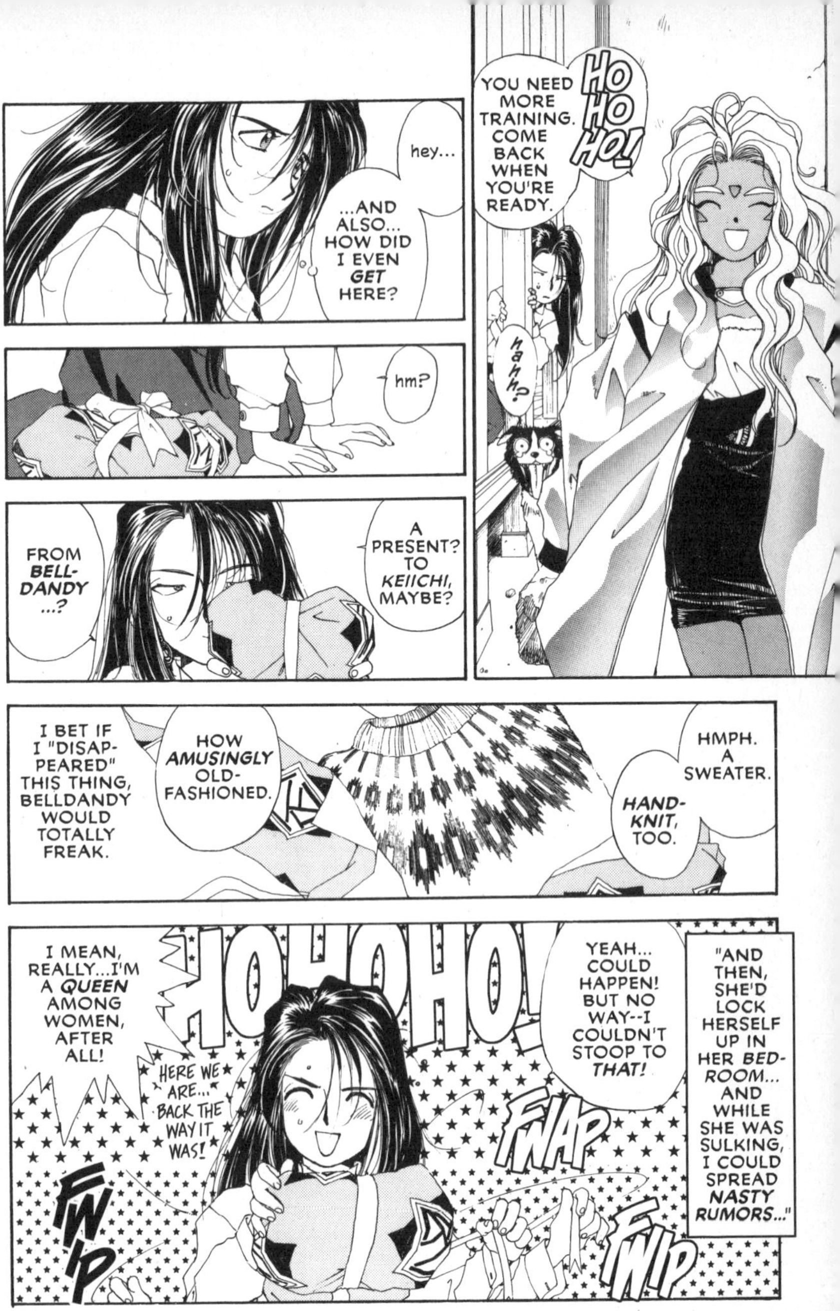
hey...
...AND ALSO... HOW DID I EVEN GET HERE?
hm?
A PRESENT? TO KEIICHI, MAYBE?
FROM BELLDANDY ...?
HO HO HO!
YOU NEED MORE TRAINING. COME BACK WHEN YOU'RE READY.
hahh?
HMPH. A SWEATER.
HAND-KNIT, TOO.
HOW AMUSINGLY OLD-FASHIONED.
I BET IF I "DISAPPEARED" THIS THING, BELLDANDY WOULD TOTALLY FREAK.
"AND THEN, SHE'D LOCK HERSELF UP IN HER BEDROOM... AND WHILE SHE WAS SULKING, I COULD SPREAD NASTY RUMORS..."
YEAH... COULD HAPPEN! BUT NO WAY--I COULDN'T STOOP TO THAT!
HOHOHO!
I MEAN, REALLY...I'M A QUEEN AMONG WOMEN, AFTER ALL!
HERE WE ARE... BACK THE WAY IT WAS!
FWAP
FWIP
FWIP

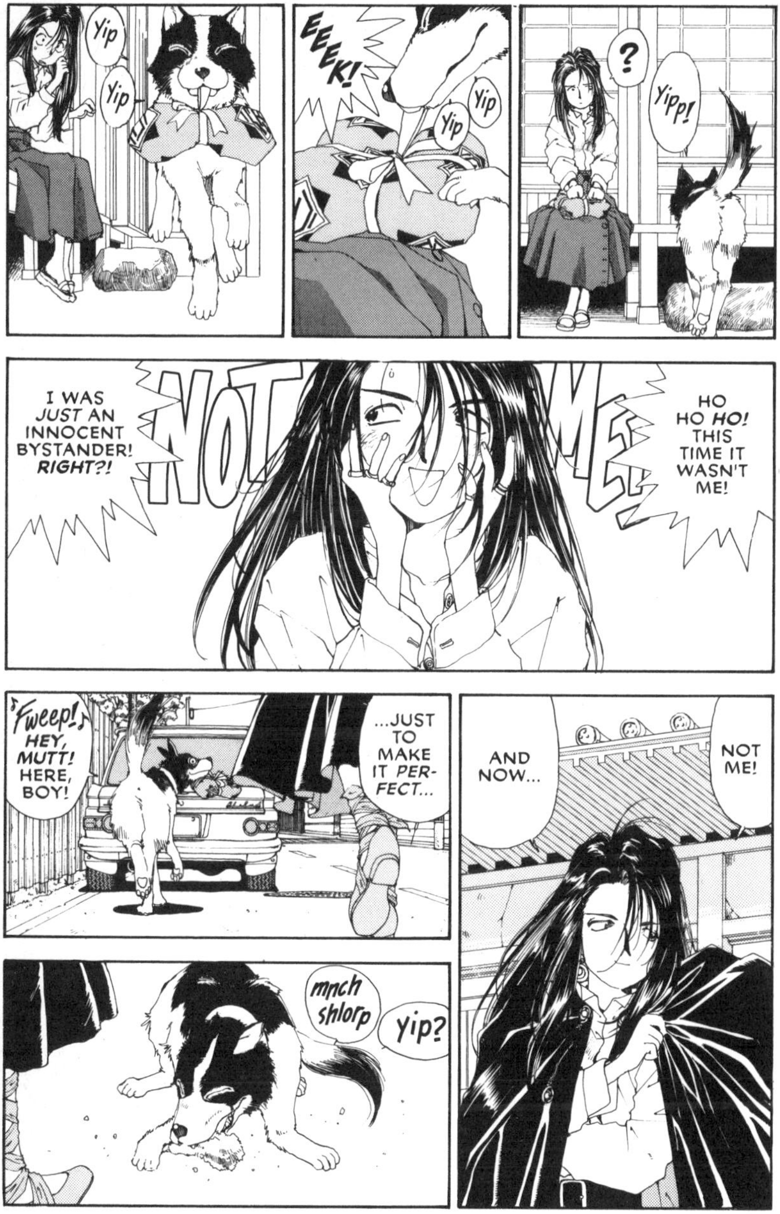
Yip
Yip
EEEK!
Yip
Yip
?
Yipp!
I WAS JUST AN INNOCENT BYSTANDER! RIGHT?!
HO HO HO! THIS TIME IT WASN'T ME!
Fweep!
HEY, MUTT! HERE, BOY!
...JUST TO MAKE IT PERFECT...
AND NOW...
NOT ME!
mnch shlorp
yip?

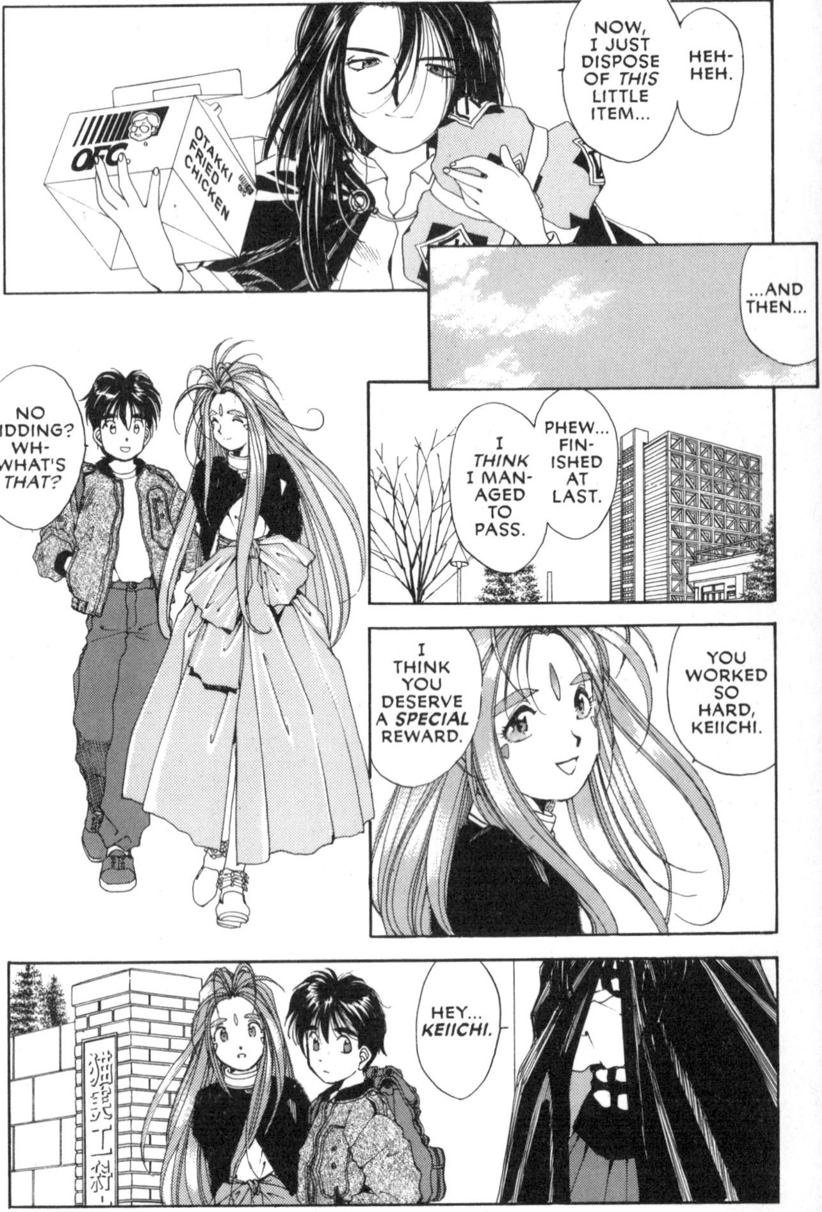
OFC
OTAKKI FRIED CHICKEN
NOW, I JUST DISPOSE OF *THIS* LITTLE ITEM...
HEH-HEH.
...AND THEN...
PHEW... FIN-ISHED AT LAST.
I *THINK* I MAN-AGED TO PASS.
YOU WORKED SO HARD, KEIICHI.
I THINK YOU DESERVE A *SPECIAL* REWARD.
NO KIDDING? WH-WHAT'S *THAT?*
HEY... ***KEIICHI.***

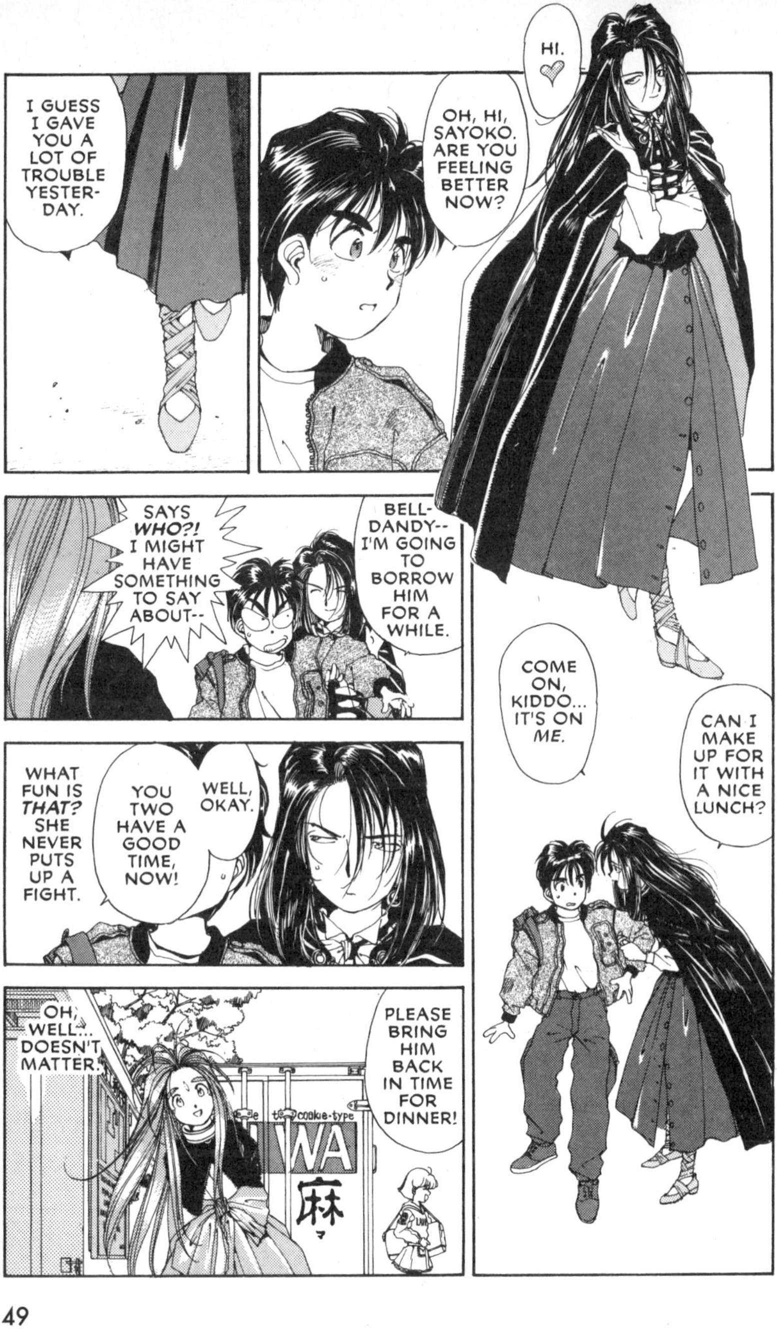
HI. ♡
OH, HI, SAYOKO. ARE YOU FEELING BETTER NOW?
I GUESS I GAVE YOU A LOT OF TROUBLE YESTER-DAY.
CAN I MAKE UP FOR IT WITH A NICE LUNCH?
COME ON, KIDDO... IT'S ON *ME.*
BELL-DANDY-- I'M GOING TO BORROW HIM FOR A WHILE.
SAYS *WHO?!* I MIGHT HAVE SOMETHING TO SAY ABOUT--
WELL, OKAY.
YOU TWO HAVE A GOOD TIME, NOW!
WHAT FUN IS *THAT?* SHE NEVER PUTS UP A FIGHT.
PLEASE BRING HIM BACK IN TIME FOR DINNER!
OH, WELL... DOESN'T MATTER.
cookie-type
WA
麻

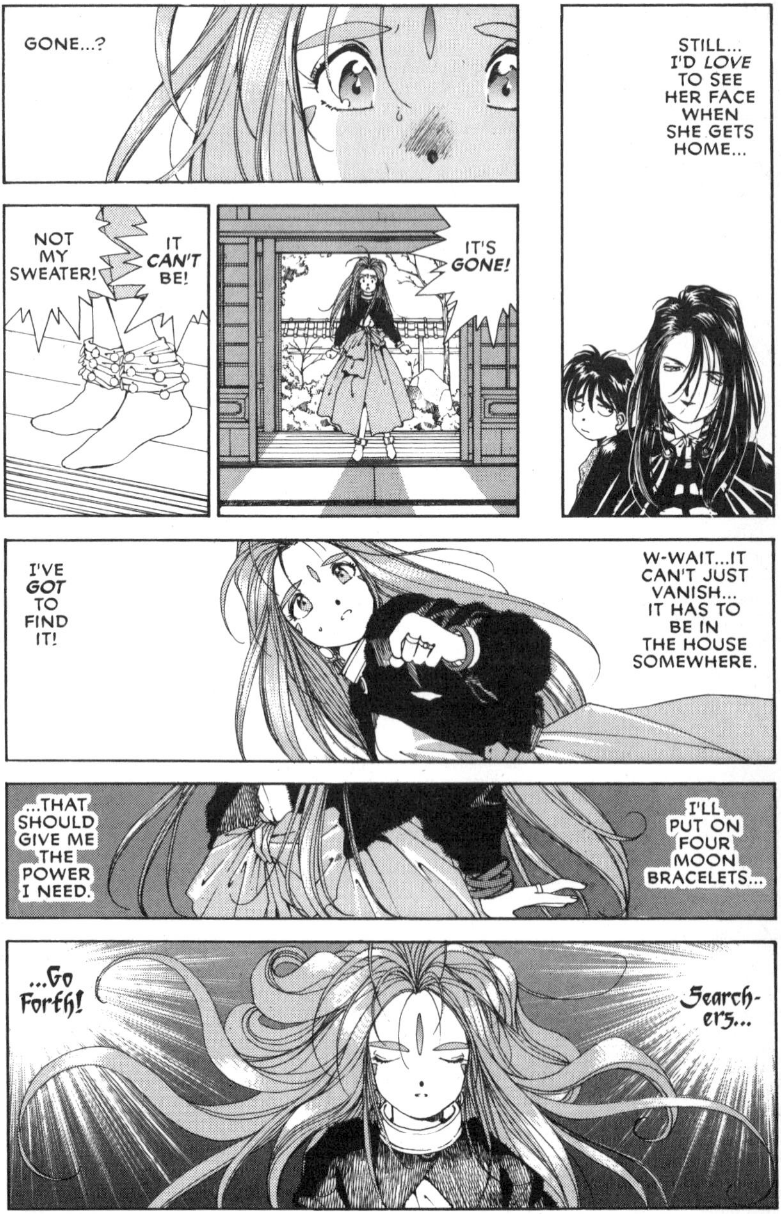
GONE...?
NOT MY SWEATER!
IT CAN'T BE!
IT'S GONE!
STILL... I'D LOVE TO SEE HER FACE WHEN SHE GETS HOME...
I'VE GOT TO FIND IT!
W-WAIT...IT CAN'T JUST VANISH... IT HAS TO BE IN THE HOUSE SOMEWHERE.
I'LL PUT ON FOUR MOON BRACELETS...
...THAT SHOULD GIVE ME THE POWER I NEED.
Searchers...
...Go Forth!

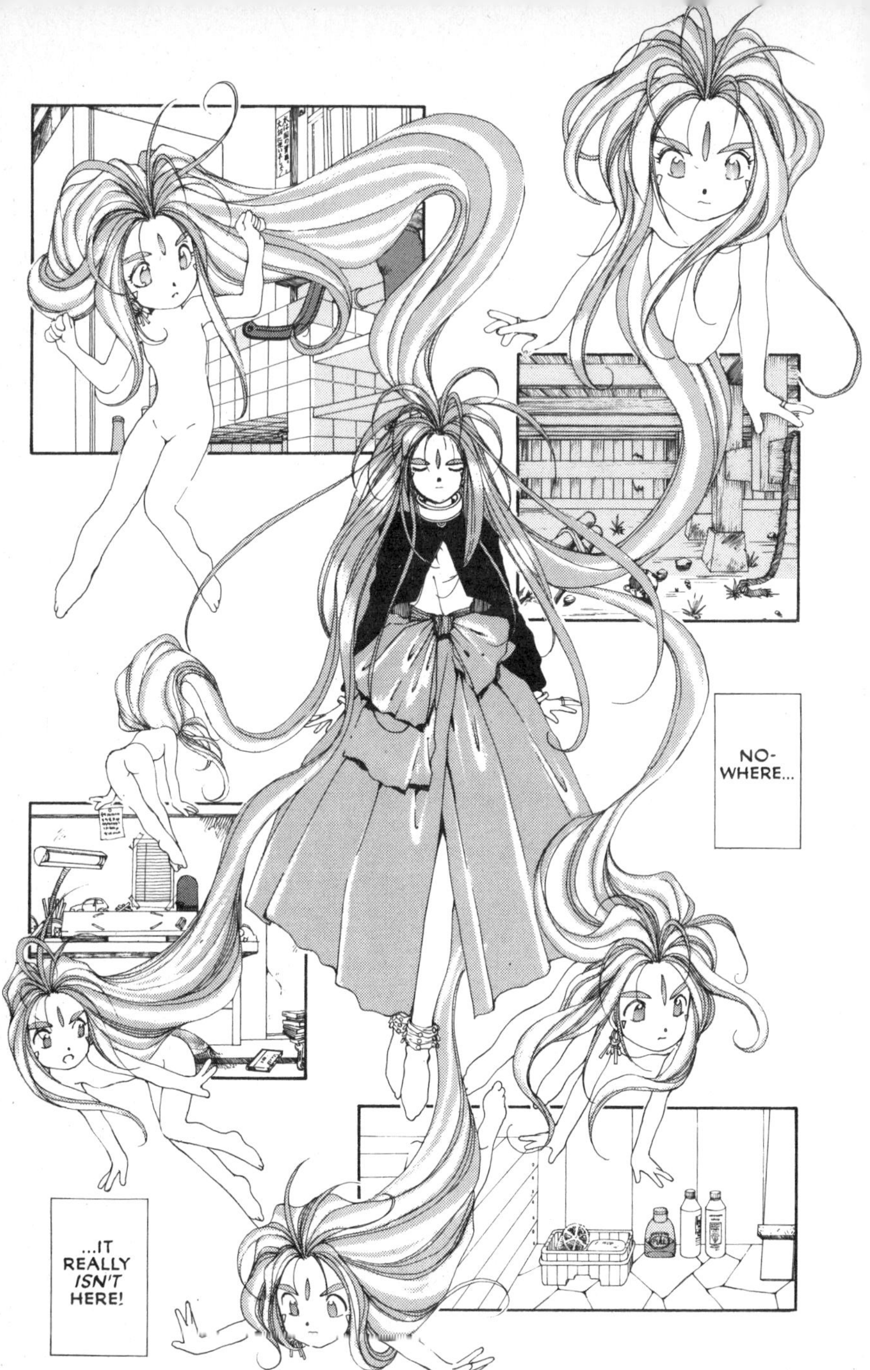
NO-WHERE...
...IT REALLY *ISN'T* HERE!

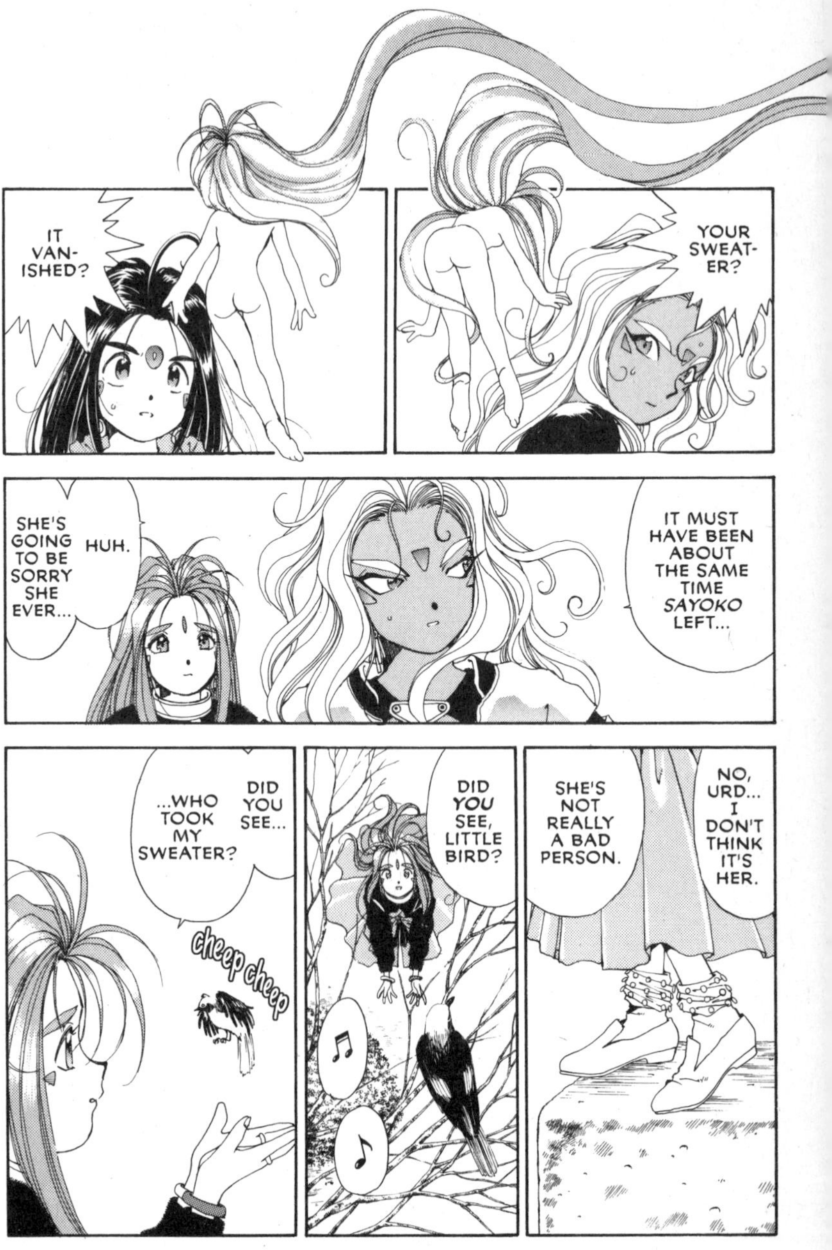
YOUR SWEATER?
IT VANISHED?
IT MUST HAVE BEEN ABOUT THE SAME TIME SAYOKO LEFT...
HUH.
SHE'S GOING TO BE SORRY SHE EVER...
NO, URD... I DON'T THINK IT'S HER.
SHE'S NOT REALLY A BAD PERSON.
DID YOU SEE, LITTLE BIRD?
DID YOU SEE...
...WHO TOOK MY SWEATER?
cheep cheep

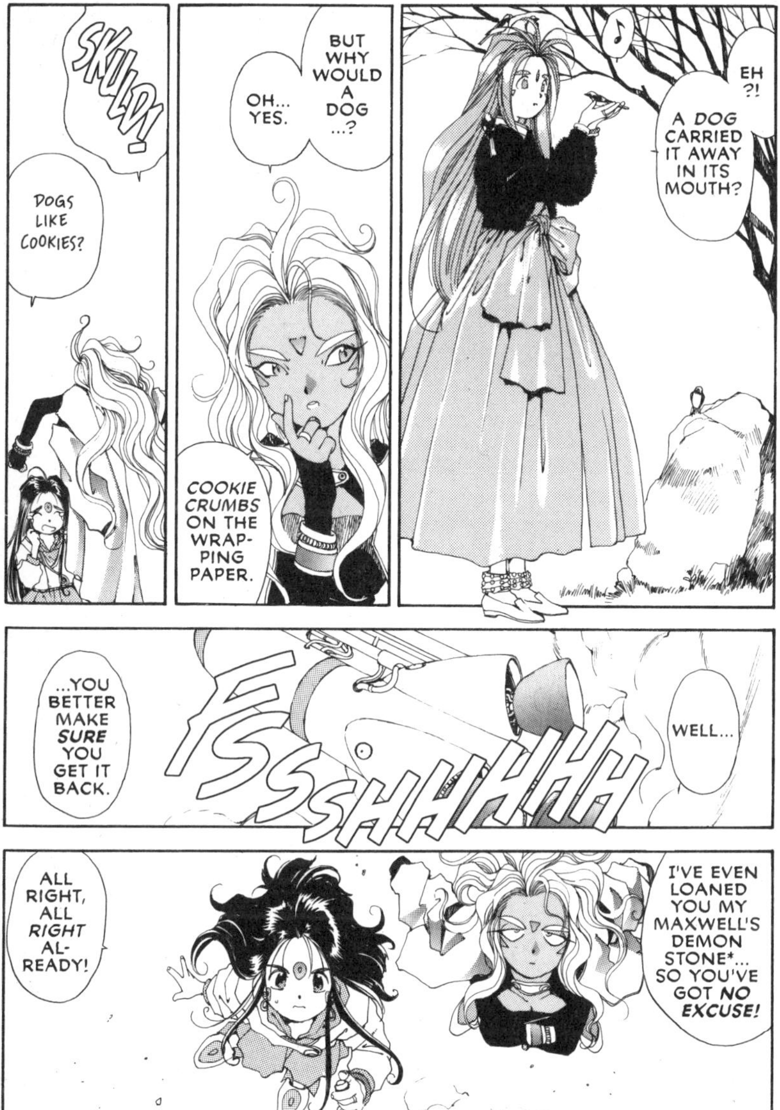
EH ?!
A *DOG* CARRIED IT AWAY IN ITS MOUTH?
BUT WHY WOULD A DOG ...?
OH... YES.
COOKIE CRUMBS ON THE WRAP-PING PAPER.
SKULD!
DOGS LIKE COOKIES?
WELL...
FSSSHHHHHH
...YOU BETTER MAKE ***SURE*** YOU GET IT BACK.
I'VE EVEN LOANED YOU MY MAXWELL'S DEMON STONE*... SO YOU'VE GOT ***NO EXCUSE!***
ALL RIGHT, ALL *RIGHT* AL-READY!

*SEE OH MY GODDESS! VOL. 3 P. 120-122!**

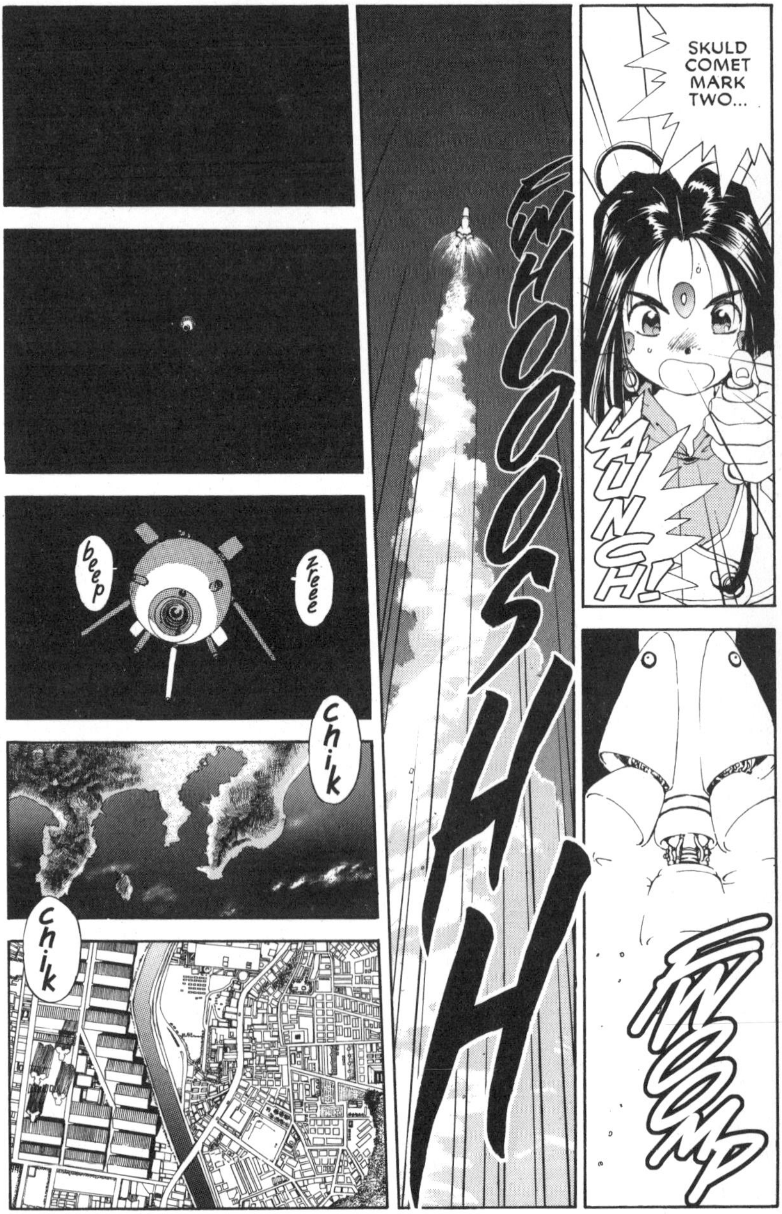

SKULD COMET MARK TWO...
LAUNCH!
FWOOOMP
FWHOOOOOSHHH
beep
zreee
chik
chik

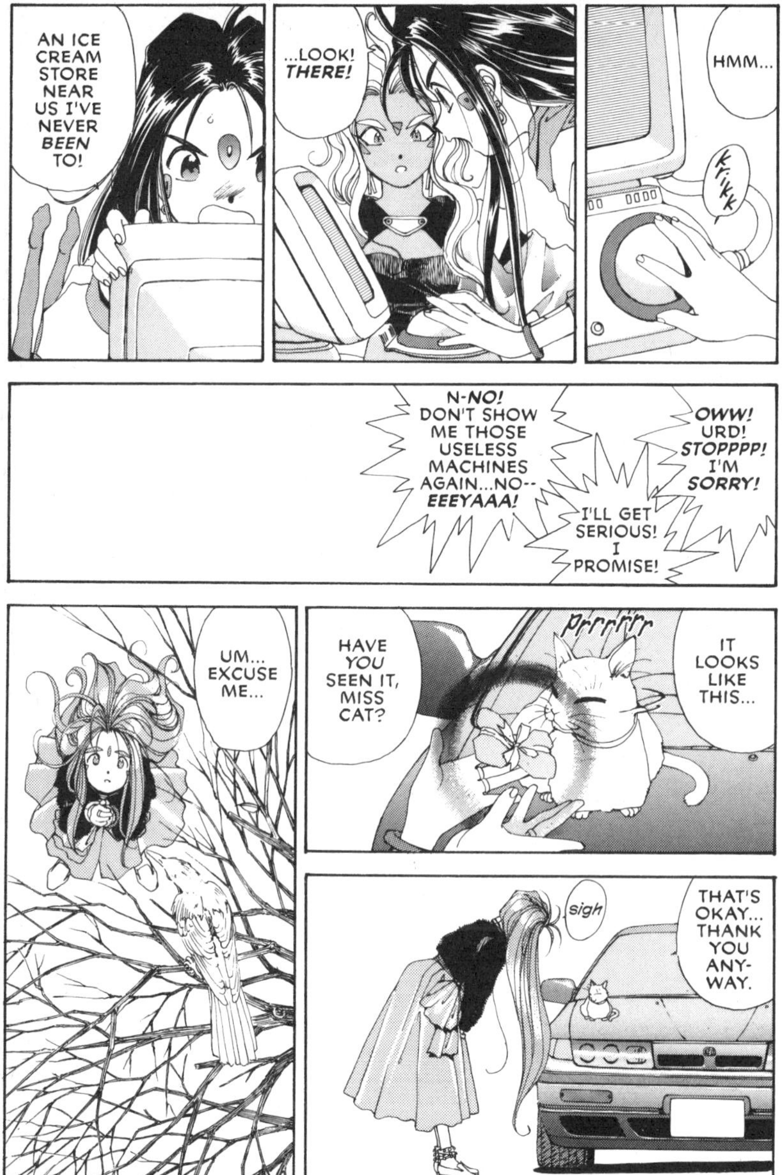
AN ICE CREAM STORE NEAR US I'VE NEVER *BEEN* TO!
...LOOK! *THERE!*
HMM...
krikk
N-*NO!* DON'T SHOW ME THOSE USELESS MACHINES AGAIN...NO-- *EEEYAAA!*
OWW! URD! *STOPPPP!* I'M *SORRY!*
I'LL GET SERIOUS! I PROMISE!
UM... EXCUSE ME...
HAVE *YOU* SEEN IT, MISS CAT?
Prrrrrr
IT LOOKS LIKE THIS...
sigh
THAT'S OKAY... THANK YOU ANYWAY.

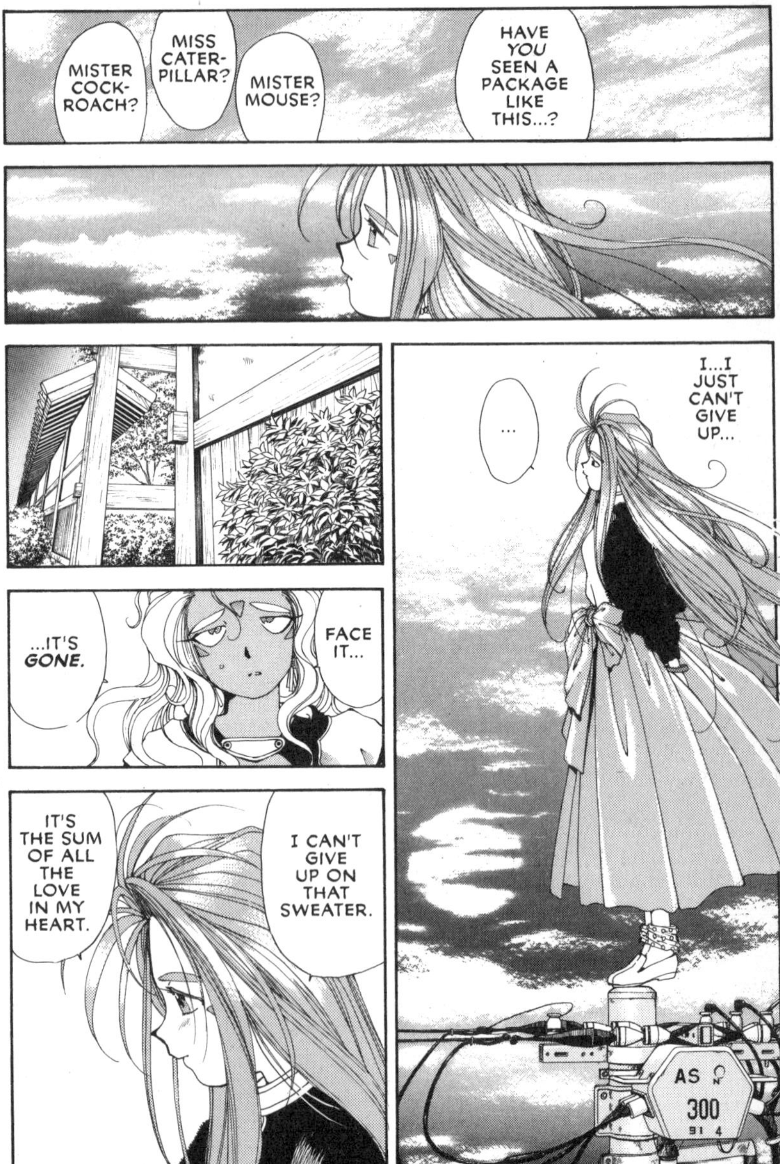
MISTER COCK-ROACH?
MISS CATER-PILLAR?
MISTER MOUSE?
HAVE *YOU* SEEN A PACKAGE LIKE THIS...?
...
I...I JUST CAN'T GIVE UP...
FACE IT...
...IT'S ***GONE.***
I CAN'T GIVE UP ON THAT SWEATER.
IT'S THE SUM OF ALL THE LOVE IN MY HEART.
AS
300

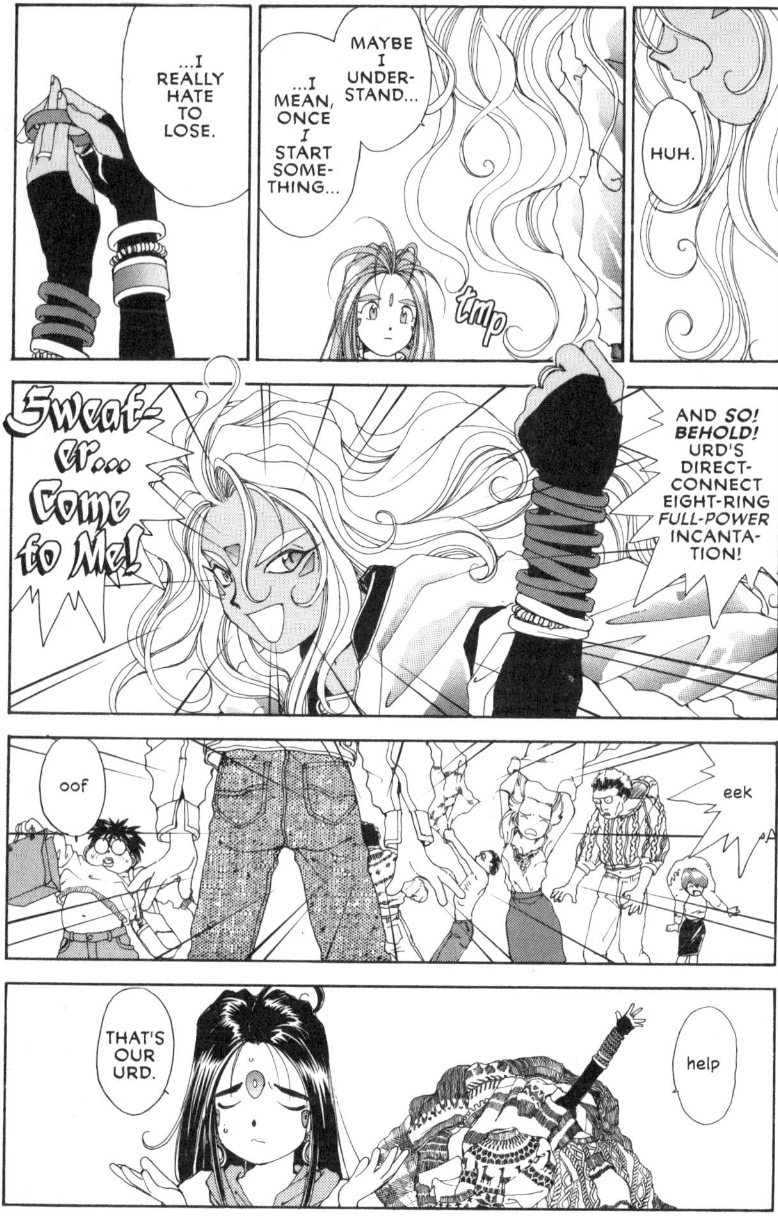
...I REALLY HATE TO LOSE.
MAYBE I UNDERSTAND...
...I MEAN, ONCE I START SOMETHING...
tmp
HUH.
Sweat-er... Come to Me!
AND SO! BEHOLD! URD'S DIRECT-CONNECT EIGHT-RING FULL-POWER INCANTATION!
oof
eek
THAT'S OUR URD.
help

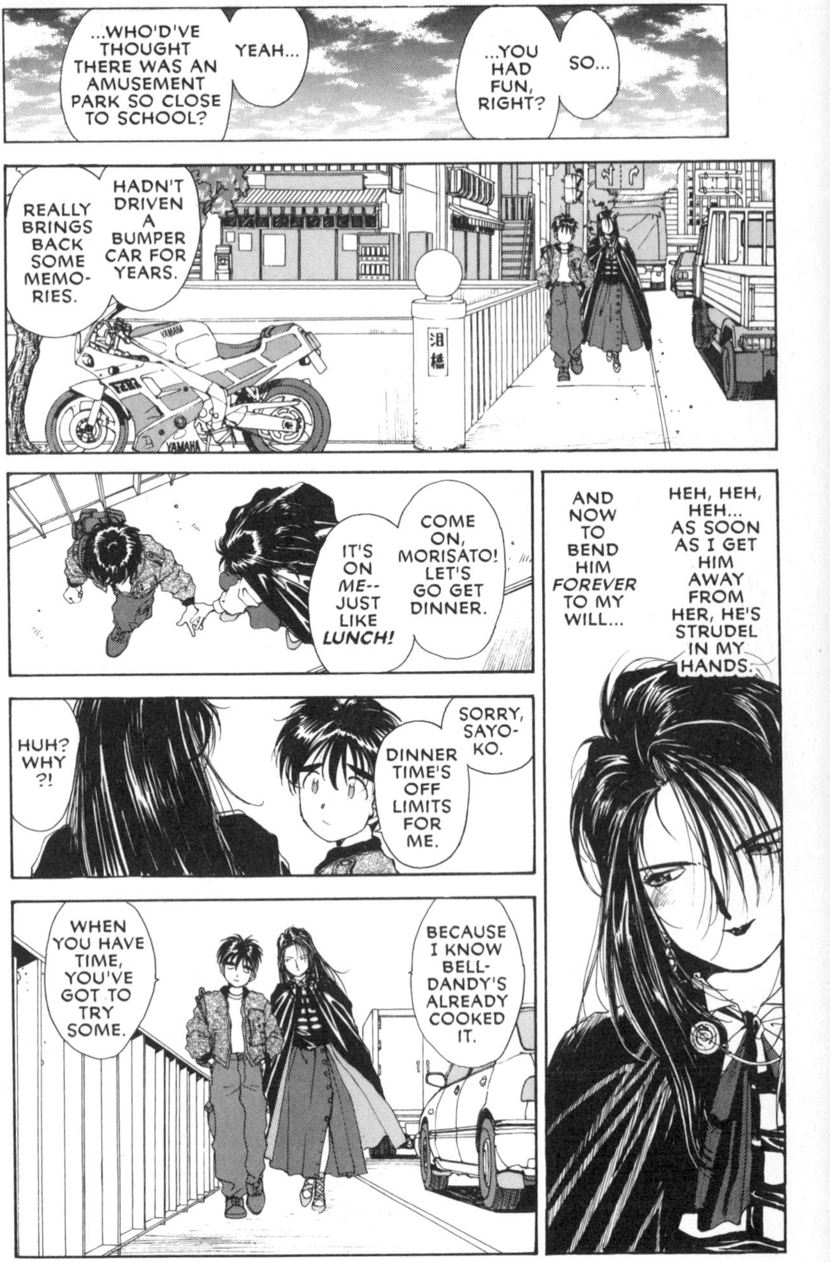
SO...
...YOU HAD FUN, RIGHT?
YEAH...
...WHO'D'VE THOUGHT THERE WAS AN AMUSEMENT PARK SO CLOSE TO SCHOOL?
HADN'T DRIVEN A BUMPER CAR FOR YEARS.
REALLY BRINGS BACK SOME MEMO-RIES.
HEH, HEH, HEH... AS SOON AS I GET HIM AWAY FROM HER, HE'S STRUDEL IN MY HANDS.
AND NOW TO BEND HIM *FOREVER* TO MY WILL...
COME ON, MORISATO! LET'S GO GET DINNER.
IT'S ON *ME*-- JUST LIKE ***LUNCH!***
SORRY, SAYO-KO.
DINNER TIME'S OFF LIMITS FOR ME.
HUH? WHY ?!
BECAUSE I KNOW BELL-DANDY'S ALREADY COOKED IT.
WHEN YOU HAVE TIME, YOU'VE GOT TO TRY SOME.

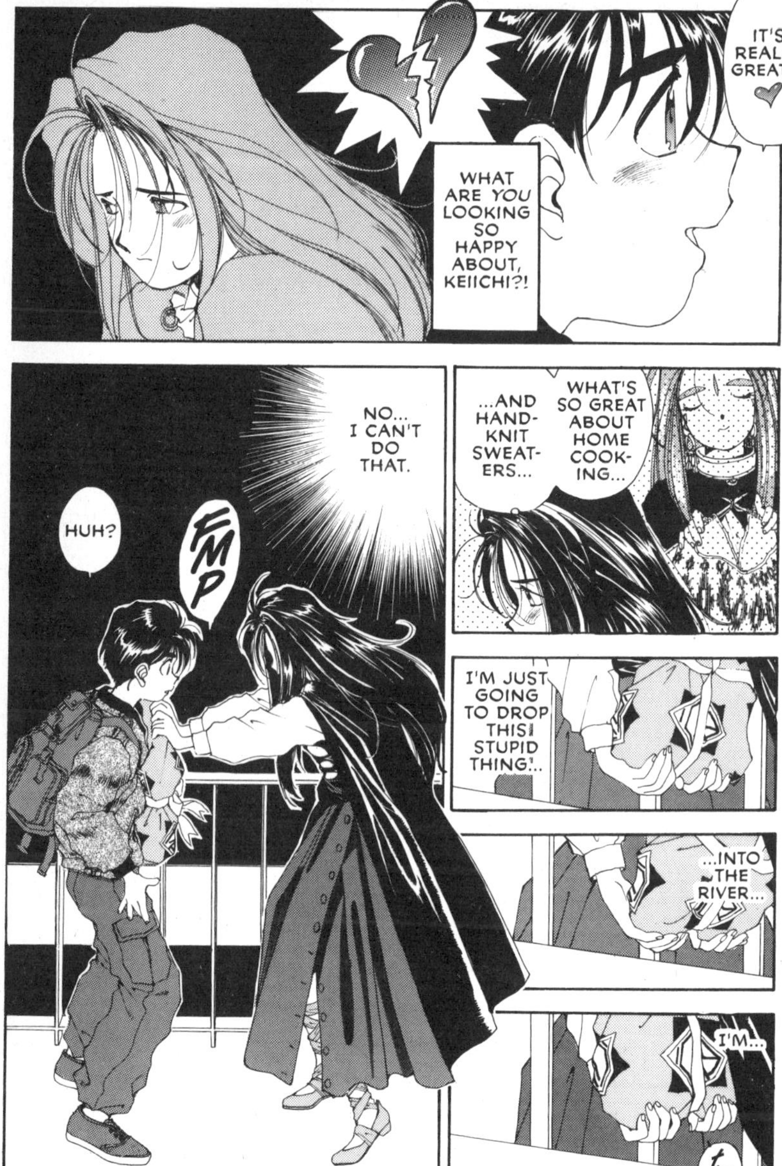
IT'S REALLY GREAT--!
WHAT ARE *YOU* LOOKING SO HAPPY ABOUT, KEIICHI?!
WHAT'S SO GREAT ABOUT HOME COOKING...
...AND HAND-KNIT SWEATERS...
I'M JUST GOING TO DROP THIS STUPID THING...
...INTO THE RIVER...
I'M...
tmp
NO... I CAN'T DO THAT.
FMP
HUH?

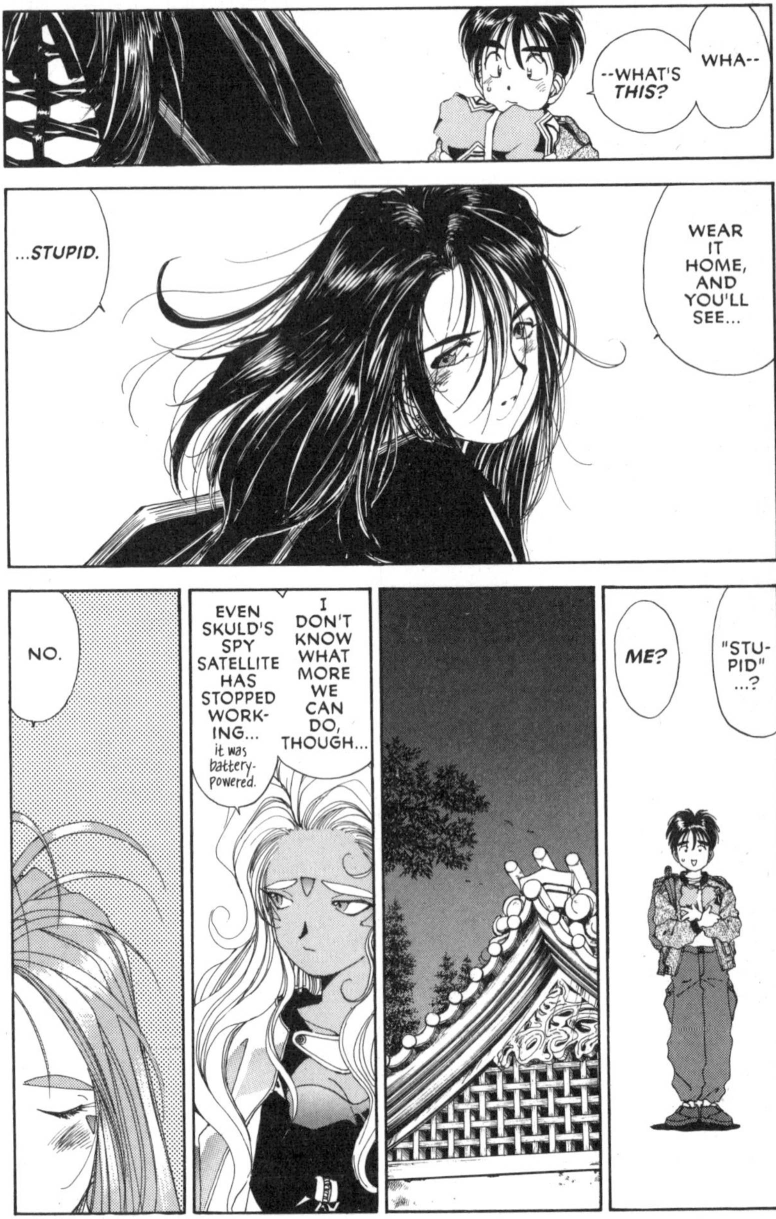
WHA--
--WHAT'S *THIS?*
WEAR IT HOME, AND YOU'LL SEE...
...*STUPID.*
"STUPID" ...?
ME?
I DON'T KNOW WHAT MORE WE CAN DO, THOUGH...
EVEN SKULD'S SPY SATELLITE HAS STOPPED WORKING...
it was battery-powered.
NO.

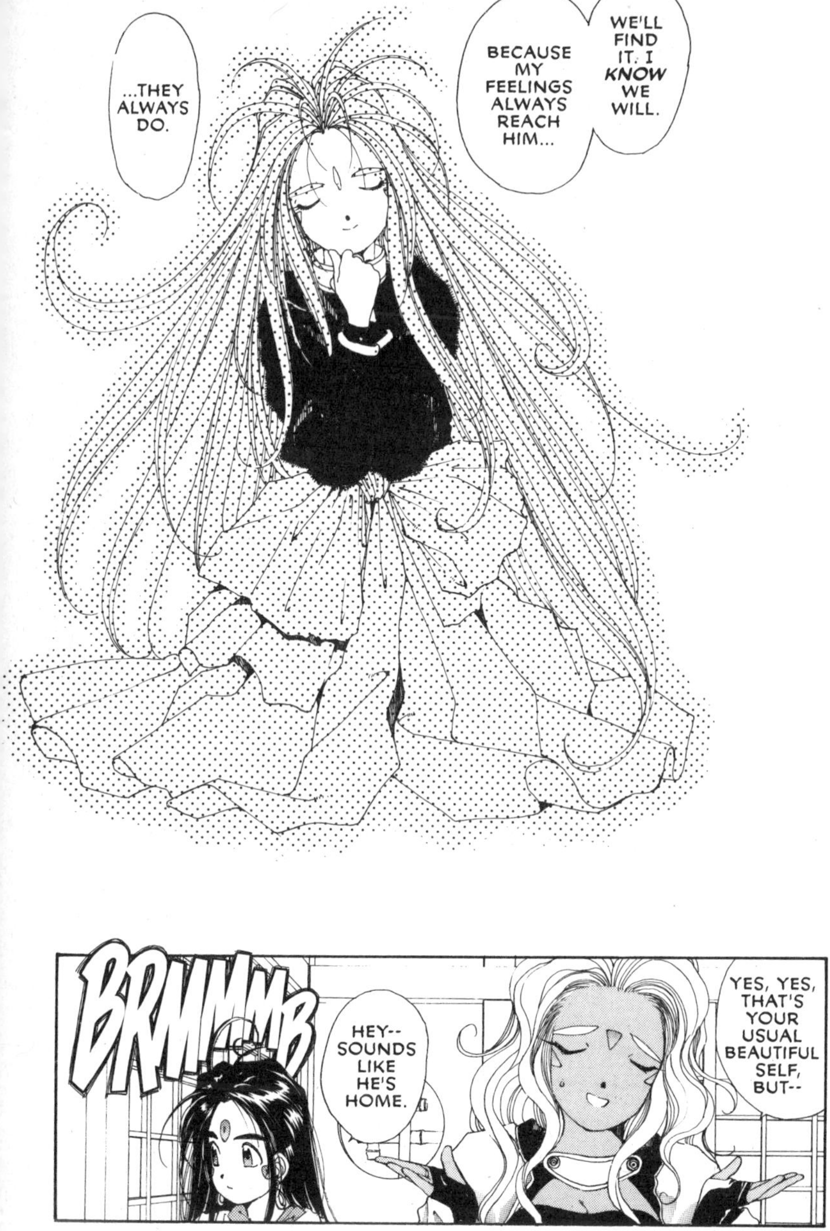
WE'LL FIND IT. I *KNOW* WE WILL.
BECAUSE MY FEELINGS ALWAYS REACH HIM...
...THEY ALWAYS DO.
YES, YES, THAT'S YOUR USUAL BEAUTIFUL SELF, BUT--
HEY-- SOUNDS LIKE HE'S HOME.
BRMMMB

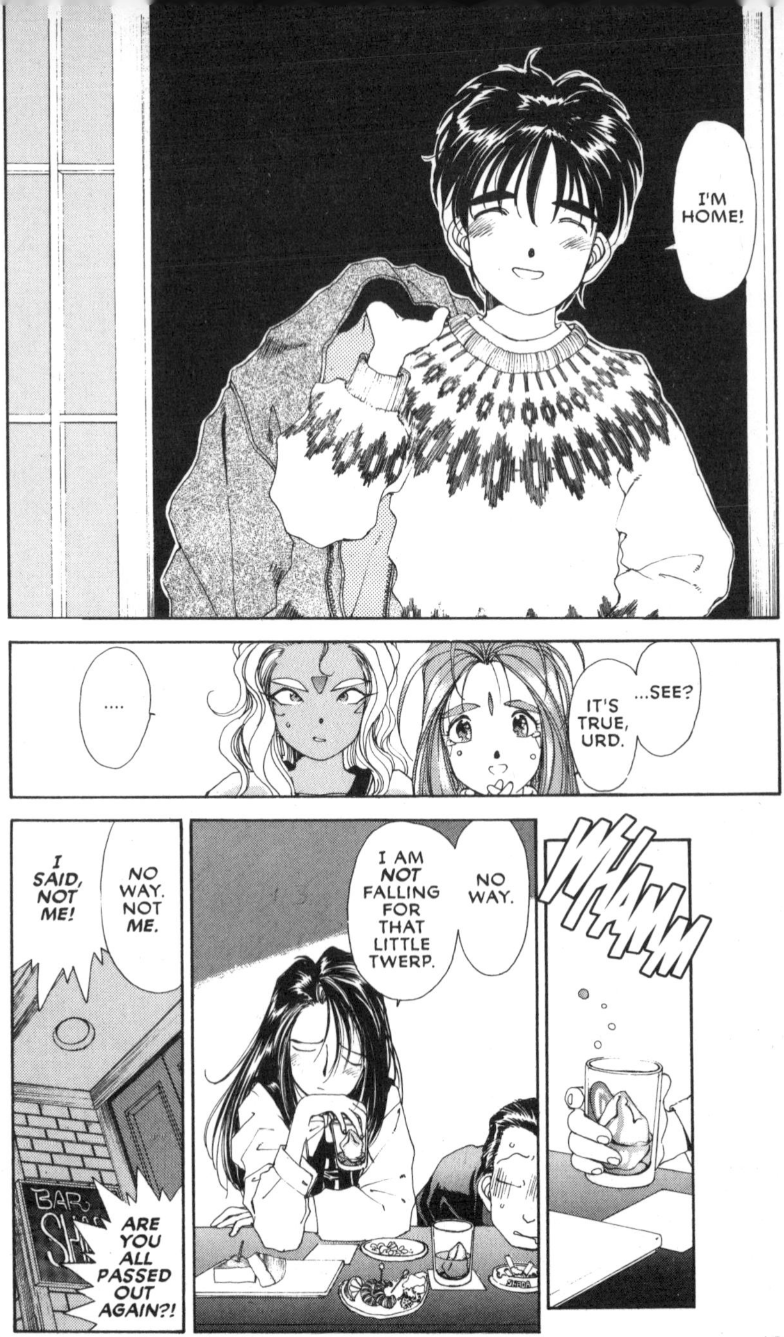
I'M HOME!
...SEE?
IT'S TRUE, URD.
....
WHAMM
NO WAY.
I AM *NOT* FALLING FOR THAT LITTLE TWERP.
NO WAY. NOT *ME.*
I SAID, NOT ME!
BAR
ARE YOU ALL PASSED OUT AGAIN?!

THE ADVENTURES OF MINI-URD

Now with added MINI-SKULD!

◆ STORMWRACK--A TALE OF BASEBALL ◆

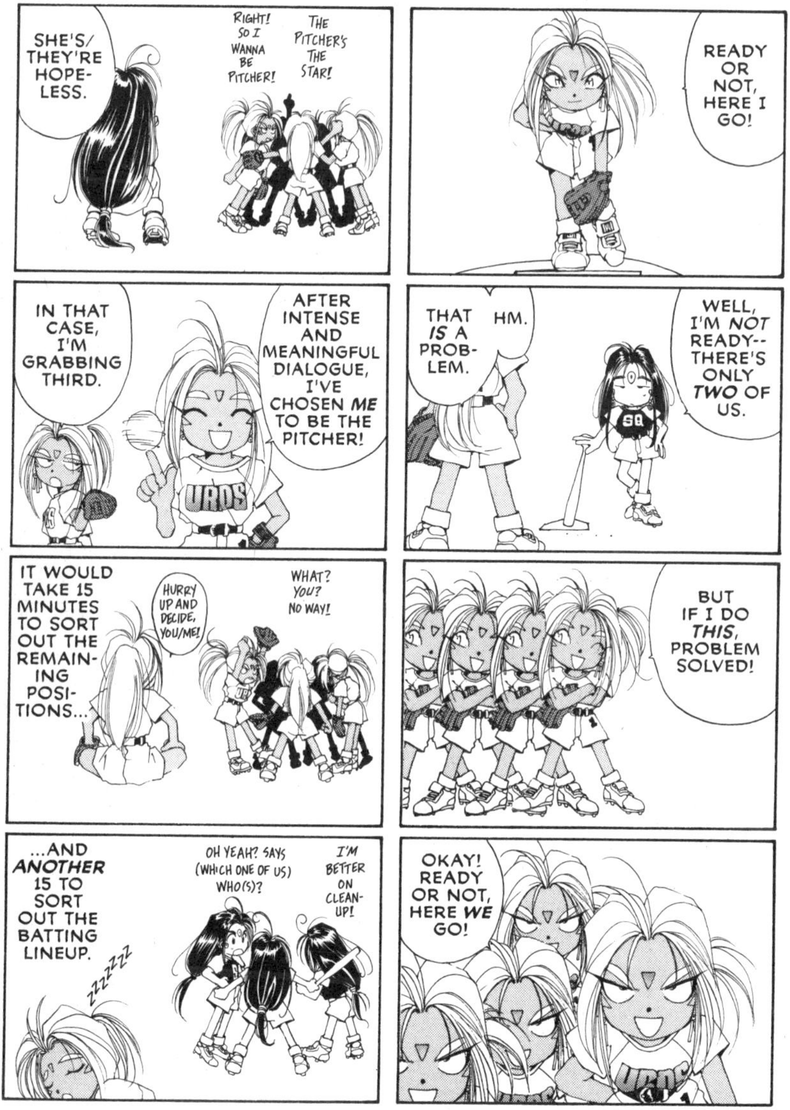

SHE'S/ THEY'RE HOPE- LESS.
RIGHT! SO I WANNA BE PITCHER!
THE PITCHER'S THE STAR!
READY OR NOT, HERE I GO!
AFTER INTENSE AND MEANINGFUL DIALOGUE, I'VE CHOSEN *ME* TO BE THE PITCHER!
IN THAT CASE, I'M GRABBING THIRD.
WELL, I'M *NOT* READY-- THERE'S ONLY *TWO* OF US.
HM.
THAT *IS* A PROB- LEM.
IT WOULD TAKE 15 MINUTES TO SORT OUT THE REMAIN- ING POSI- TIONS...
HURRY UP AND DECIDE, YOU/ME!
WHAT? YOU? NO WAY!
BUT IF I DO *THIS*, PROBLEM SOLVED!
...AND *ANOTHER* 15 TO SORT OUT THE BATTING LINEUP.
OH YEAH? SAYS (WHICH ONE OF US) WHO(S)?
I'M BETTER ON CLEAN- UP!
ZZZZZZZ
OKAY! READY OR NOT, HERE *WE* GO!

◆ STORMWRACK--A TALE OF BASEBALL (PART DEUX) ◆

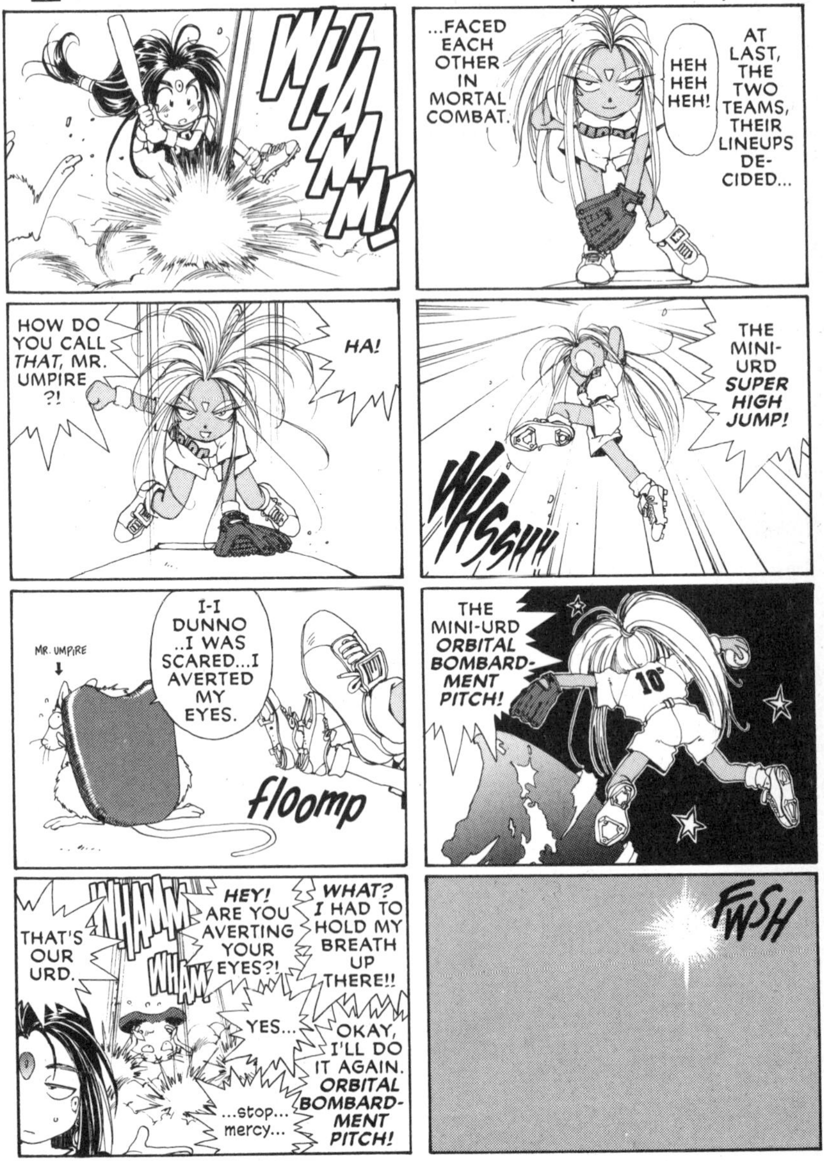
AT LAST, THE TWO TEAMS, THEIR LINEUPS DECIDED...
HEH HEH HEH!
...FACED EACH OTHER IN MORTAL COMBAT.
THE MINI-URD *SUPER HIGH JUMP!*
WHSSHH
THE MINI-URD *ORBITAL BOMBARDMENT PITCH!*
FWSH
WHAMM!
HA!
HOW DO YOU CALL *THAT*, MR. UMPIRE?!
I-I DUNNO ..I WAS SCARED...I AVERTED MY EYES.
MR. UMPIRE
floomp
WHAT? I HAD TO HOLD MY BREATH UP THERE!!
HEY! ARE YOU AVERTING YOUR EYES?!
WHAMM
WHAM
THAT'S OUR URD.
YES...
OKAY, I'LL DO IT AGAIN. *ORBITAL BOMBARDMENT PITCH!*
...stop... mercy...

◊STORMWRACK--A TALE OF BASEBALL (PART DER DRITTE)◊

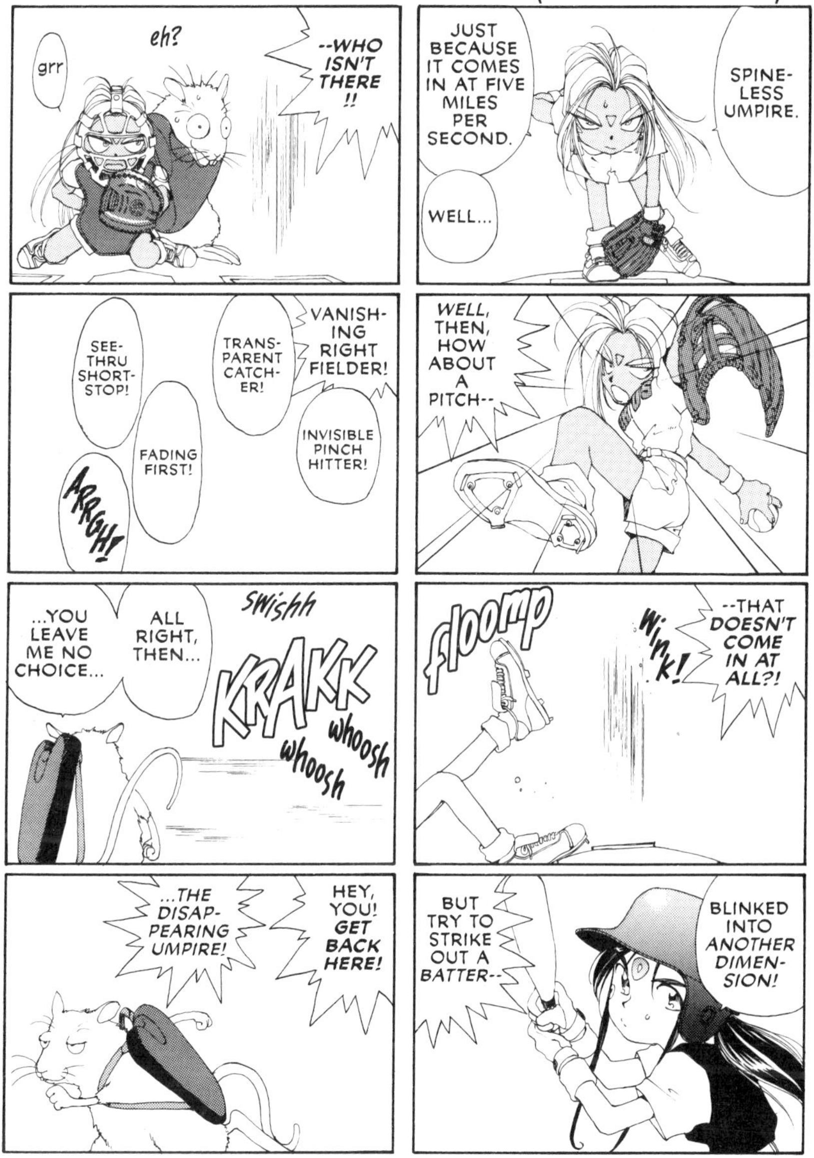
SPINE-LESS UMPIRE.
JUST BECAUSE IT COMES IN AT FIVE MILES PER SECOND.
WELL...
WELL, THEN, HOW ABOUT A PITCH--
--THAT DOESN'T COME IN AT ALL?!
Wink!
floomp
BLINKED INTO ANOTHER DIMEN-SION!
BUT TRY TO STRIKE OUT A BATTER--
--WHO ISN'T THERE!!
eh?
grr
VANISH-ING RIGHT FIELDER!
TRANS-PARENT CATCH-ER!
SEE-THRU SHORT-STOP!
INVISIBLE PINCH HITTER!
FADING FIRST!
ARRGH!
ALL RIGHT, THEN...
...YOU LEAVE ME NO CHOICE...
SWishh
KRAKK
whoosh
whoosh
HEY, YOU! GET BACK HERE!
...THE DISAP-PEARING UMPIRE!

STORMWRACK--A TALE OF BASEBALL (WHATEVER COMES AFTER THAT)

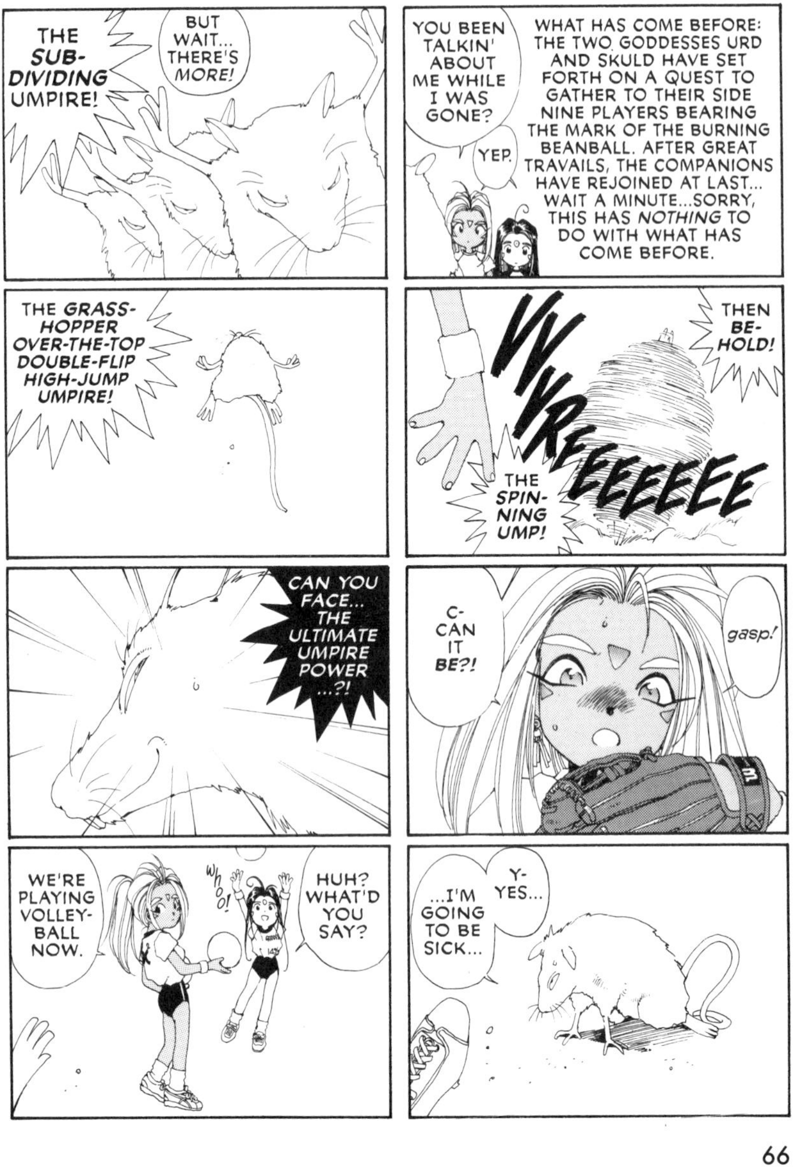
WHAT HAS COME BEFORE: THE TWO GODDESSES URD AND SKULD HAVE SET FORTH ON A QUEST TO GATHER TO THEIR SIDE NINE PLAYERS BEARING THE MARK OF THE BURNING BEANBALL. AFTER GREAT TRAVAILS, THE COMPANIONS HAVE REJOINED AT LAST... WAIT A MINUTE...SORRY, THIS HAS *NOTHING* TO DO WITH WHAT HAS COME BEFORE.
YOU BEEN TALKIN' ABOUT ME WHILE I WAS GONE?
YEP.
THEN *BE-HOLD!*
VVVREEEEEEE
THE *SPIN-NING UMP!*
gasp!
C-CAN IT *BE?!*
Y-YES...
...I'M GOING TO BE SICK...
BUT WAIT... THERE'S *MORE!*
THE *SUB-DIVIDING* UMPIRE!
THE *GRASS-HOPPER OVER-THE-TOP DOUBLE-FLIP HIGH-JUMP UMPIRE!*
CAN YOU FACE... THE ULTIMATE UMPIRE POWER ...?!
HUH? WHAT'D YOU SAY?
Whoo!
WE'RE PLAYING VOLLEY-BALL NOW.

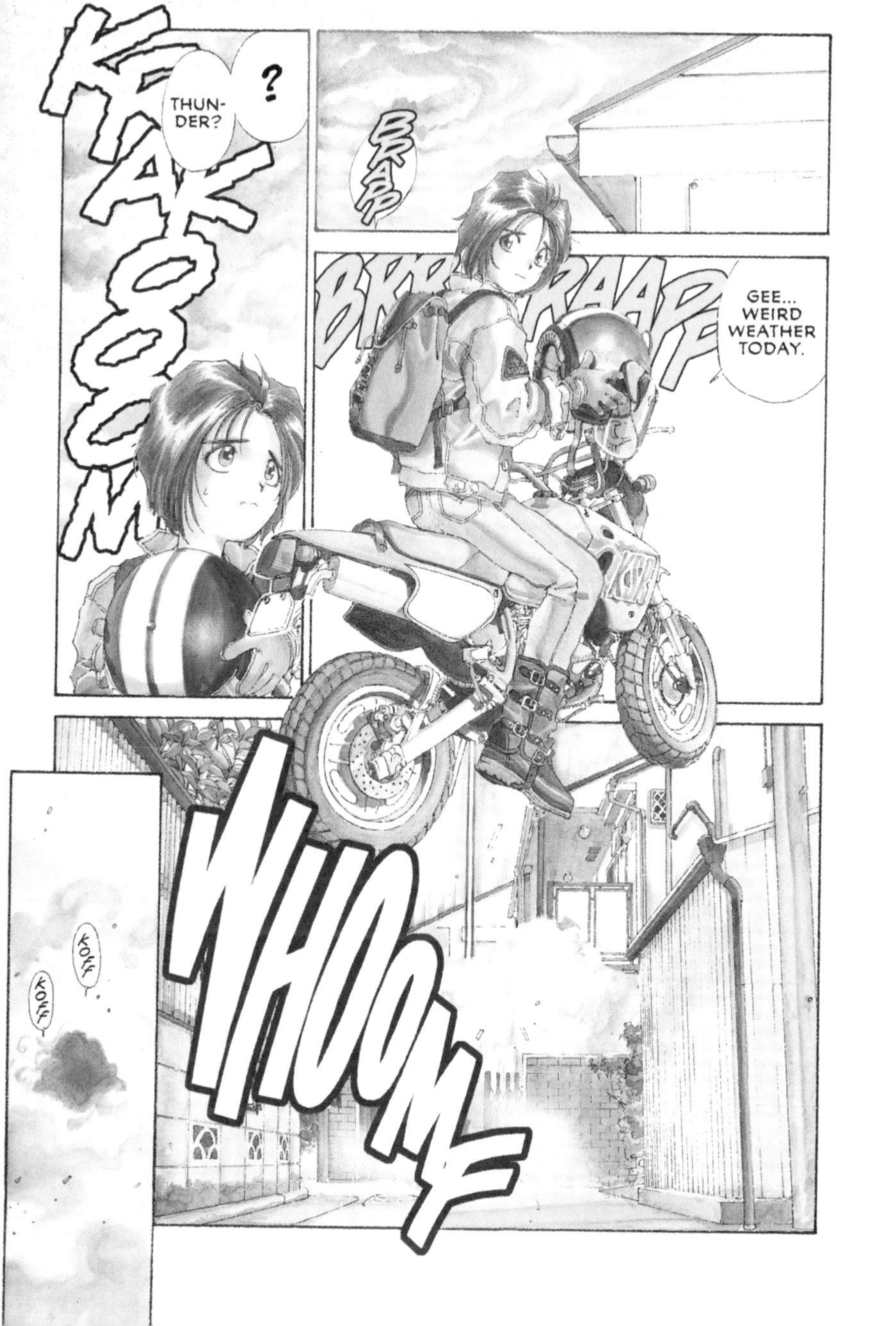
KRAKOOOOM
THUN-DER?
?
BRAPP
BRRRRAAPP
GEE... WEIRD WEATHER TODAY.
WHUOMF
KOFF
KOFF

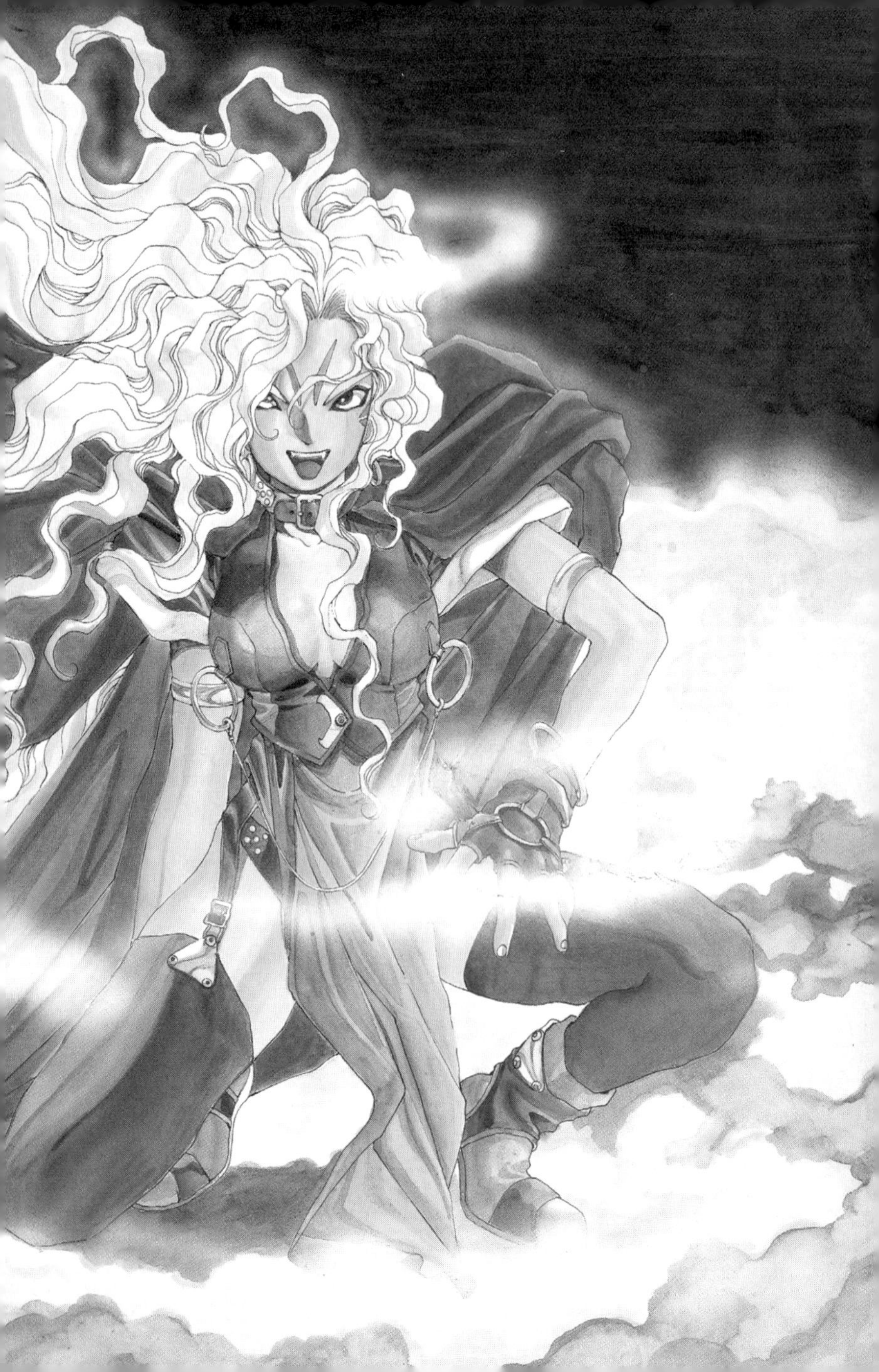

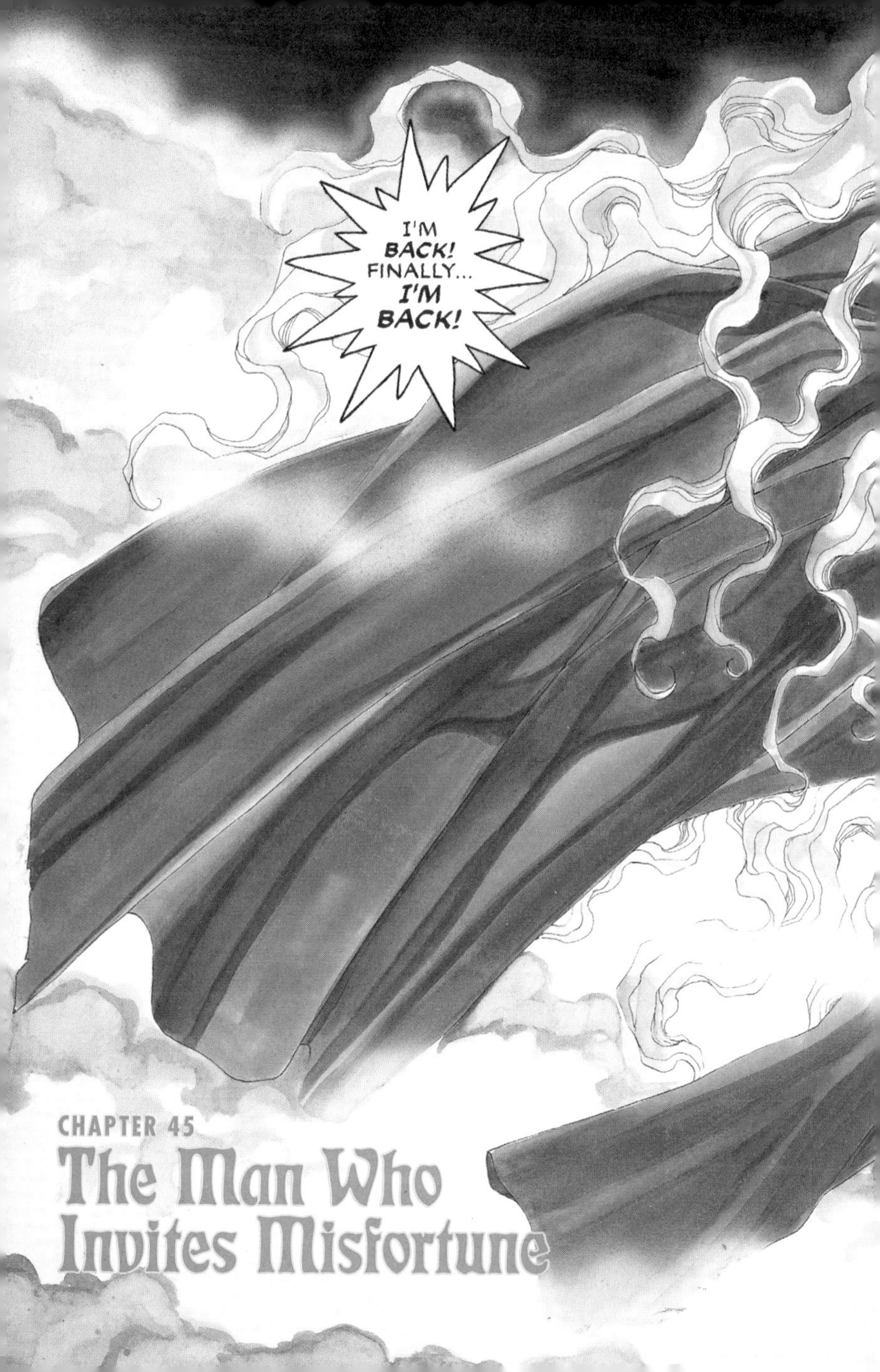
I'M BACK! FINALLY... I'M BACK!

CHAPTER 45

The Man Who Invites Misfortune

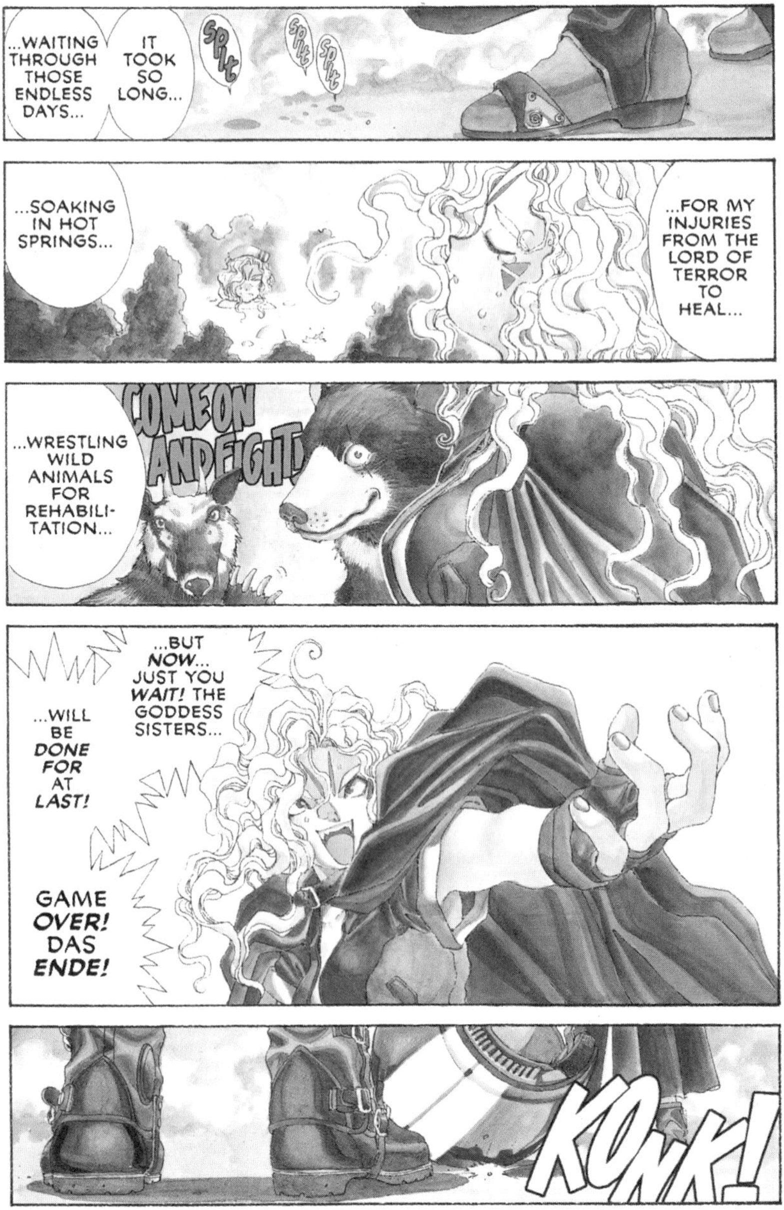
...WAITING THROUGH THOSE ENDLESS DAYS...
IT TOOK SO LONG...
spit
spit
spit
...SOAKING IN HOT SPRINGS...
...FOR MY INJURIES FROM THE LORD OF TERROR TO HEAL...
...WRESTLING WILD ANIMALS FOR REHABILI-TATION...
COME ON AND FIGHT!
...BUT NOW... JUST YOU WAIT! THE GODDESS SISTERS...
...WILL BE DONE FOR AT LAST!
GAME OVER! DAS ENDE!
KONK!

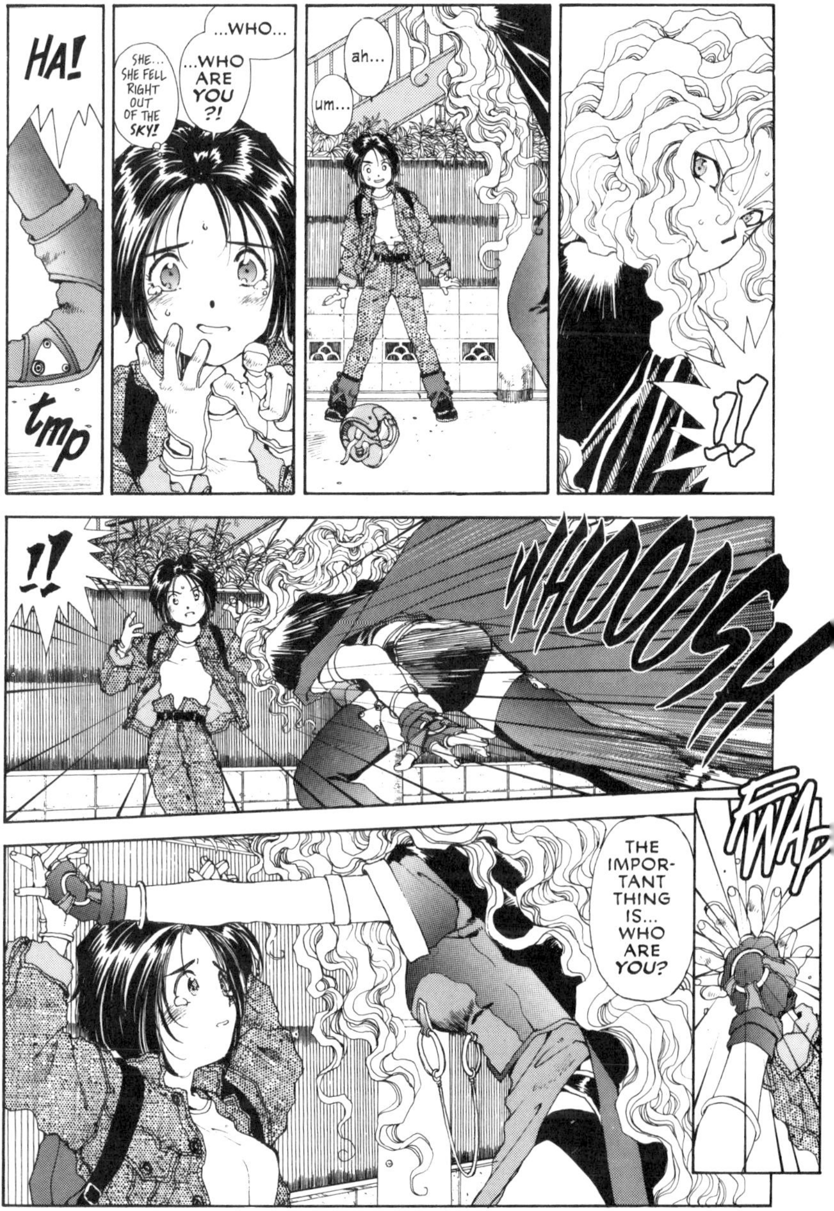
HA!
tmp
SHE... SHE FELL RIGHT OUT OF THE SKY!
...WHO...
...WHO ARE YOU?!
ah...
um...
!!
!!
WHOOOSH
FWAP
THE IMPORTANT THING IS... WHO ARE YOU?

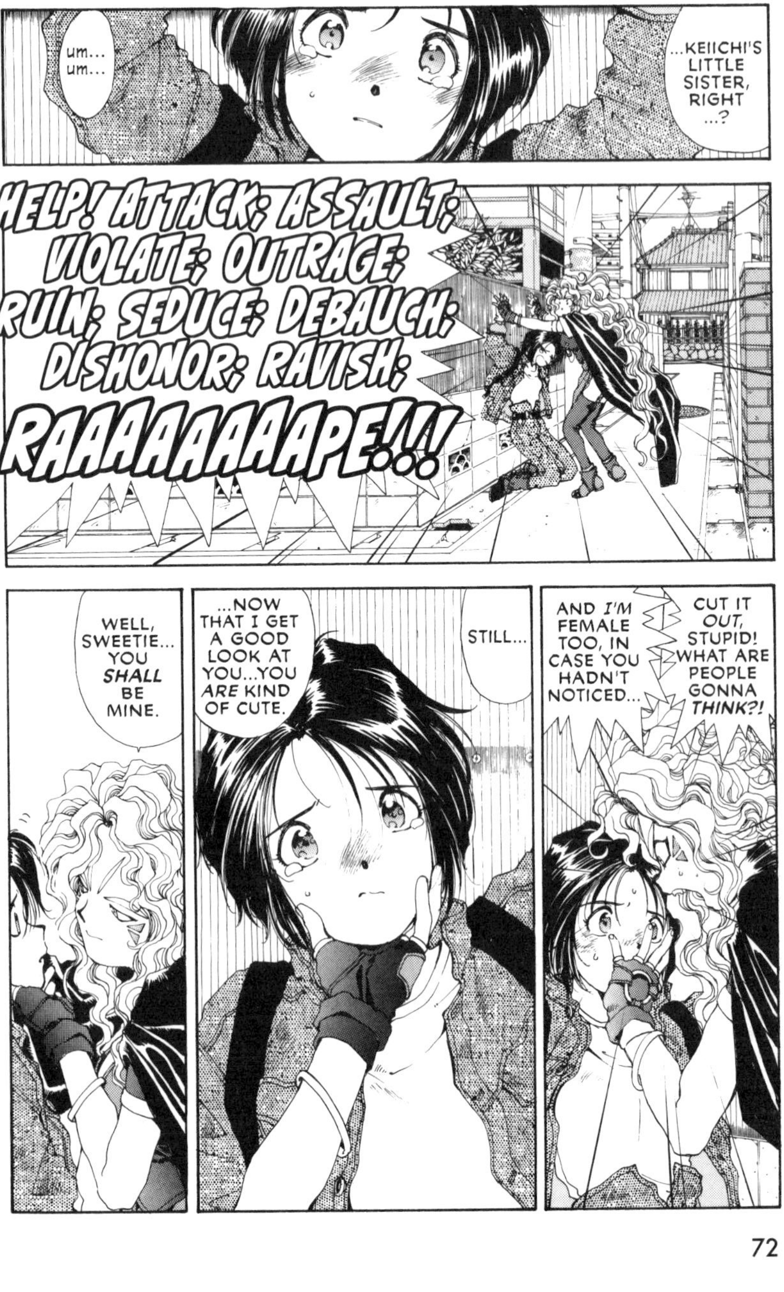
...KEIICHI'S LITTLE SISTER, RIGHT ...?
um... um...
HELP! ATTACK; ASSAULT; VIOLATE; OUTRAGE; RUIN; SEDUCE; DEBAUCH; DISHONOR; RAVISH;
RAAAAAAAAAPE!!!
CUT IT OUT, STUPID! WHAT ARE PEOPLE GONNA THINK?!
AND I'M FEMALE TOO, IN CASE YOU HADN'T NOTICED...
STILL...
...NOW THAT I GET A GOOD LOOK AT YOU...YOU ARE KIND OF CUTE.
WELL, SWEETIE... YOU SHALL BE MINE.

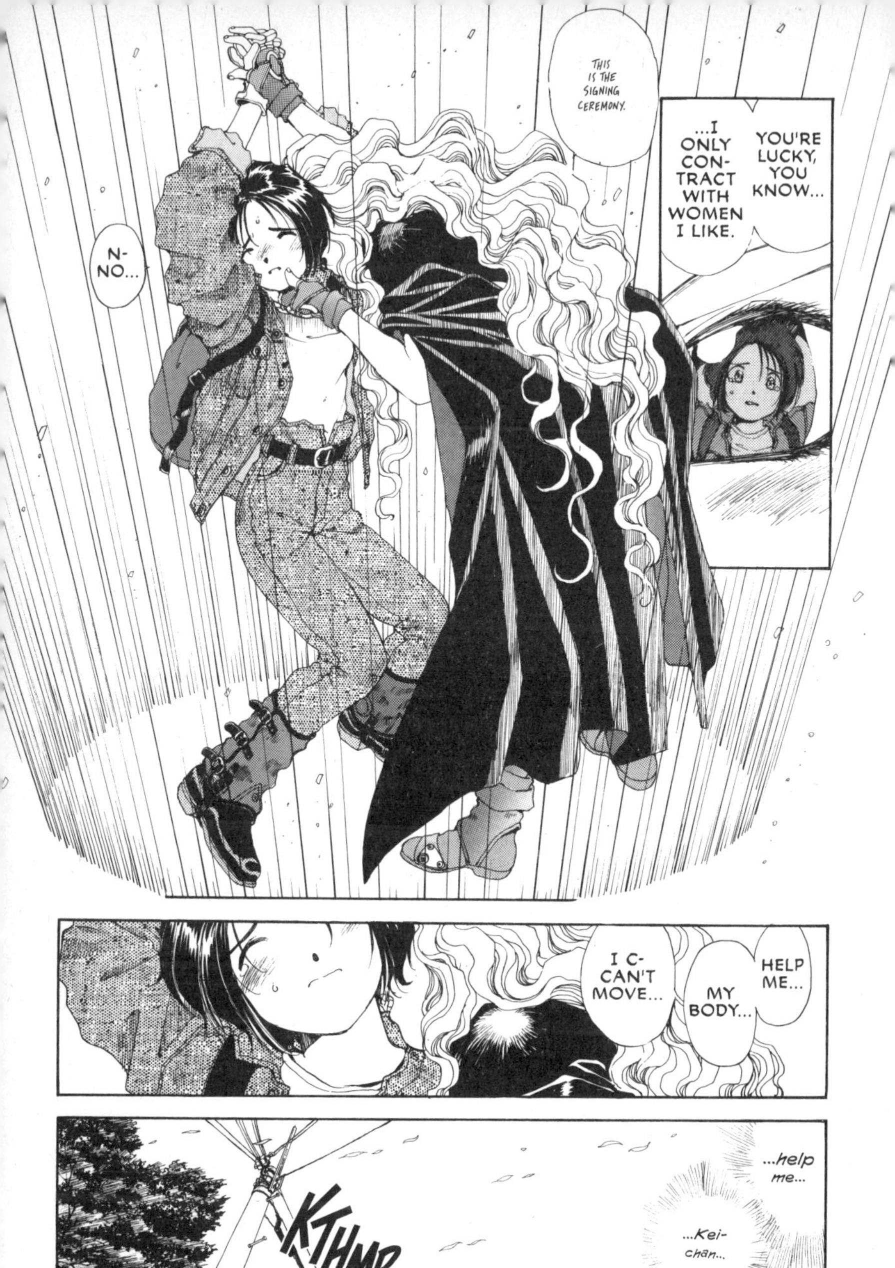
N-NO...
THIS IS THE SIGNING CEREMONY.
YOU'RE LUCKY, YOU KNOW...
...I ONLY CONTRACT WITH WOMEN I LIKE.
I C-CAN'T MOVE...
MY BODY...
HELP ME...
KTHMP
...help me...
...Kei-chan...

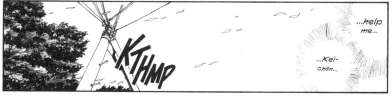

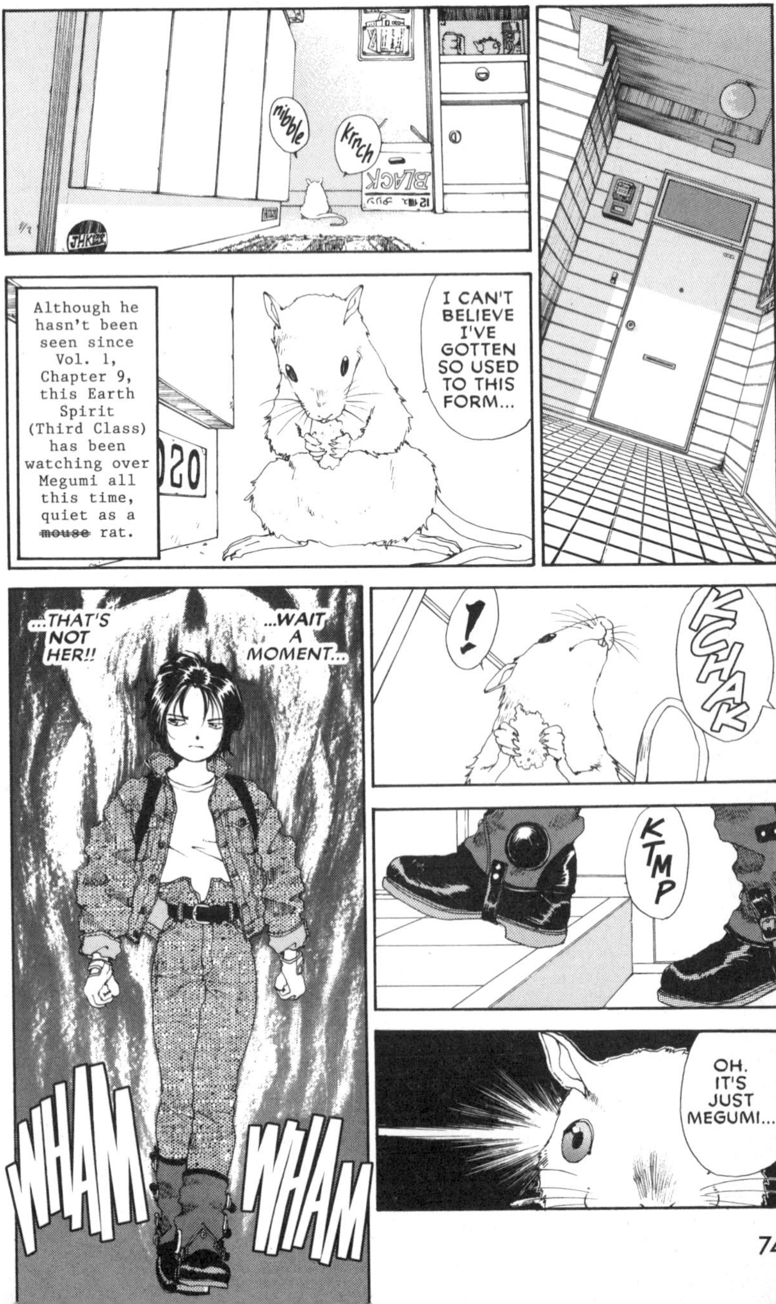
nibble
krnch
Although he hasn't been seen since Vol. 1, Chapter 9, this Earth Spirit (Third Class) has been watching over Megumi all this time, quiet as a ~~mouse~~ rat.
I CAN'T BELIEVE I'VE GOTTEN SO USED TO THIS FORM...
!
KCHAK
KTMP
OH. IT'S JUST MEGUMI...
...WAIT A MOMENT...
...THAT'S NOT HER!!
WHAM
WHAM

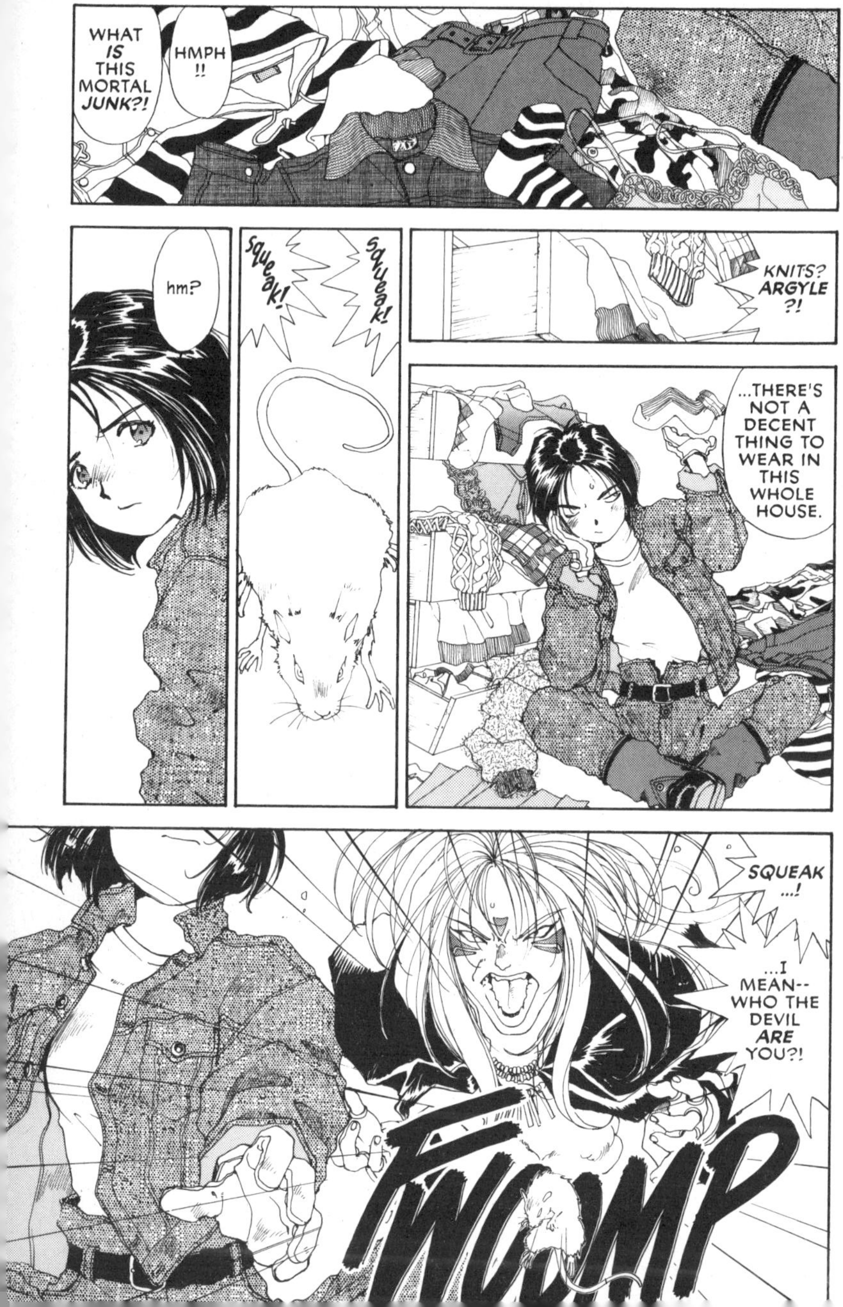
WHAT IS THIS MORTAL JUNK?!
HMPH !!
hm?
squeak!
squeak!
KNITS? ARGYLE ?!
...THERE'S NOT A DECENT THING TO WEAR IN THIS WHOLE HOUSE.
SQUEAK ...!
...I MEAN-- WHO THE DEVIL ARE YOU?!
TWOMP

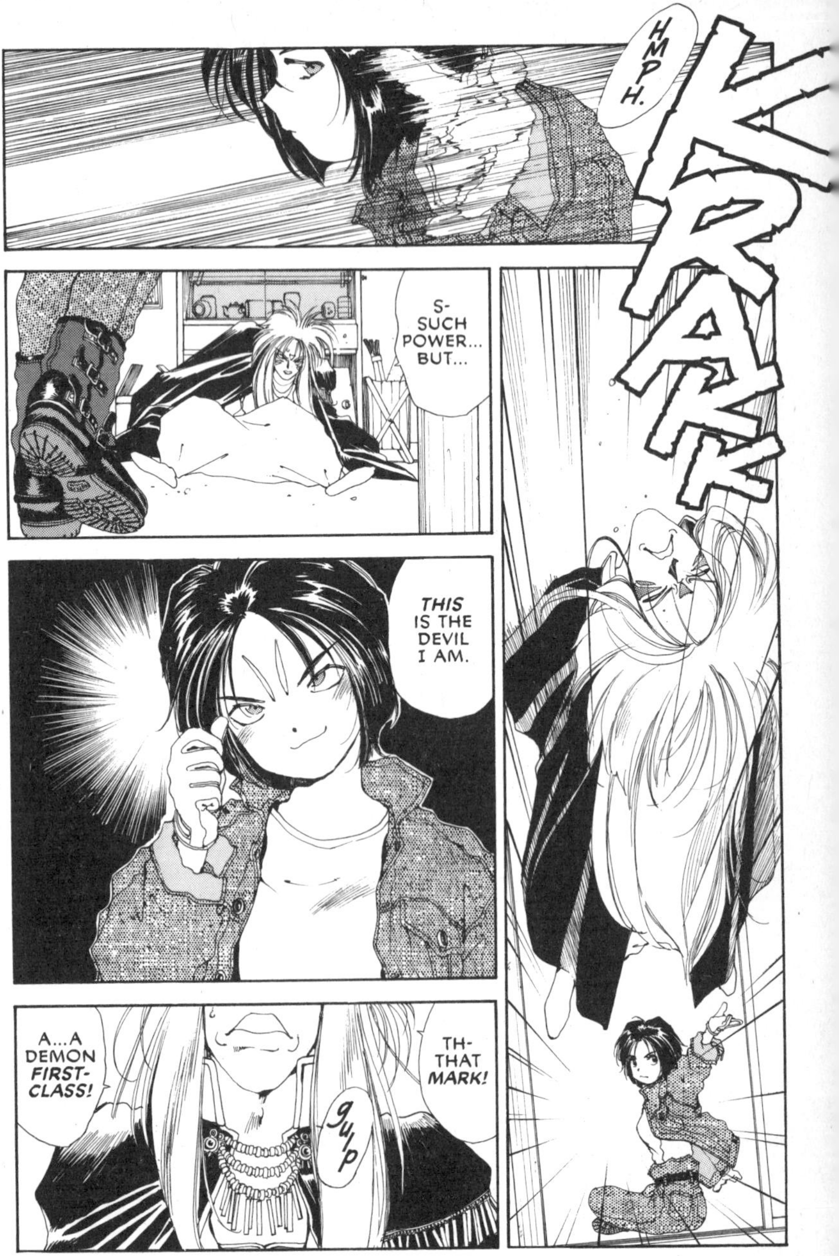
KRAK
HMPH.
S-SUCH POWER... BUT...
THIS IS THE DEVIL I AM.
TH-THAT MARK!
gulp
A...A DEMON FIRST-CLASS!

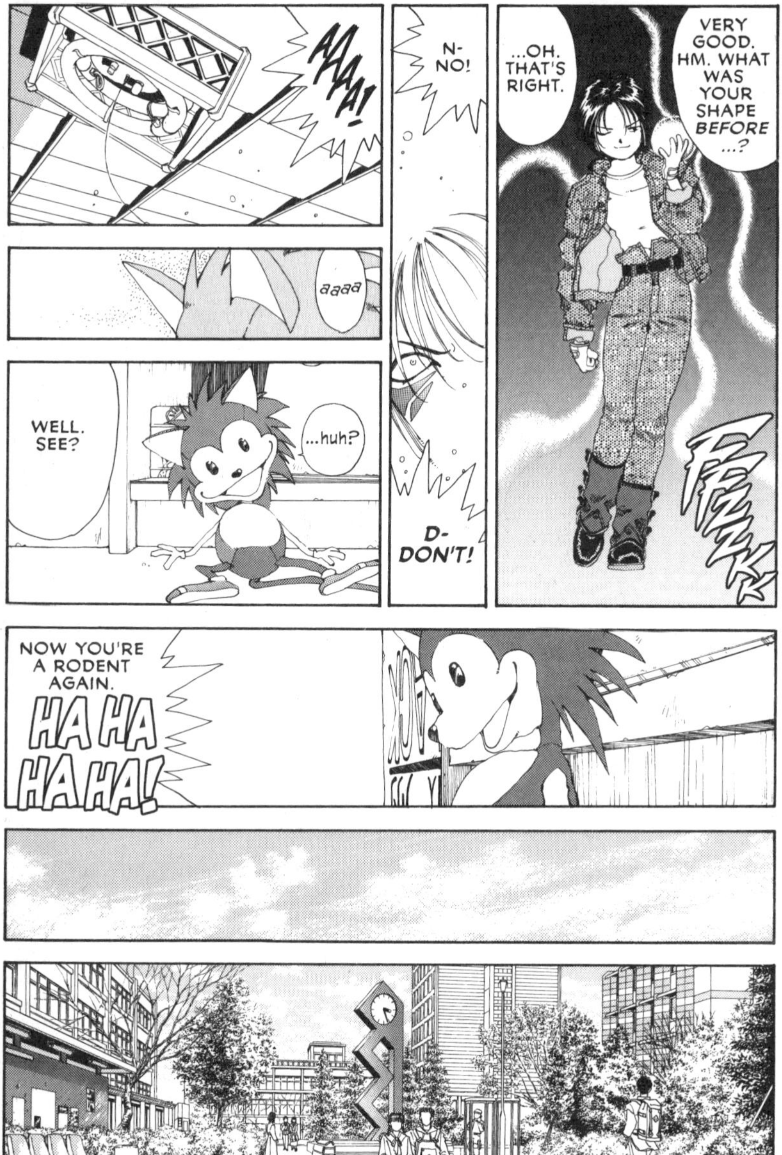
VERY GOOD. HM. WHAT WAS YOUR SHAPE BEFORE ...?
...OH. THAT'S RIGHT.
N-NO!
D-DON'T!
FZZZK
AAAAA!
aaaa
WELL. SEE?
...huh?
NOW YOU'RE A RODENT AGAIN.
HA HA HA HA!

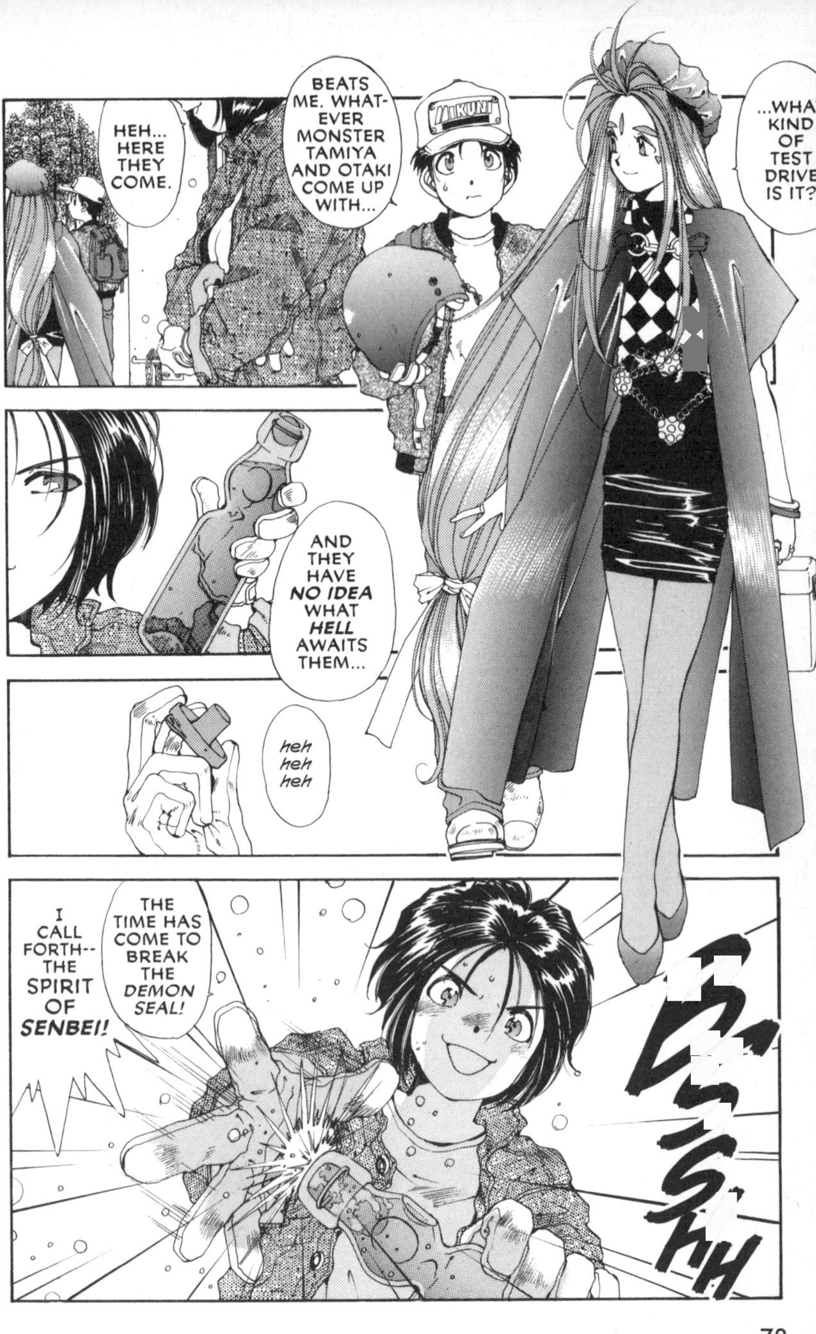
...WHAT KIND OF TEST DRIVE IS IT?
BEATS ME. WHAT-EVER MONSTER TAMIYA AND OTAKI COME UP WITH...
HEH... HERE THEY COME.
AND THEY HAVE *NO IDEA* WHAT *HELL* AWAITS THEM...
heh heh heh
THE TIME HAS COME TO BREAK THE *DEMON SEAL!*
I CALL FORTH-- THE SPIRIT OF *SENBEI!*

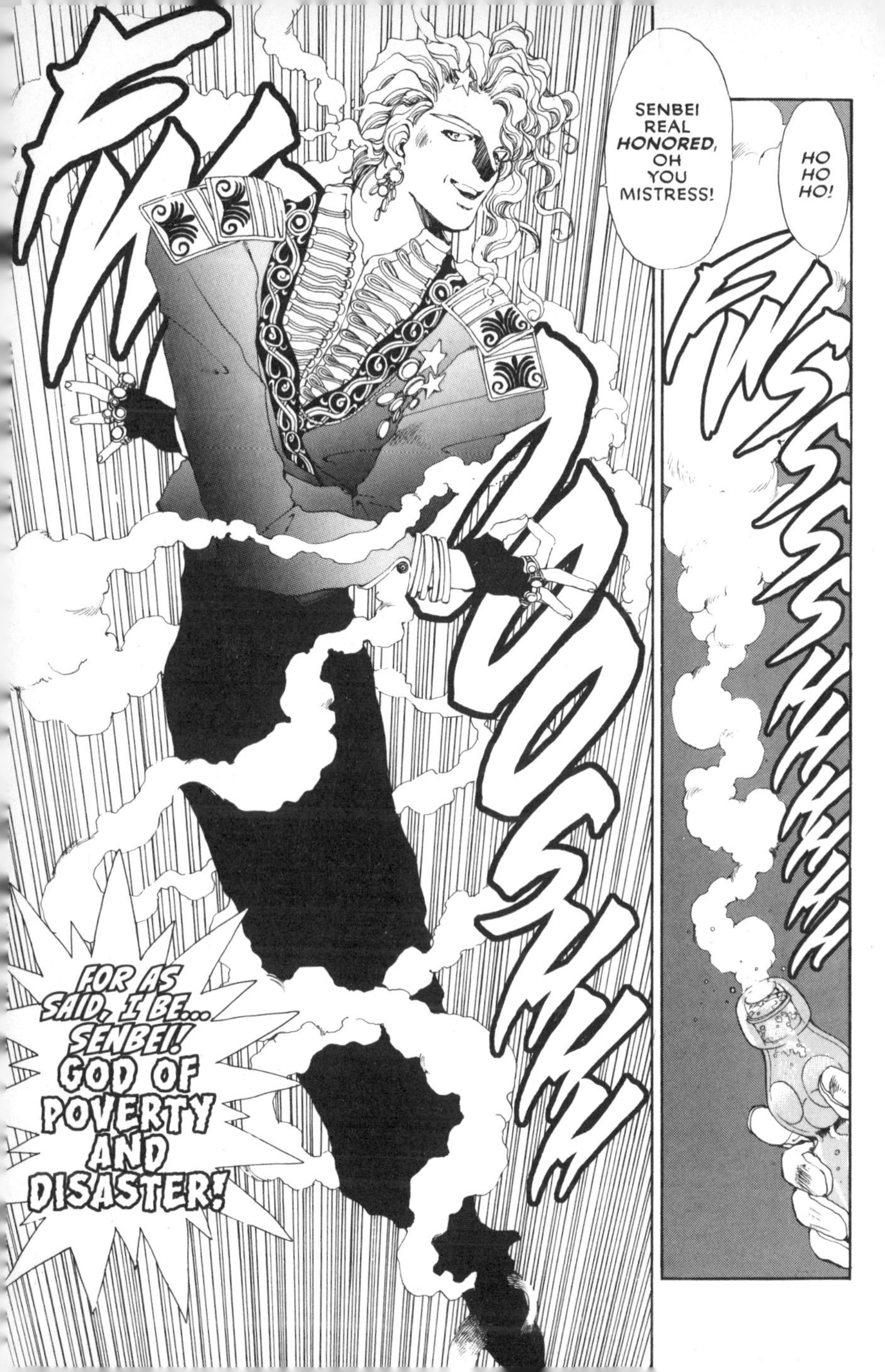
HO HO HO!
SENBEI REAL *HONORED*, OH YOU MISTRESS!
FOR AS SAID, I BE... SENBEI! GOD OF POVERTY AND DISASTER!

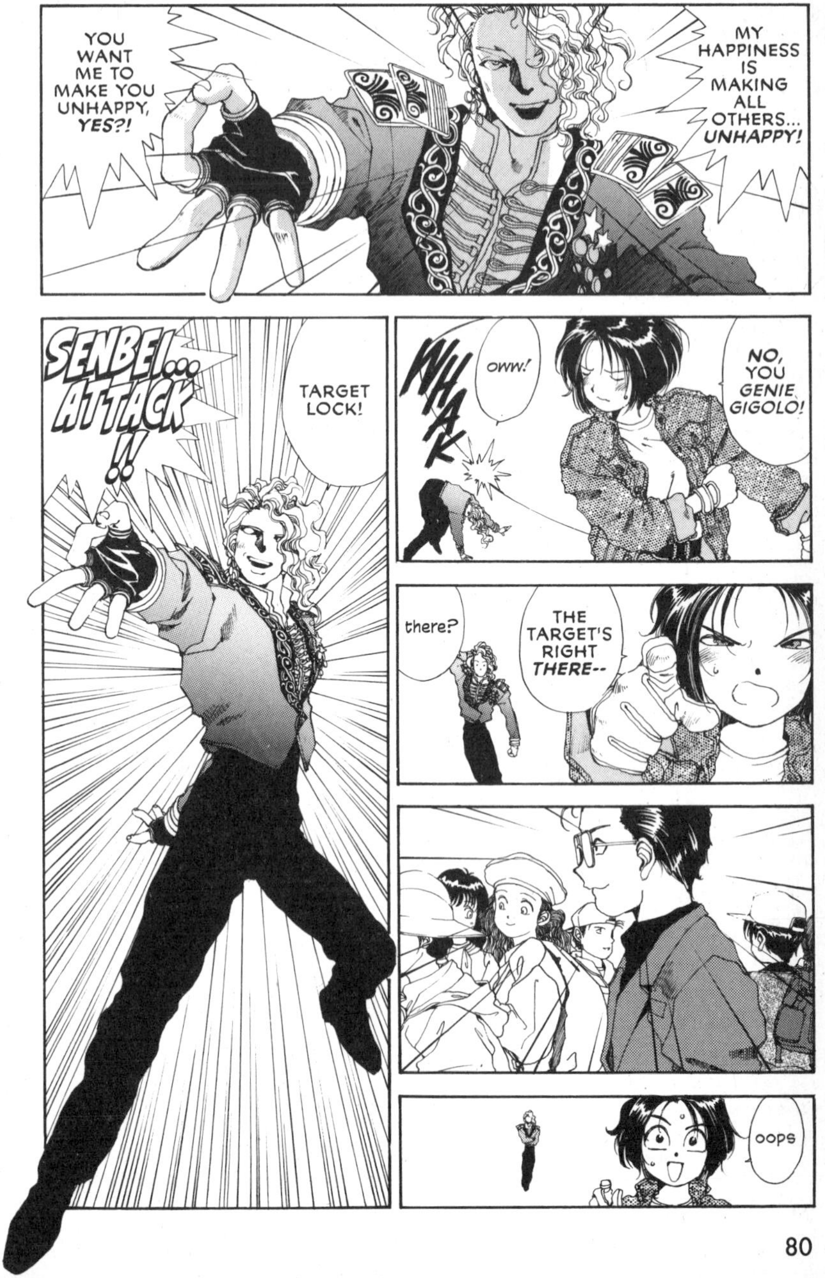
YOU WANT ME TO MAKE YOU UNHAPPY, *YES?!*
MY HAPPINESS IS MAKING ALL OTHERS... *UNHAPPY!*
SENBEI... ATTACK!!
TARGET LOCK!
WHAK
oww!
NO, YOU *GENIE GIGOLO!*
there?
THE TARGET'S RIGHT *THERE--*
oops

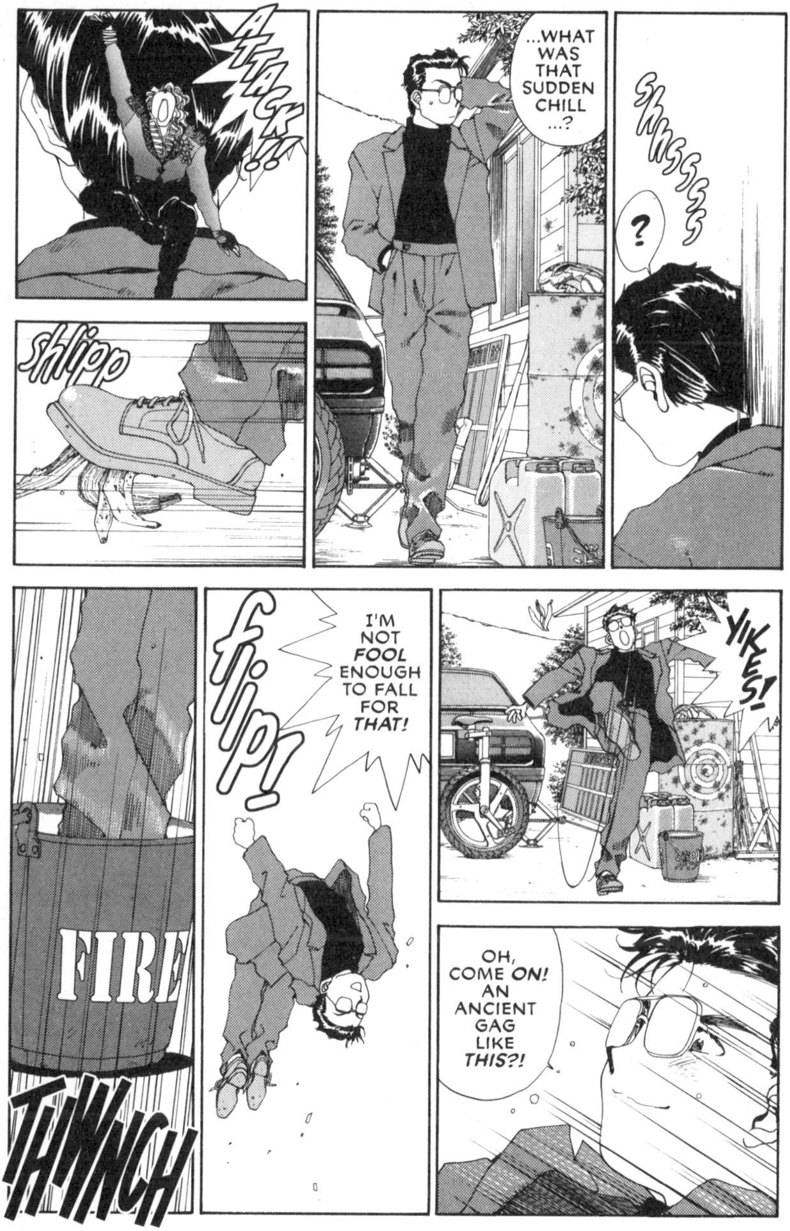
ATTACK!!
...WHAT WAS THAT SUDDEN CHILL ...?
SHHSSSS
?
shlipp
flip!
I'M NOT FOOL ENOUGH TO FALL FOR THAT!
YIKES!
FIRE
THWNCH
OH, COME ON! AN ANCIENT GAG LIKE THIS?!

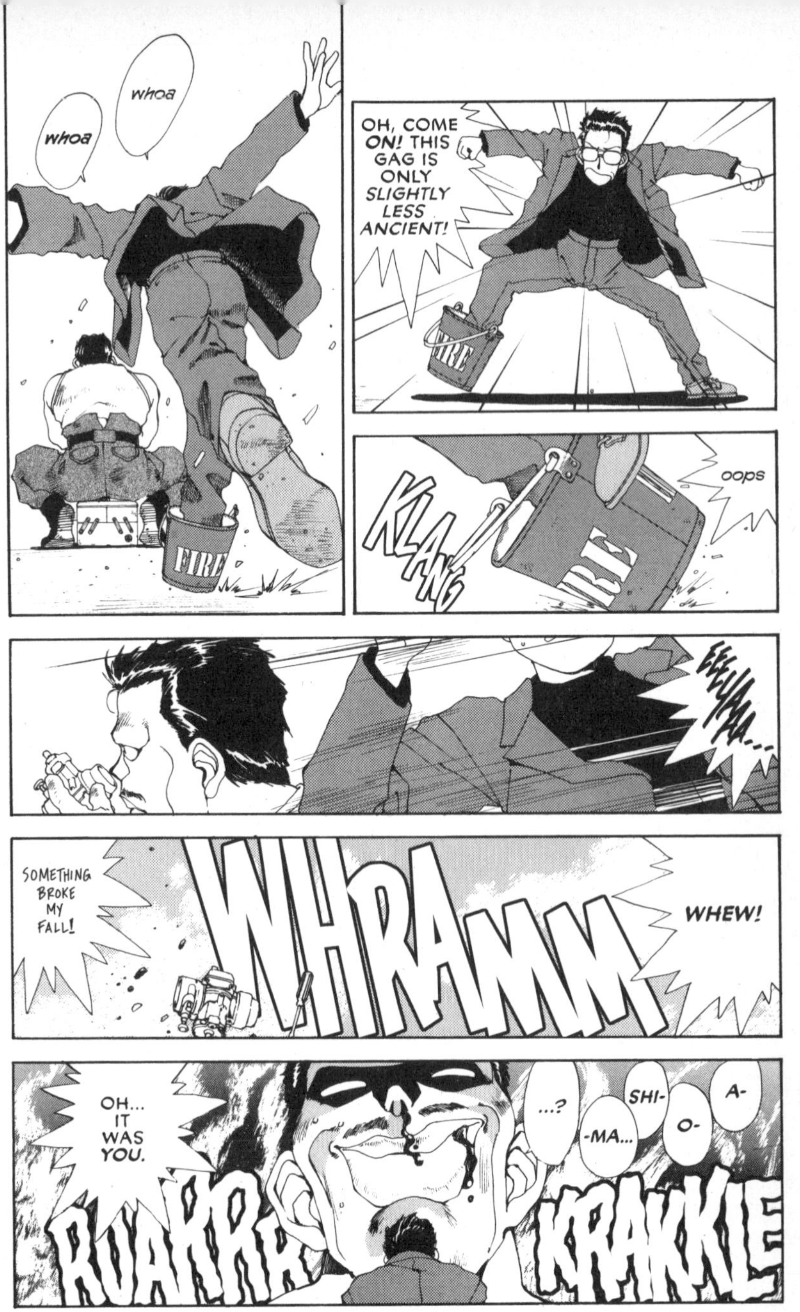
whoa
whoa
OH, COME ON! THIS GAG IS ONLY SLIGHTLY LESS ANCIENT!
FIRE
oops
KLANG
FIRE
EEEYAAA...
SOMETHING BROKE MY FALL!
WHRAMM
WHEW!
OH... IT WAS YOU.
...?
SHI-
-MA...
A-
O-
RUAKRR
KRAKKLE

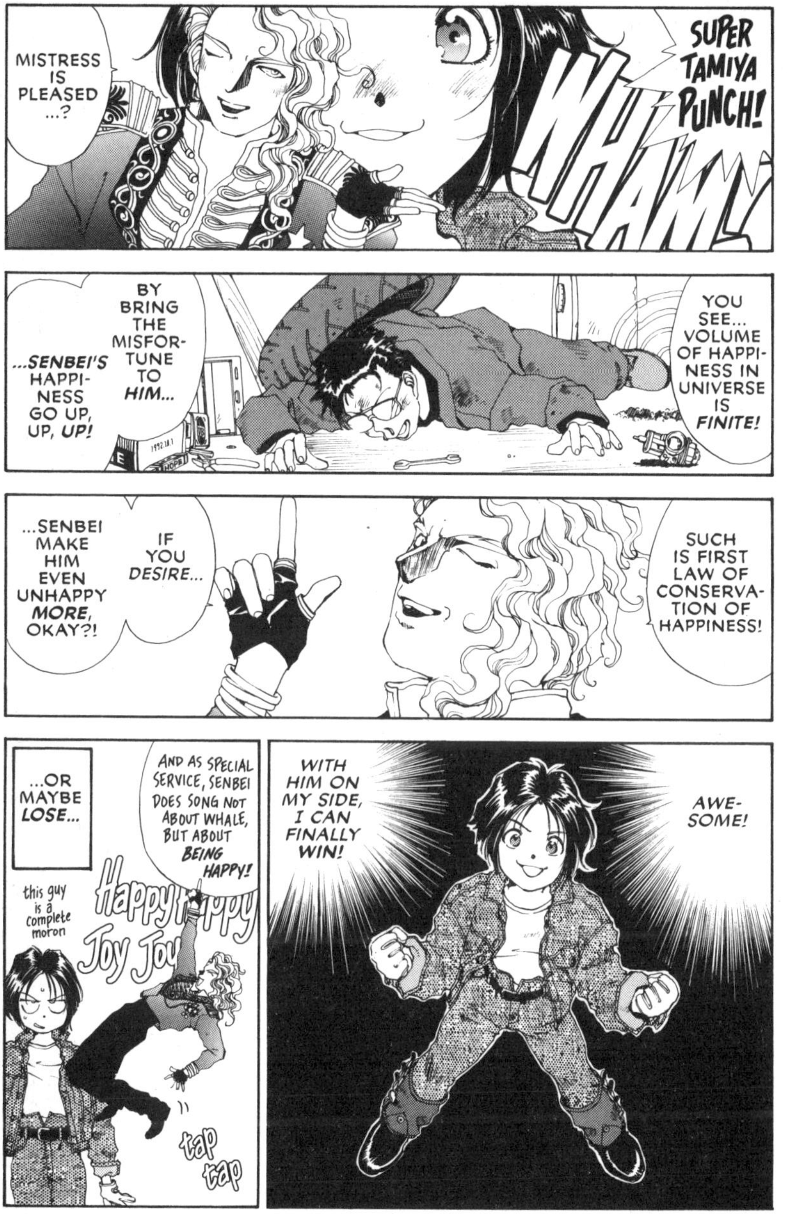
SUPER TAMIYA PUNCH!
WHAM!
MISTRESS IS PLEASED ...?
YOU SEE... VOLUME OF HAPPINESS IN UNIVERSE IS FINITE!
BY BRING THE MISFORTUNE TO HIM...
...SENBEI'S HAPPINESS GO UP, UP, UP!
SUCH IS FIRST LAW OF CONSERVATION OF HAPPINESS!
IF YOU DESIRE...
...SENBEI MAKE HIM EVEN UNHAPPY MORE, OKAY?!
AWESOME!
WITH HIM ON MY SIDE, I CAN FINALLY WIN!
AND AS SPECIAL SERVICE, SENBEI DOES SONG NOT ABOUT WHALE, BUT ABOUT BEING HAPPY!
...OR MAYBE LOSE...
Happy Happy
Joy Joy
this guy is a complete moron
tap tap

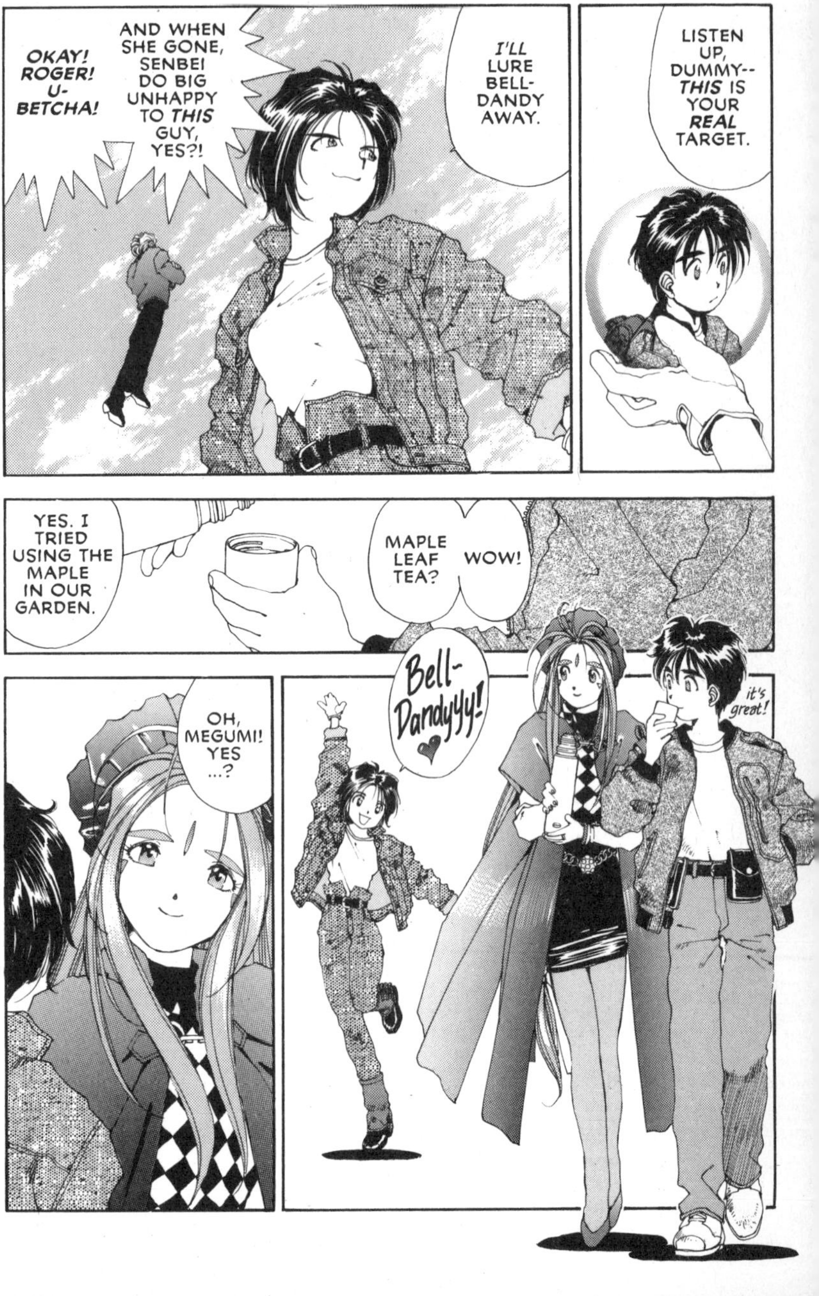
LISTEN UP, DUMMY-- THIS IS YOUR REAL TARGET.
I'LL LURE BELL-DANDY AWAY.
AND WHEN SHE GONE, SENBEI DO BIG UNHAPPY TO THIS GUY, YES?!
OKAY! ROGER! U-BETCHA!
WOW!
MAPLE LEAF TEA?
YES. I TRIED USING THE MAPLE IN OUR GARDEN.
it's great!
Bell-Dandyyy!
OH, MEGUMI! YES ...?

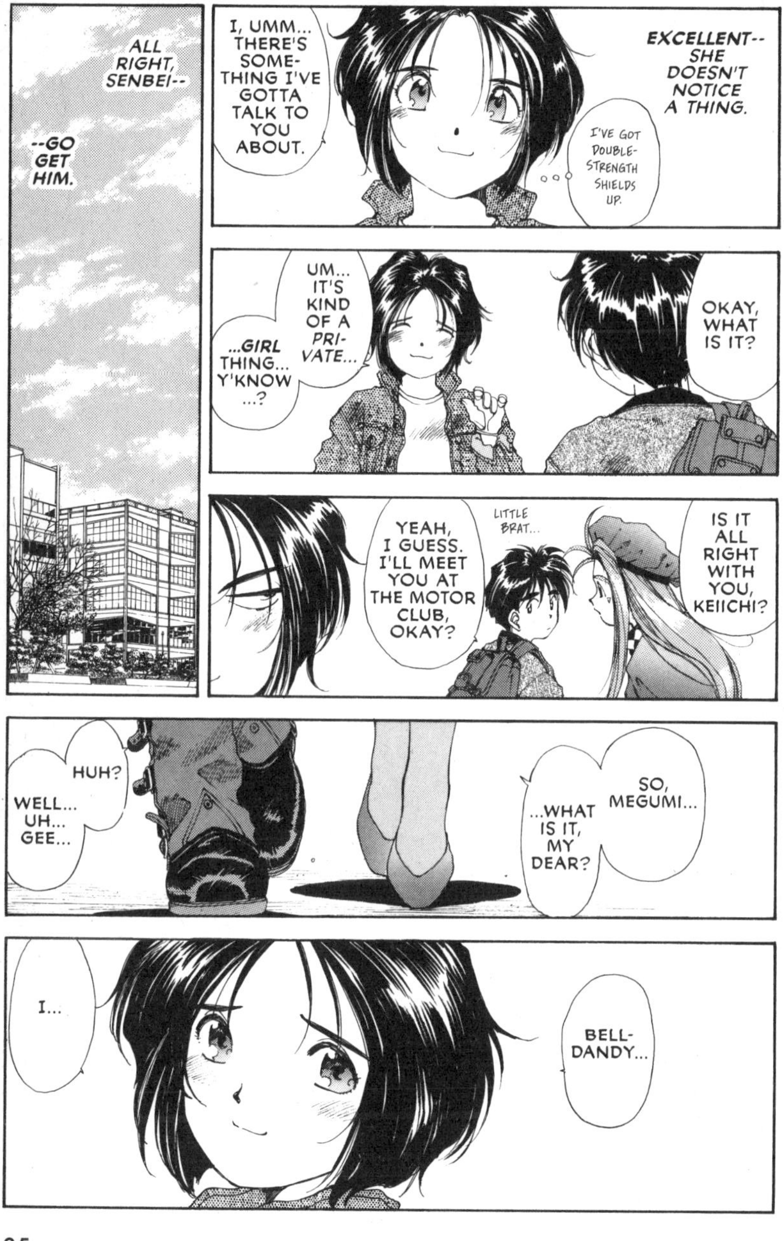
ALL RIGHT, SENBEI--
--GO GET HIM.
I, UMM... THERE'S SOMETHING I'VE GOTTA TALK TO YOU ABOUT.
I'VE GOT DOUBLE-STRENGTH SHIELDS UP.
EXCELLENT-- SHE DOESN'T NOTICE A THING.
OKAY, WHAT IS IT?
UM... IT'S KIND OF A PRIVATE...
...GIRL THING... Y'KNOW ...?
IS IT ALL RIGHT WITH YOU, KEIICHI?
YEAH, I GUESS. I'LL MEET YOU AT THE MOTOR CLUB, OKAY?
LITTLE BRAT...
SO, MEGUMI...
...WHAT IS IT, MY DEAR?
HUH?
WELL... UH... GEE...
BELL-DANDY...
I...

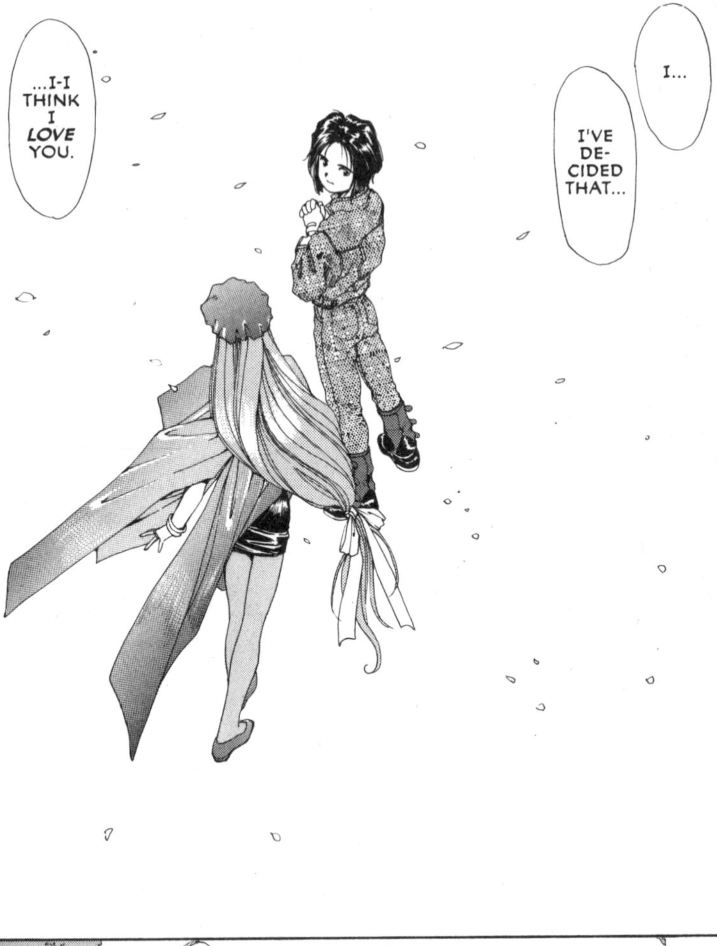
I...
I'VE DE-CIDED THAT...
...I-I THINK I *LOVE* YOU.

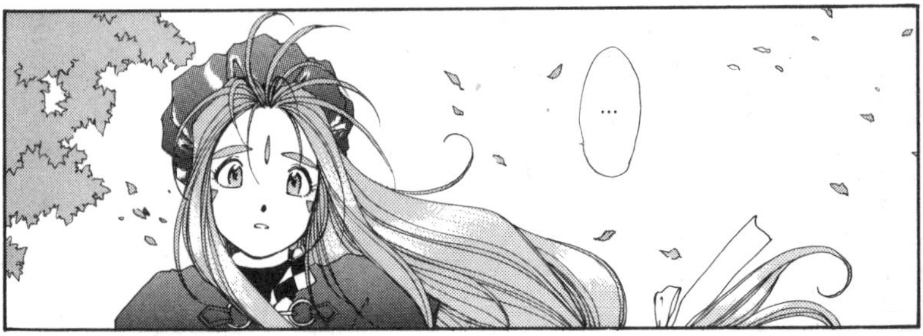
...

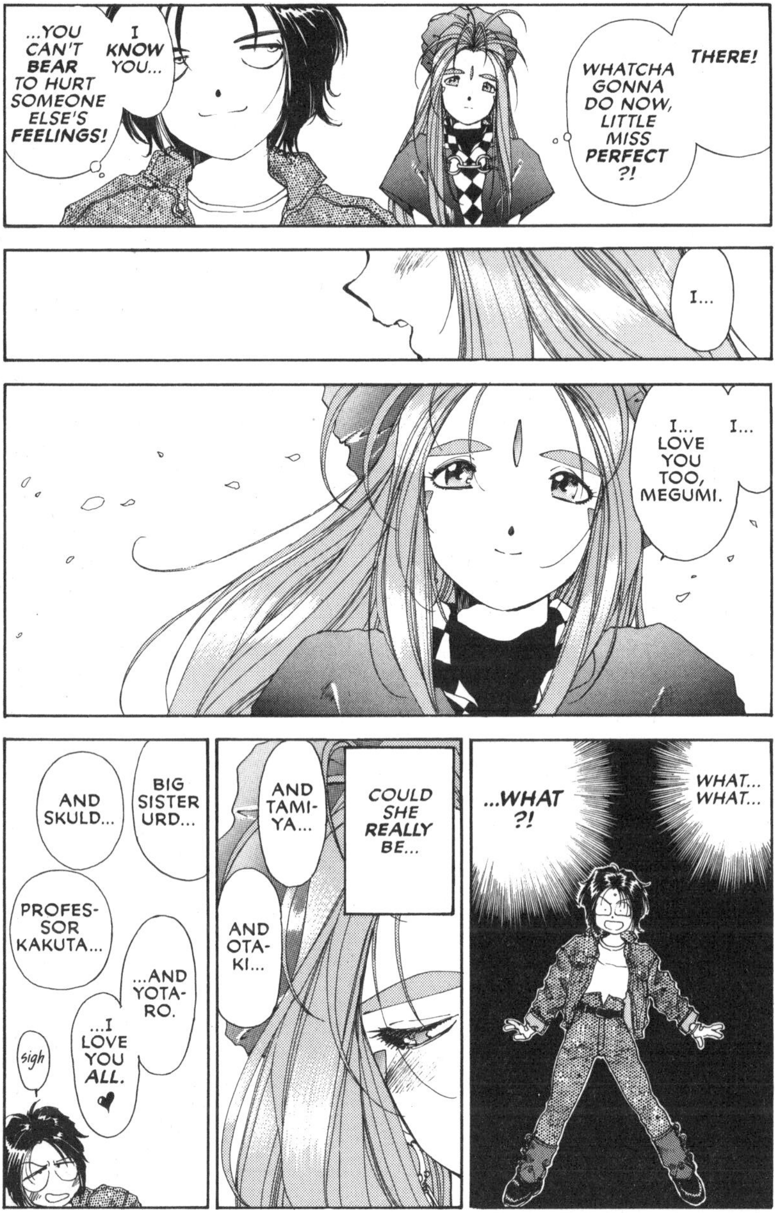
I KNOW YOU...
...YOU CAN'T BEAR TO HURT SOMEONE ELSE'S FEELINGS!
THERE!
WHATCHA GONNA DO NOW, LITTLE MISS PERFECT ?!
I...
I... I... LOVE YOU TOO, MEGUMI.
BIG SISTER URD...
AND SKULD...
PROFES-SOR KAKUTA...
...AND YOTA-RO.
...I LOVE YOU ALL. ♥
sigh
AND TAMI-YA...
AND OTA-KI...
COULD SHE REALLY BE...
...WHAT ?!
WHAT... WHAT...

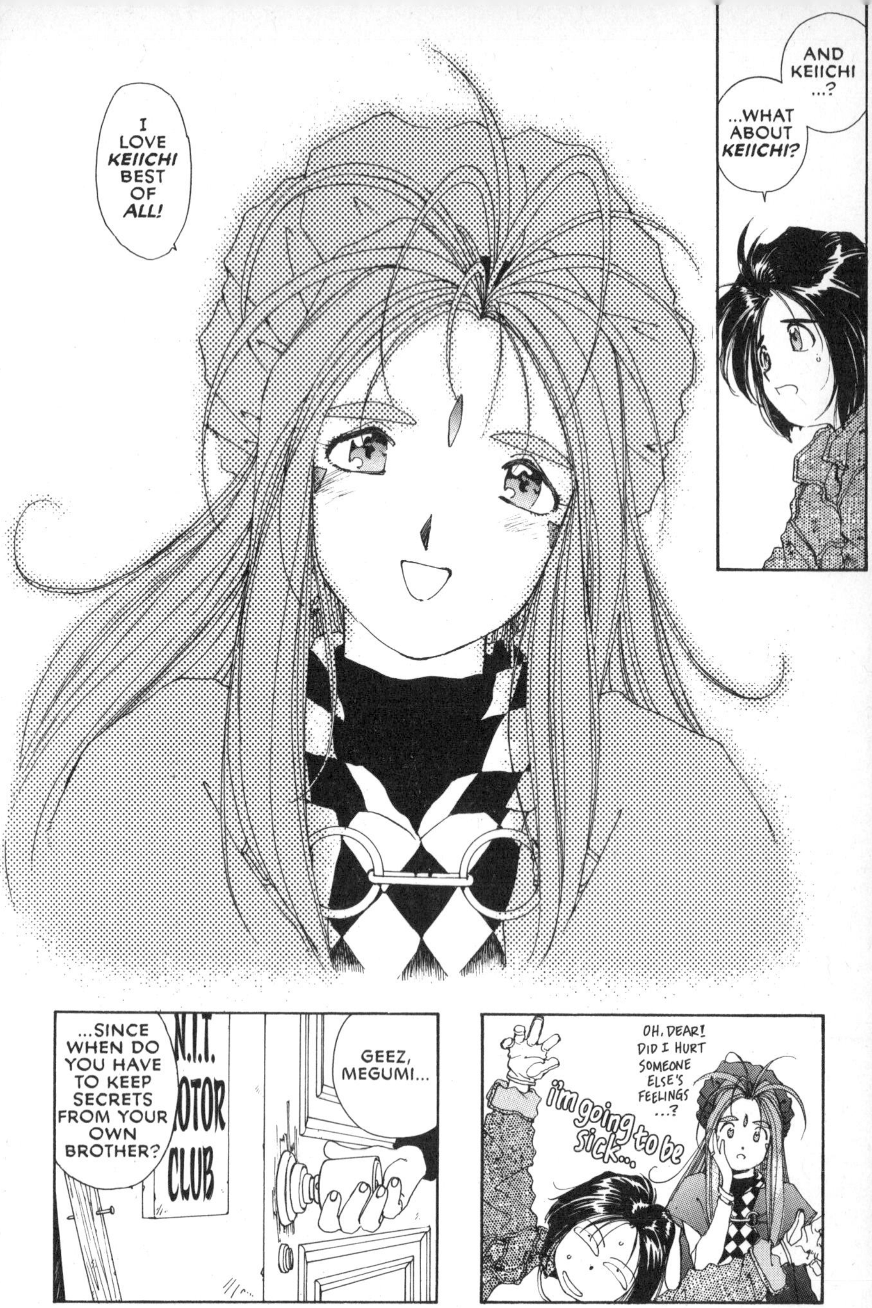
AND KEIICHI ...?
...WHAT ABOUT KEIICHI?
I LOVE KEIICHI BEST OF ALL!
GEEZ, MEGUMI...
...SINCE WHEN DO YOU HAVE TO KEEP SECRETS FROM YOUR OWN BROTHER?
N.I.T. MOTOR CLUB
OH, DEAR! DID I HURT SOMEONE ELSE'S FEELINGS ...?
i'm going to be sick...

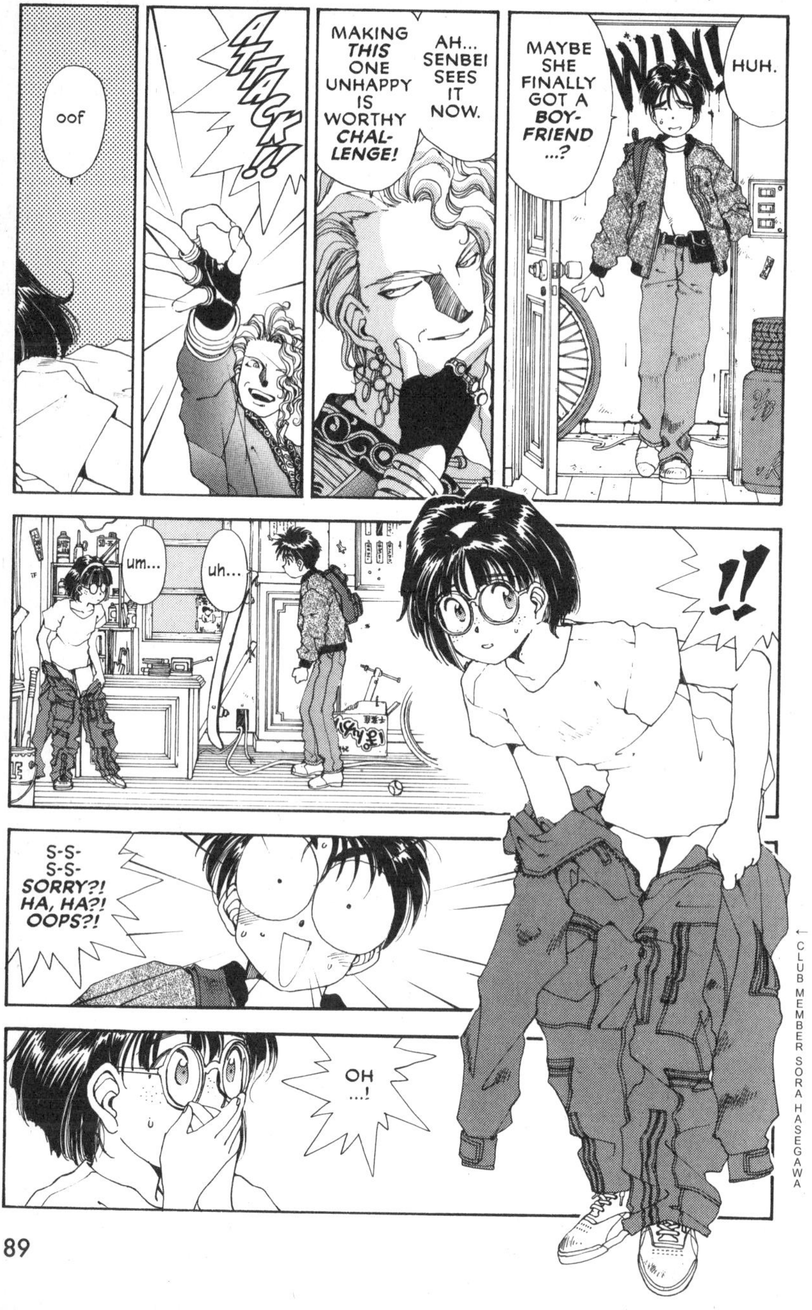
HUH.
WIN!
MAYBE SHE FINALLY GOT A BOY-FRIEND ...?
AH... SENBEI SEES IT NOW.
MAKING THIS ONE UNHAPPY IS WORTHY CHAL-LENGE!
ATTACK!!
oof
!!
uh...
um...
S-S-S-S-SORRY?! HA, HA?! OOPS?!
OH ...!
← CLUB MEMBER SORA HASEGAWA

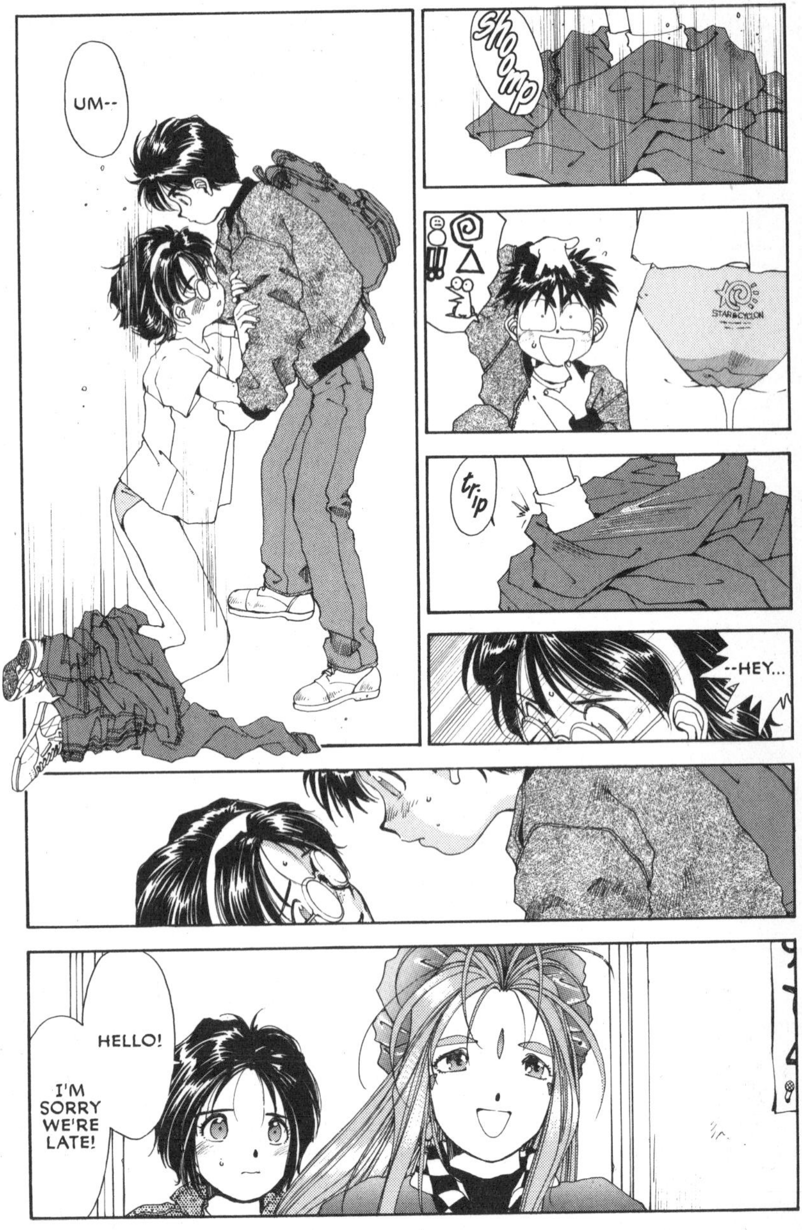
shoomp
UM--
trip
--HEY...
HELLO!
I'M SORRY WE'RE LATE!

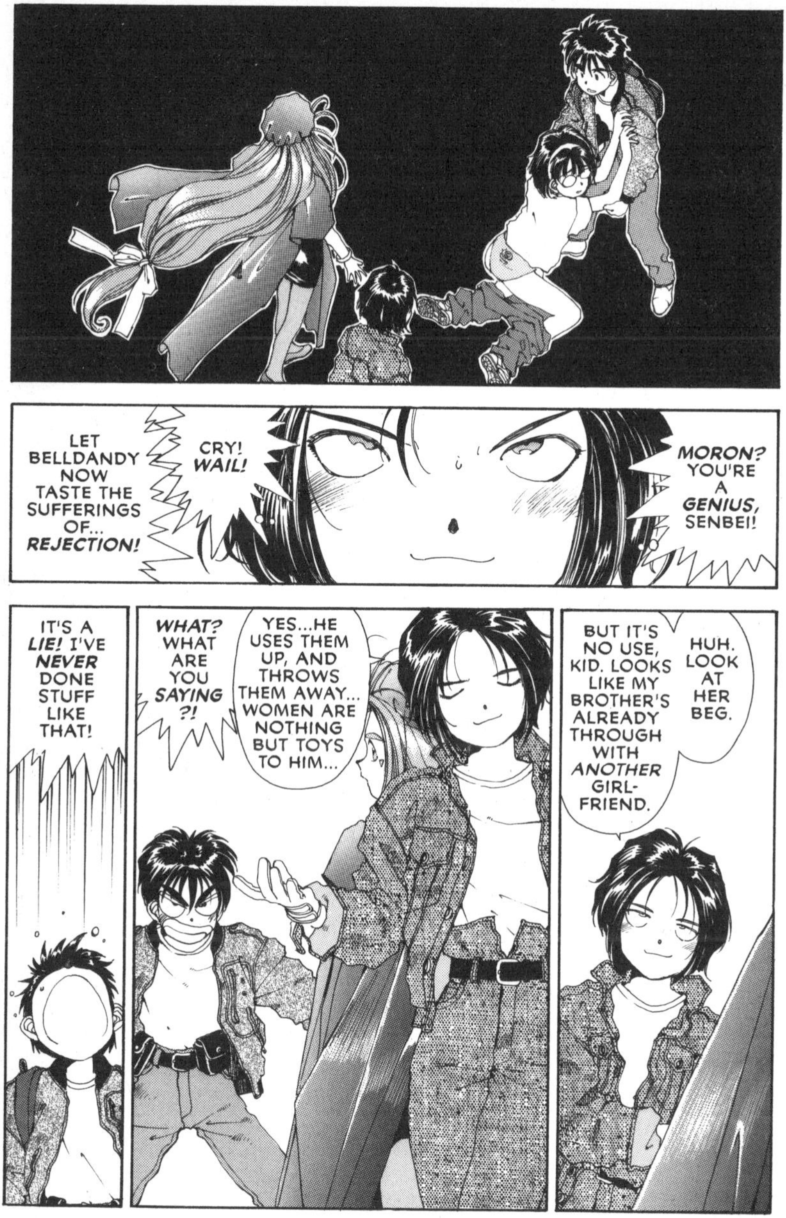
MORON? YOU'RE A GENIUS, SENBEI!
CRY! WAIL!
LET BELLDANDY NOW TASTE THE SUFFERINGS OF... REJECTION!
HUH. LOOK AT HER BEG.
BUT IT'S NO USE, KID. LOOKS LIKE MY BROTHER'S ALREADY THROUGH WITH ANOTHER GIRL-FRIEND.
YES...HE USES THEM UP, AND THROWS THEM AWAY... WOMEN ARE NOTHING BUT TOYS TO HIM...
WHAT? WHAT ARE YOU SAYING ?!
IT'S A LIE! I'VE NEVER DONE STUFF LIKE THAT!

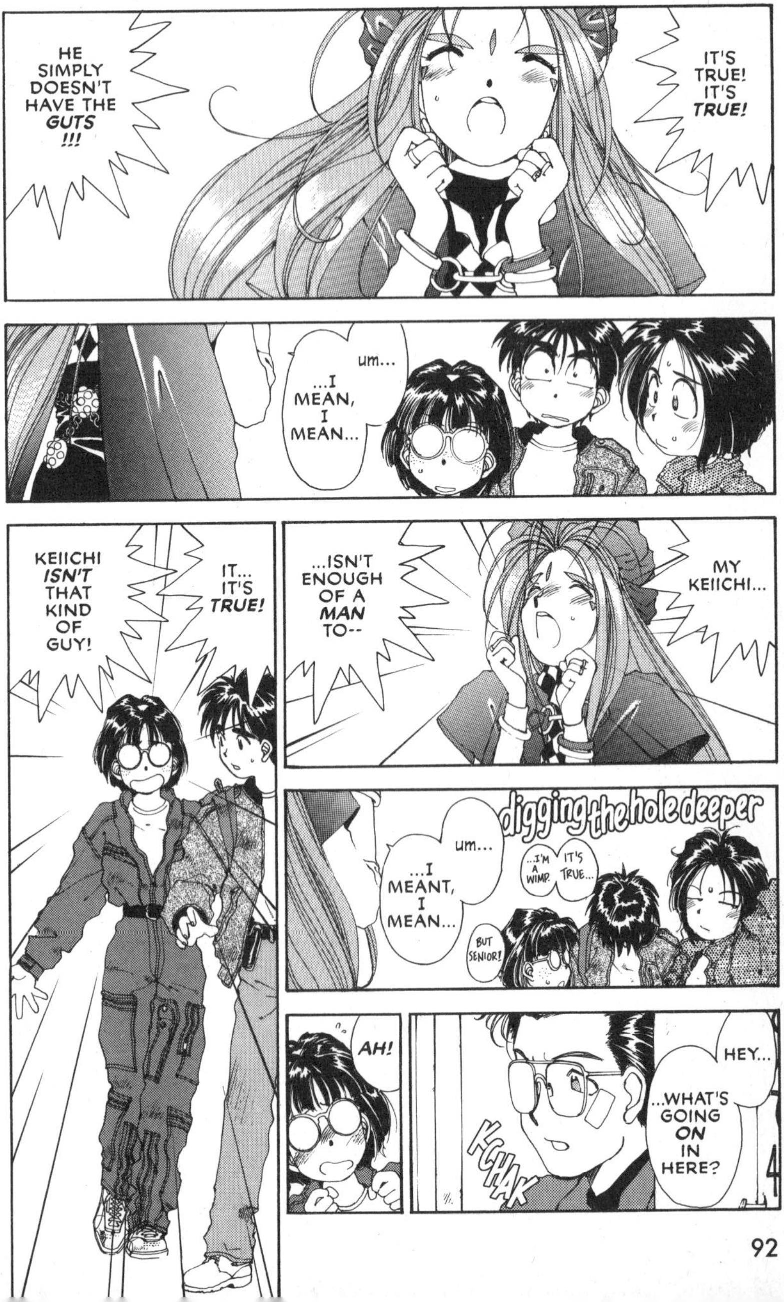
HE SIMPLY DOESN'T HAVE THE GUTS !!!
IT'S TRUE! IT'S TRUE!
um...
...I MEAN, I MEAN...
MY KEIICHI...
...ISN'T ENOUGH OF A MAN TO--
KEIICHI ISN'T THAT KIND OF GUY!
IT... IT'S TRUE!
digging the hole deeper
um...
...I MEANT, I MEAN...
...I'M A WIMP.
IT'S TRUE...
BUT SENIOR!
AH!
KCHAK
HEY...
...WHAT'S GOING ON IN HERE?

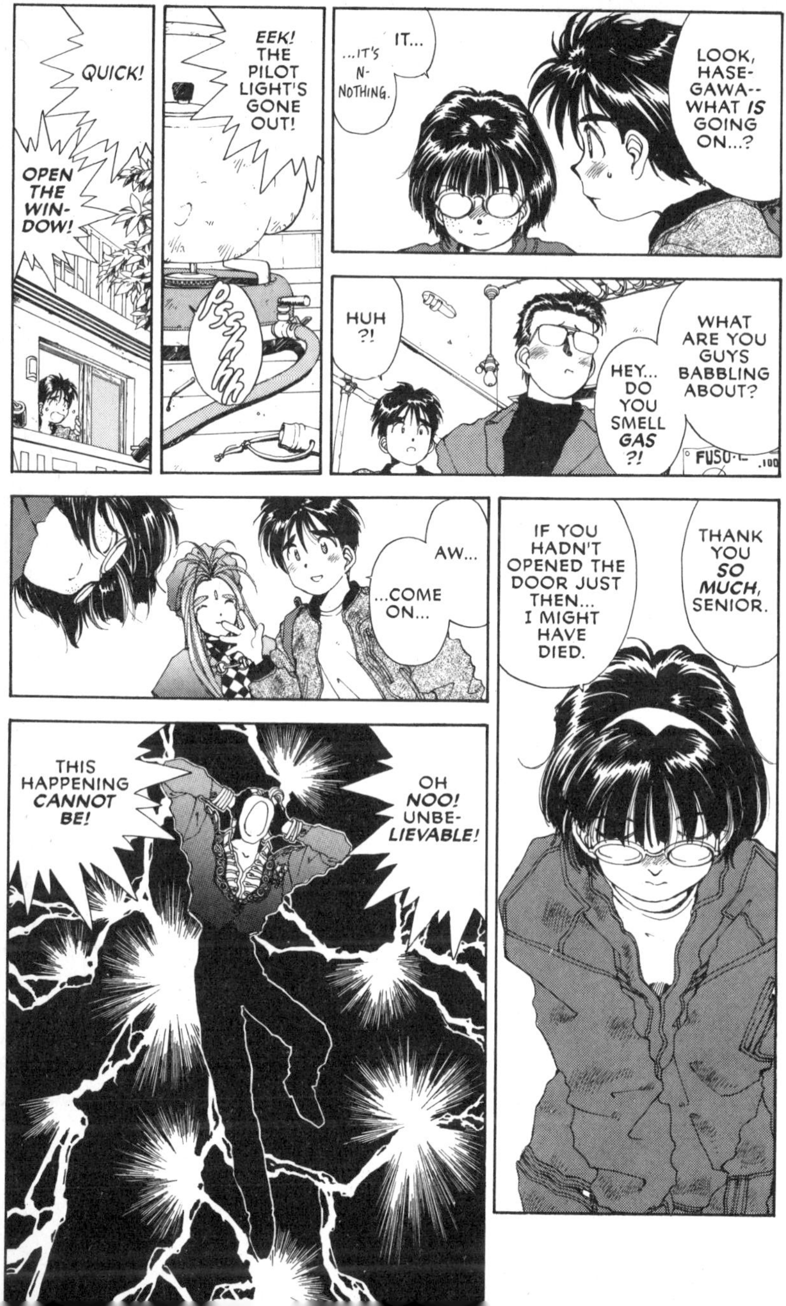
LOOK, HASE-GAWA-- WHAT *IS* GOING ON...?
IT...
...IT'S N-NOTHING.
WHAT ARE YOU GUYS BABBLING ABOUT?
HEY... DO YOU SMELL *GAS* ?!
HUH ?!
FUSO
EEK! THE PILOT LIGHT'S GONE OUT!
PSSHHH
QUICK!
OPEN THE WIN-DOW!
THANK YOU *SO MUCH*, SENIOR.
IF YOU HADN'T OPENED THE DOOR JUST THEN... I MIGHT HAVE DIED.
AW...
...COME ON...
OH *NOO!* UNBE-*LIEVABLE!*
THIS HAPPENING *CANNOT BE!*

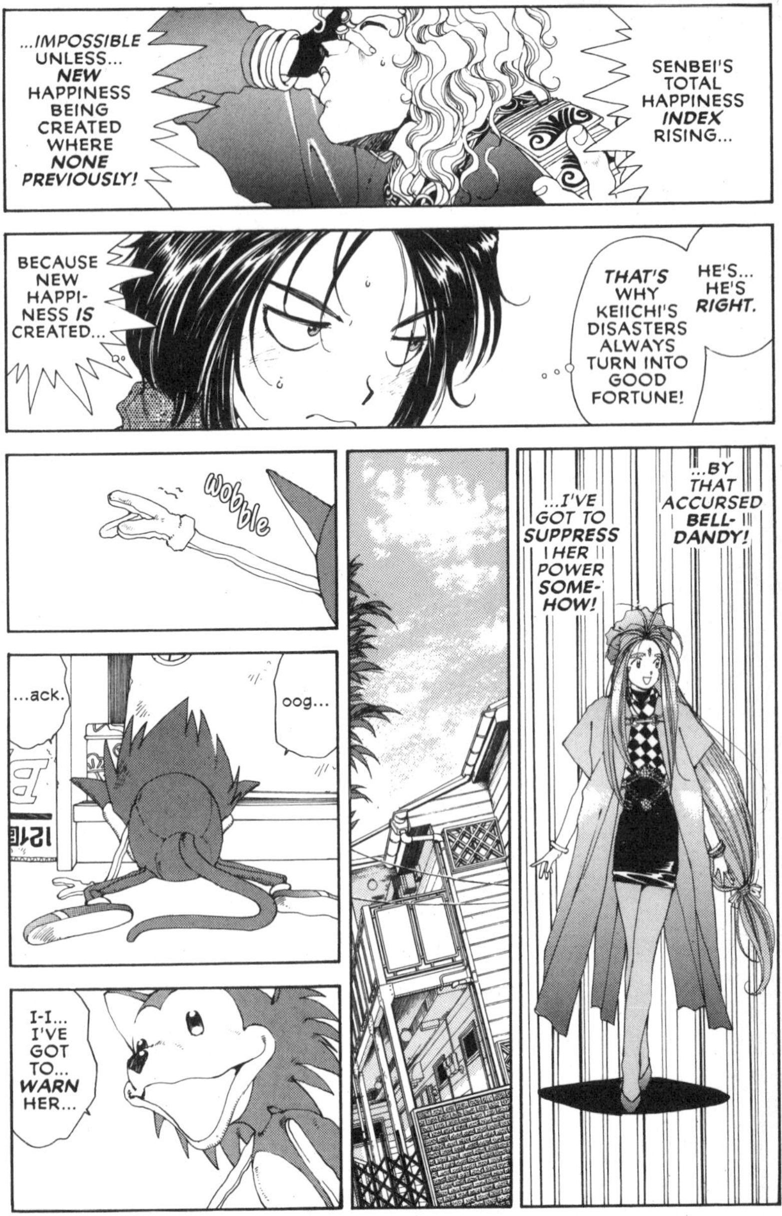
SENBEI'S TOTAL HAPPINESS INDEX RISING...
...IMPOSSIBLE UNLESS... NEW HAPPINESS BEING CREATED WHERE NONE PREVIOUSLY!
HE'S... HE'S RIGHT.
THAT'S WHY KEIICHI'S DISASTERS ALWAYS TURN INTO GOOD FORTUNE!
BECAUSE NEW HAPPINESS IS CREATED...
...BY THAT ACCURSED BELLDANDY!
...I'VE GOT TO SUPPRESS HER POWER SOMEHOW!
wobble
oog...
...ack.
I-I... I'VE GOT TO... WARN HER...

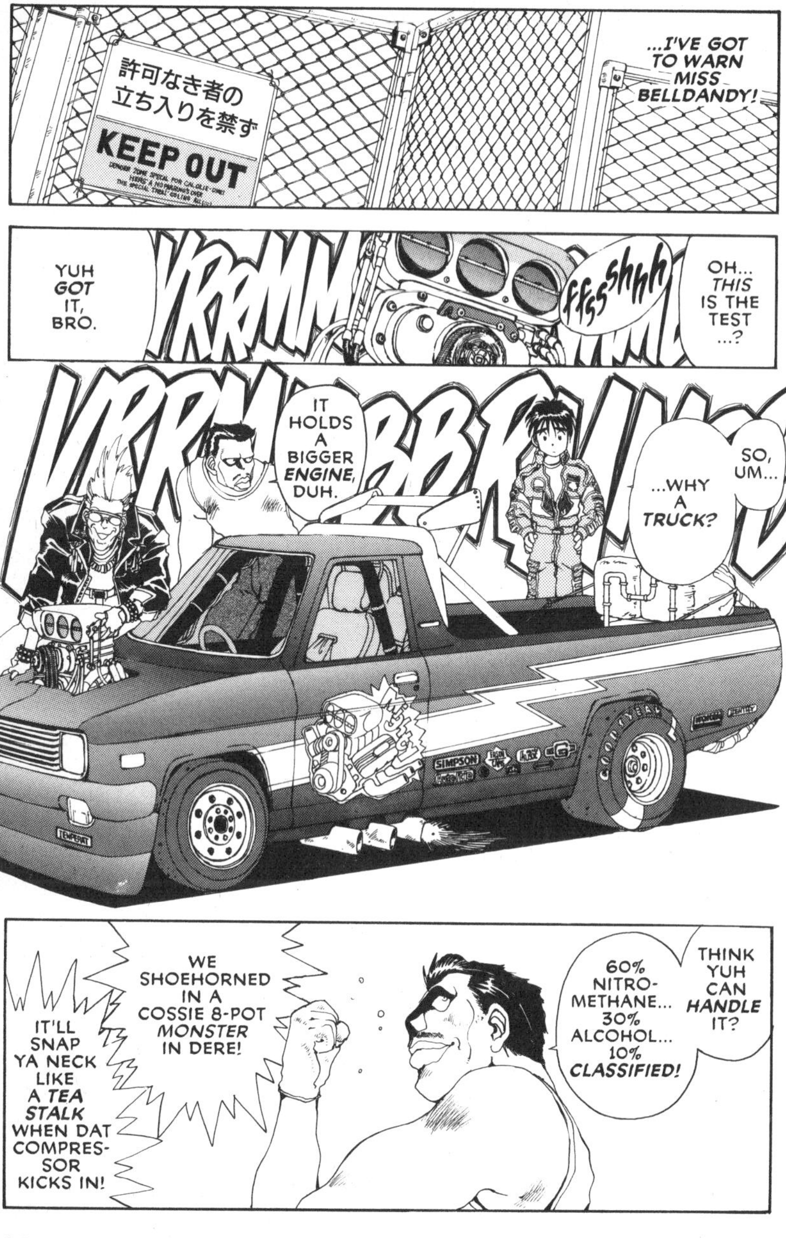
許可なき者の立ち入りを禁ず
KEEP OUT
...I'VE GOT TO WARN MISS BELLDANDY!
YUH GOT IT, BRO.
ffssshhh
OH... THIS IS THE TEST ...?
SO, UM...
...WHY A TRUCK?
IT HOLDS A BIGGER ENGINE, DUH.
SIMPSON
THINK YUH CAN HANDLE IT?
60% NITRO-METHANE... 30% ALCOHOL... 10% CLASSIFIED!
WE SHOEHORNED IN A COSSIE 8-POT MONSTER IN DERE!
IT'LL SNAP YA NECK LIKE A TEA STALK WHEN DAT COMPRES-SOR KICKS IN!

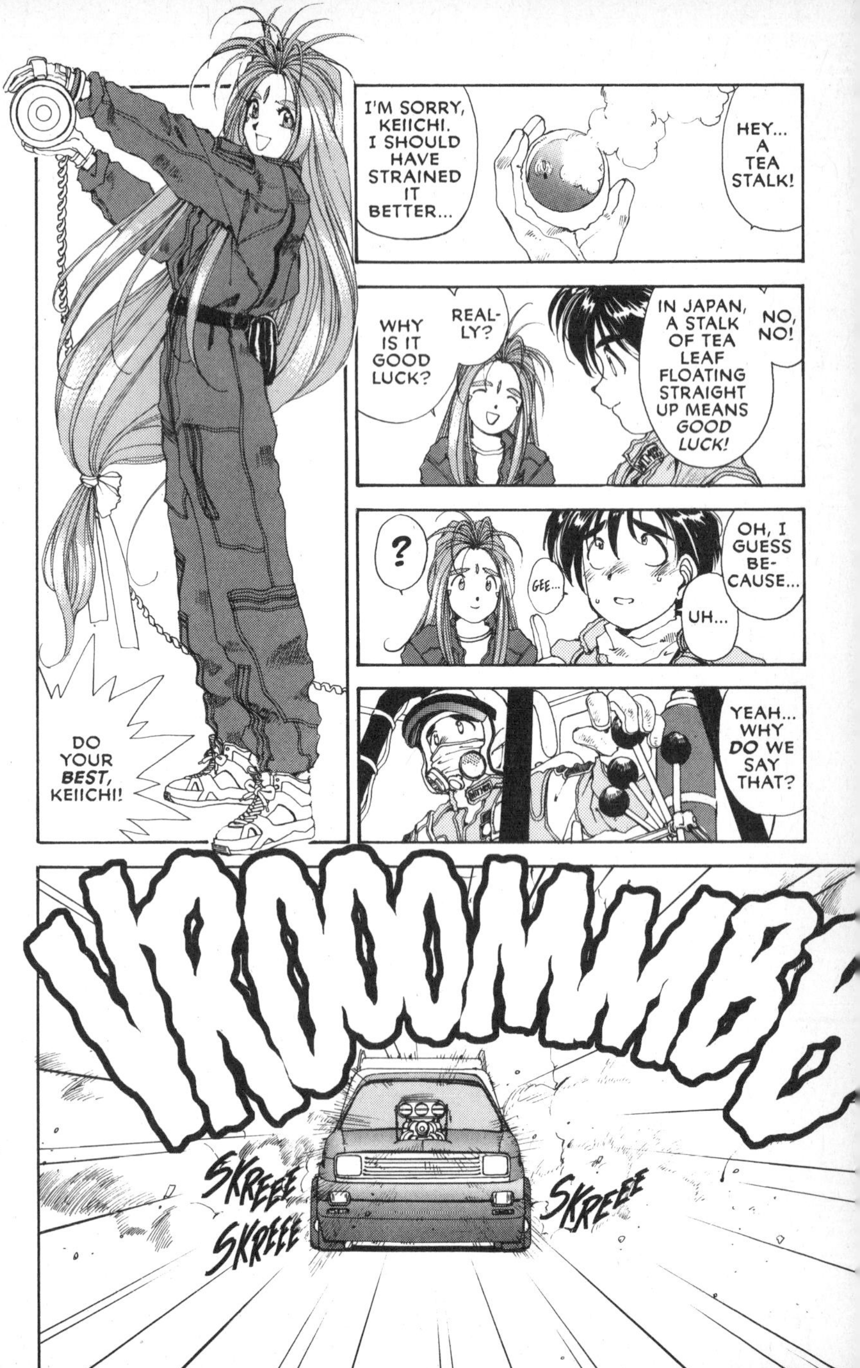

I'M SORRY, KEIICHI. I SHOULD HAVE STRAINED IT BETTER...
HEY... A TEA STALK!
NO, NO!
IN JAPAN, A STALK OF TEA LEAF FLOATING STRAIGHT UP MEANS *GOOD LUCK!*
REAL-LY?
WHY IS IT GOOD LUCK?
?
GEE...
OH, I GUESS BE-CAUSE...
UH...
YEAH... WHY *DO* WE SAY THAT?
DO YOUR *BEST,* KEIICHI!
VROOOMMB
SKREEE
SKREEE
SKREEE

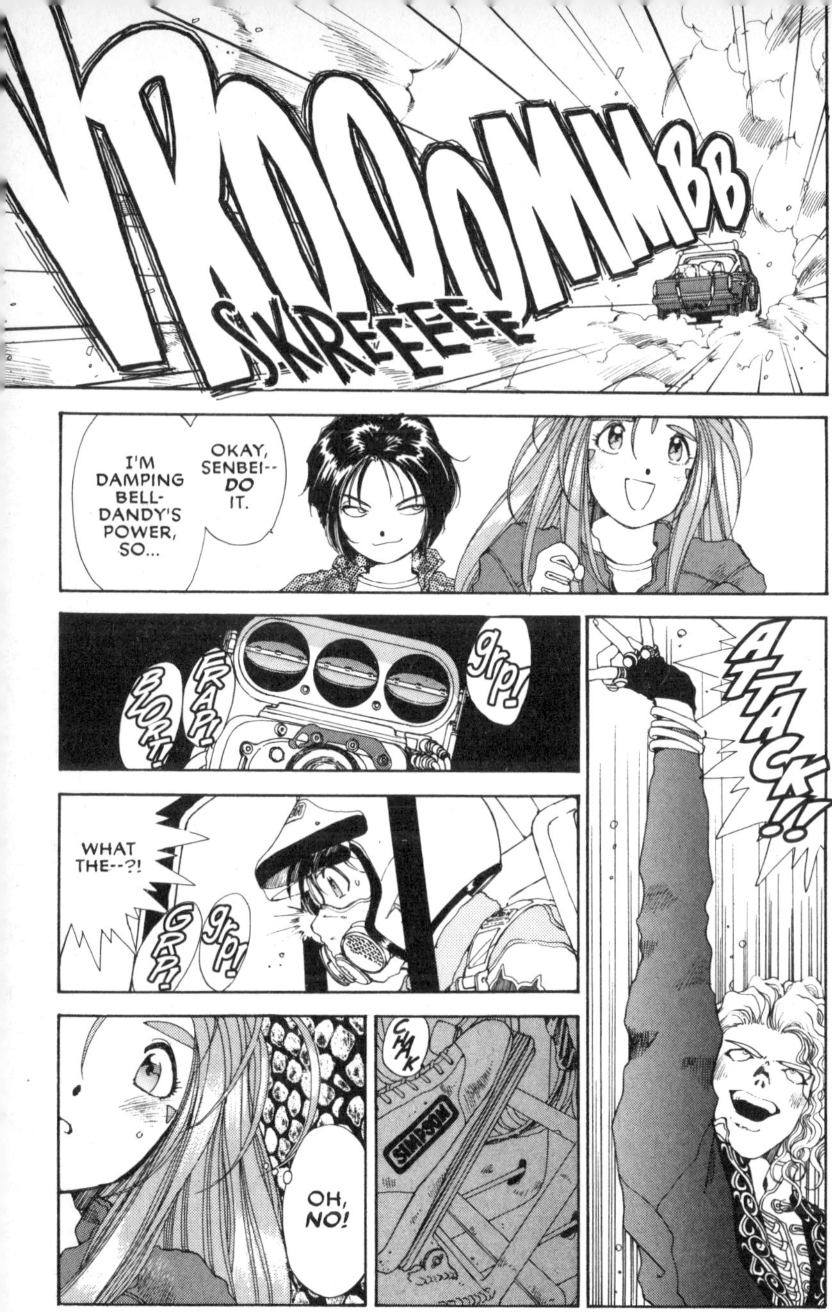
VROOOMMBB
SKREEEEE
OKAY, SENBEI-- DO IT.
I'M DAMPING BELL-DANDY'S POWER, SO...
ATTACK!!
grp!
FRAP!
BLORT!
WHAT THE--?!
grp!
GRP!
CHAK
SIMPSON
OH, NO!

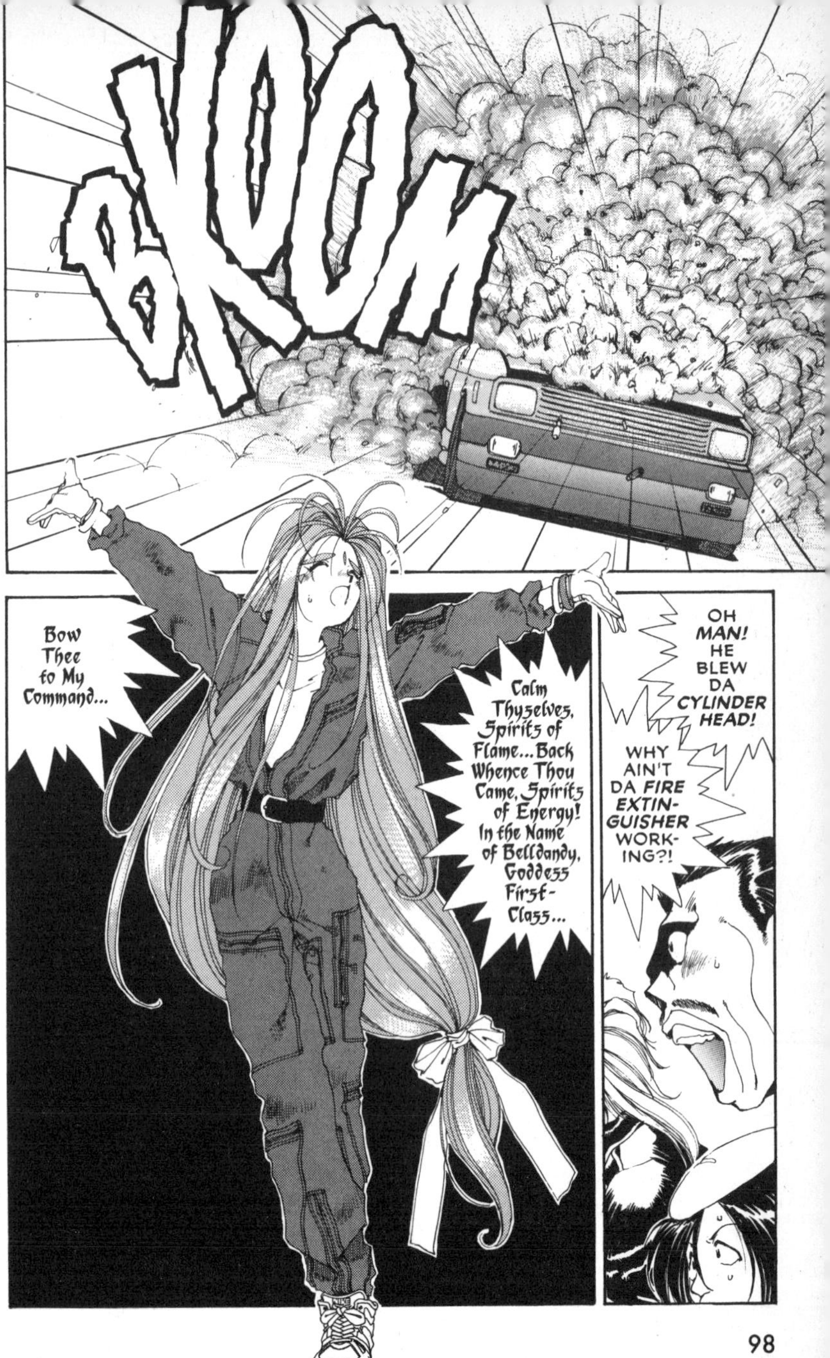

BKOOM
Bow Thee to My Command...
Calm Thyselves, Spirits of Flame... Back Whence Thou Came, Spirits of Energy! In the Name of Belldandy, Goddess First-Class...
OH MAN! HE BLEW DA CYLINDER HEAD!
WHY AIN'T DA FIRE EXTIN-GUISHER WORK-ING?!

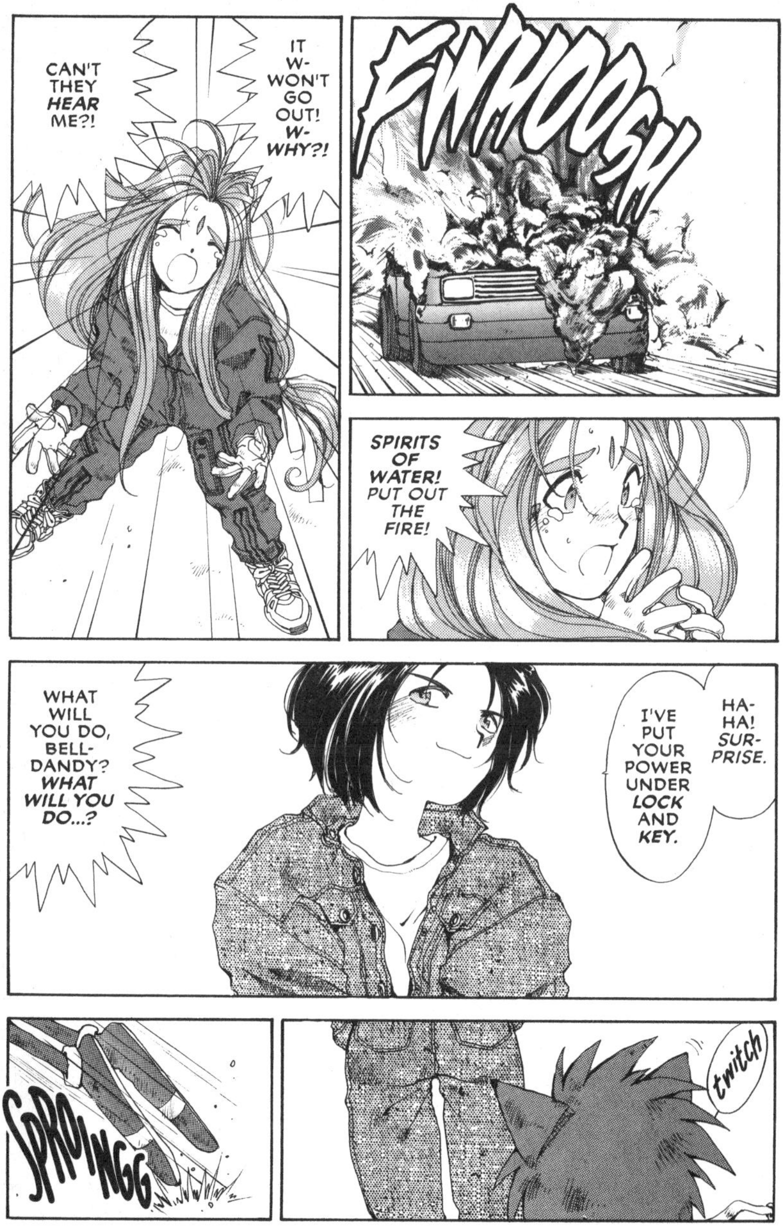
CAN'T THEY HEAR ME?!
IT W-WON'T GO OUT! W-WHY?!
FWHOOSH
SPIRITS OF WATER! PUT OUT THE FIRE!
HA-HA! SUR-PRISE.
I'VE PUT YOUR POWER UNDER LOCK AND KEY.
WHAT WILL YOU DO, BELL-DANDY? WHAT WILL YOU DO...?
SPROINGG
twitch

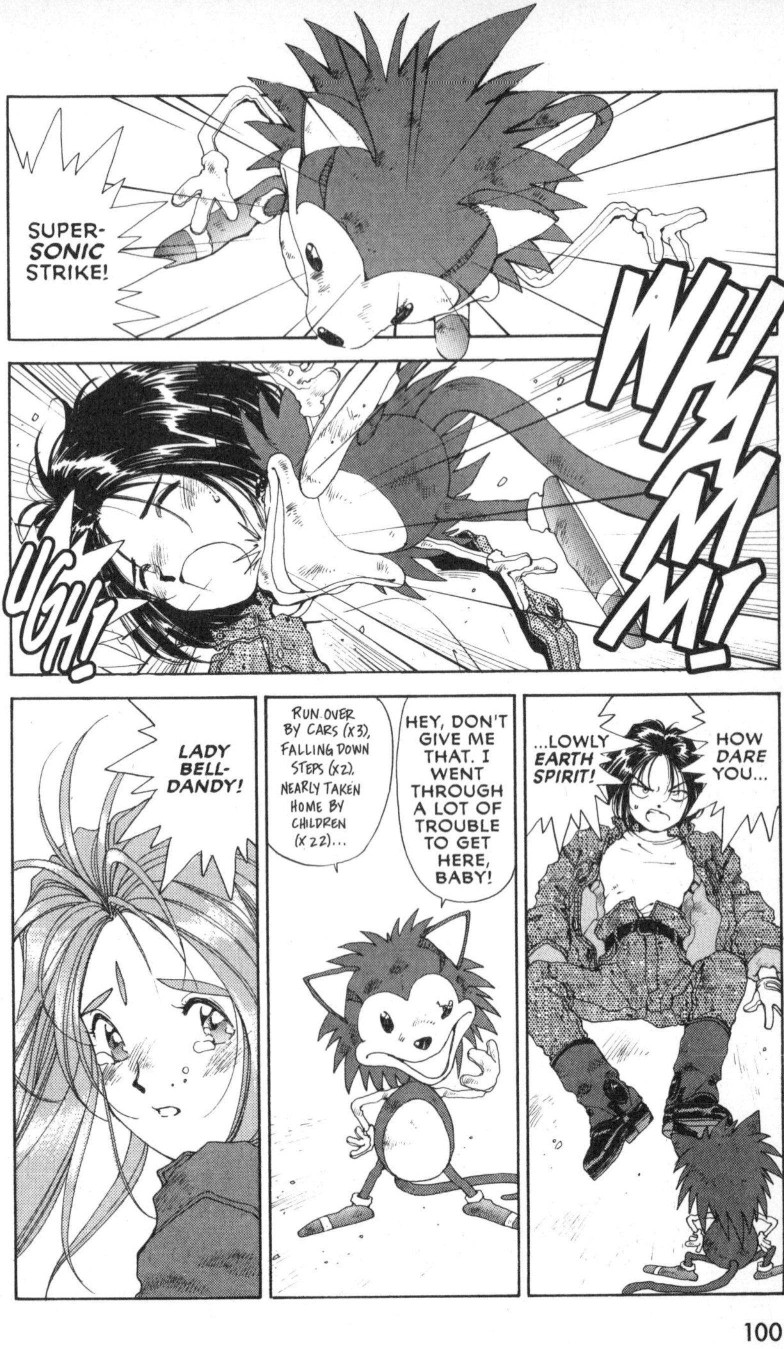
SUPER-SONIC STRIKE!
WHAMMM!
UGH!
LADY BELL-DANDY!
RUN OVER BY CARS (x3), FALLING DOWN STEPS (x2), NEARLY TAKEN HOME BY CHILDREN (x22)...
HEY, DON'T GIVE ME THAT. I WENT THROUGH A LOT OF TROUBLE TO GET HERE, BABY!
HOW DARE YOU...
...LOWLY EARTH SPIRIT!

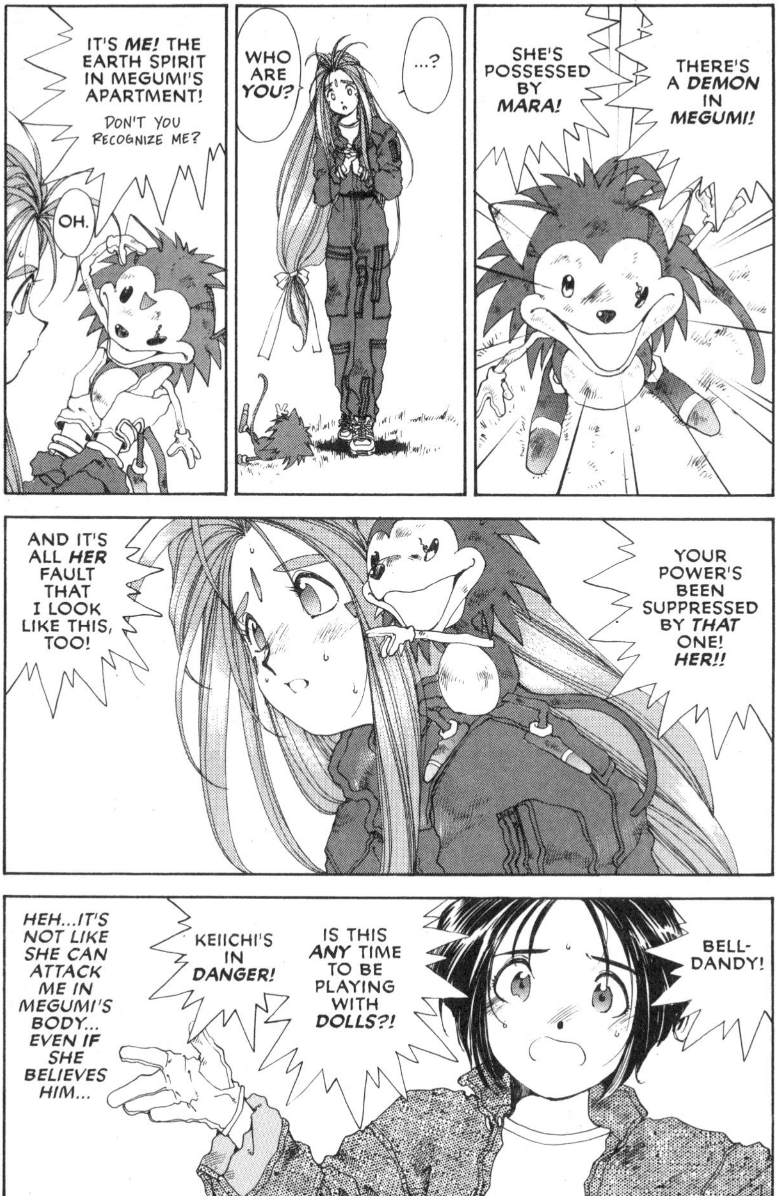
IT'S ME! THE EARTH SPIRIT IN MEGUMI'S APARTMENT!
DON'T YOU RECOGNIZE ME?
OH.
WHO ARE YOU?
...?
SHE'S POSSESSED BY MARA!
THERE'S A DEMON IN MEGUMI!
AND IT'S ALL HER FAULT THAT I LOOK LIKE THIS, TOO!
YOUR POWER'S BEEN SUPPRESSED BY THAT ONE! HER!!
HEH...IT'S NOT LIKE SHE CAN ATTACK ME IN MEGUMI'S BODY... EVEN IF SHE BELIEVES HIM...
KEIICHI'S IN DANGER!
IS THIS ANY TIME TO BE PLAYING WITH DOLLS?!
BELL-DANDY!

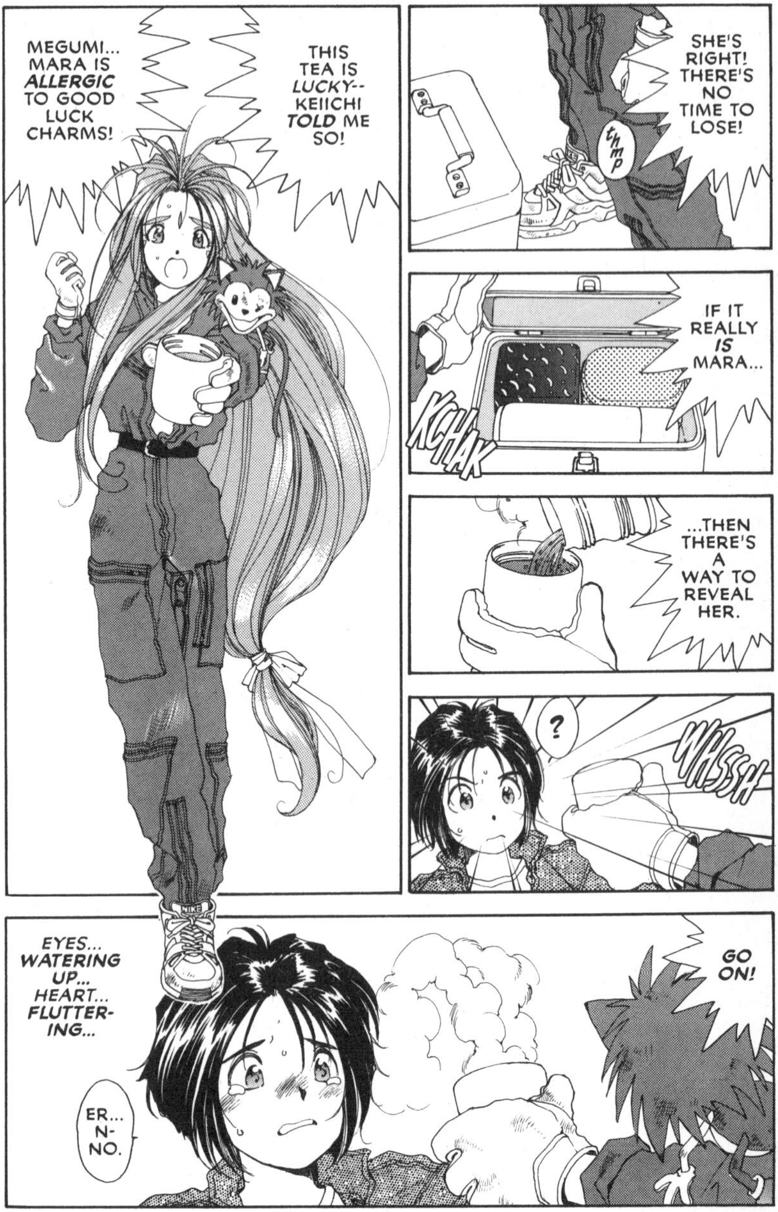
THIS TEA IS LUCKY-- KEIICHI TOLD ME SO!
MEGUMI... MARA IS ALLERGIC TO GOOD LUCK CHARMS!
SHE'S RIGHT! THERE'S NO TIME TO LOSE!
thmp
IF IT REALLY IS MARA...
KCHAK
...THEN THERE'S A WAY TO REVEAL HER.
WHSSH
?
GO ON!
EYES... WATERING UP... HEART... FLUTTERING...
ER... N-NO.

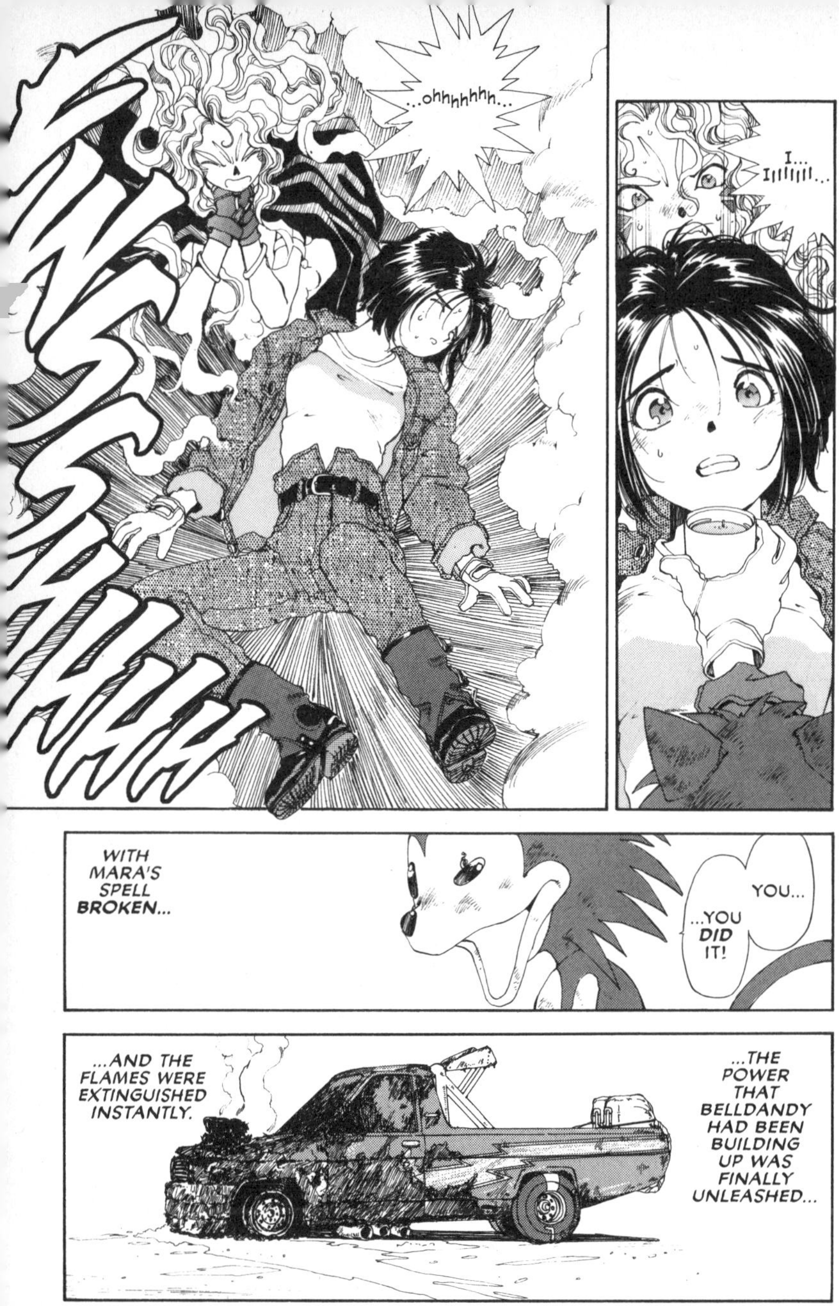
...ohhhhhhh...
I... Iiiiiiii...
WITH MARA'S SPELL **BROKEN**...
YOU... ...YOU **DID** IT!
...AND THE FLAMES WERE EXTINGUISHED INSTANTLY.
...THE POWER THAT BELLDANDY HAD BEEN BUILDING UP WAS FINALLY UNLEASHED...

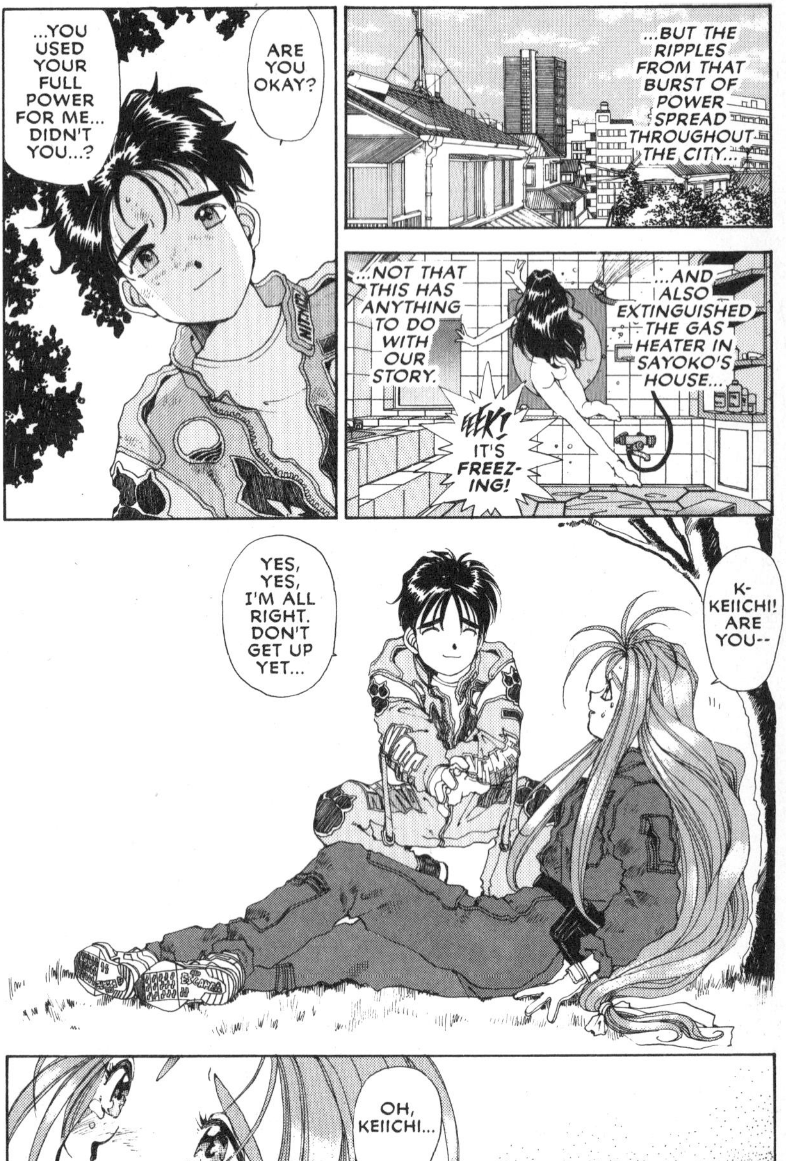
...YOU USED YOUR FULL POWER FOR ME... DIDN'T YOU...?
ARE YOU OKAY?
...BUT THE RIPPLES FROM THAT BURST OF POWER SPREAD THROUGHOUT THE CITY...
...AND ALSO EXTINGUISHED THE GAS HEATER IN SAYOKO'S HOUSE...
EEEK! IT'S FREEZING!
...NOT THAT THIS HAS ANYTHING TO DO WITH OUR STORY.
K-KEIICHI! ARE YOU--
YES, YES, I'M ALL RIGHT. DON'T GET UP YET...
OH, KEIICHI...

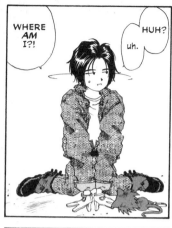

I THOUGHT... I THOUGHT YOU WERE GOING TO DIE...
WHOA!
HUH?
uh.
WHERE AM I?!
THE PARKING LOT BEHIND THE SCHOOL ?!
WHA--? HOW DID I GET HERE?!
OH, NO! COULD IT BE...
DID I SLEEP-WALK? OR WORSE... SLEEP-PARK...?
HM ...?
...WHAT'S THIS THING?

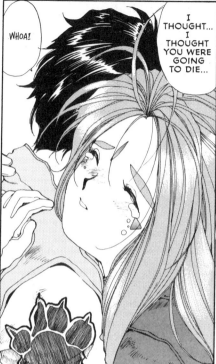

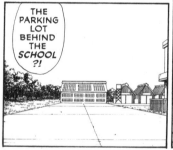

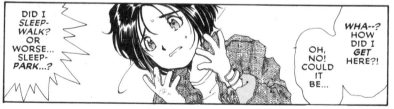

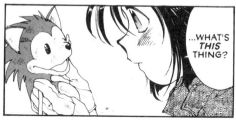

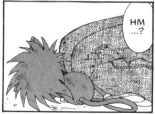

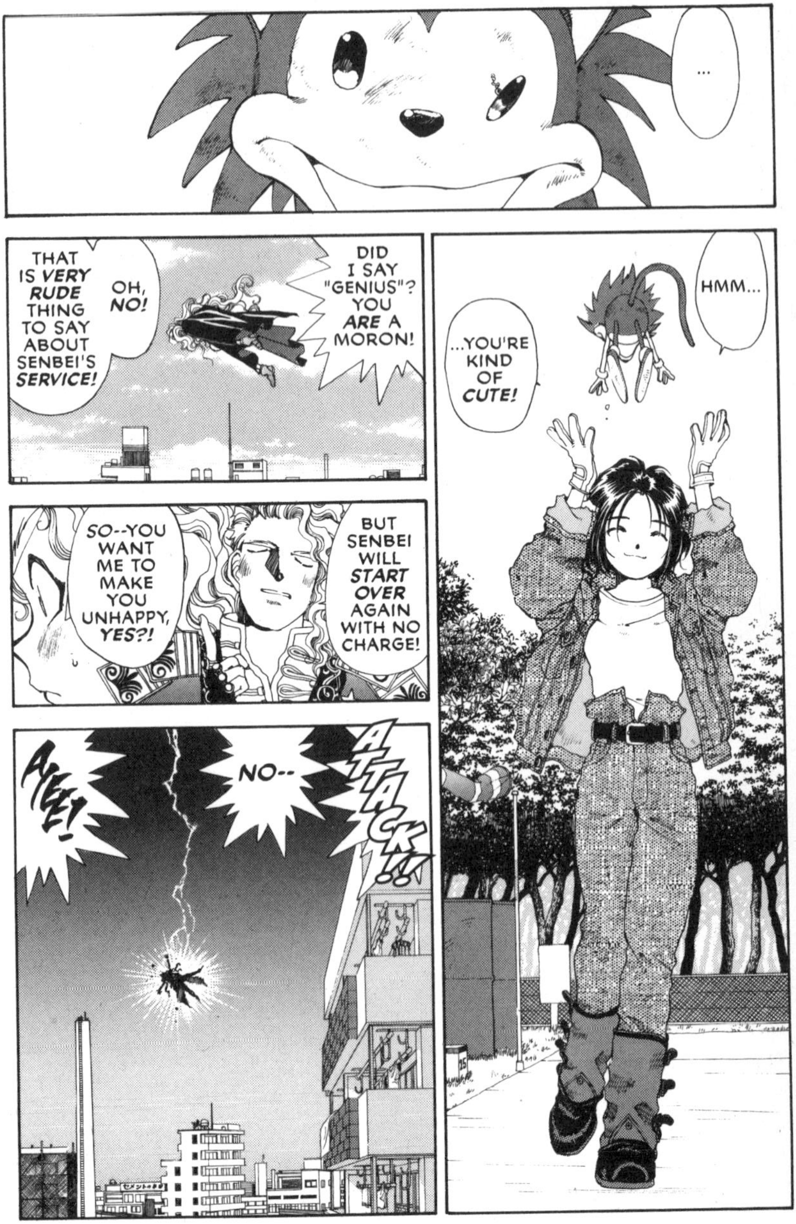
...
HMM...
...YOU'RE KIND OF CUTE!
DID I SAY "GENIUS"? YOU ARE A MORON!
OH, NO!
THAT IS VERY RUDE THING TO SAY ABOUT SENBEI'S SERVICE!
BUT SENBEI WILL START OVER AGAIN WITH NO CHARGE!
SO--YOU WANT ME TO MAKE YOU UNHAPPY, YES?!
ATTACK!!
NO--
AIEE!

CHAPTER 46

Thank You

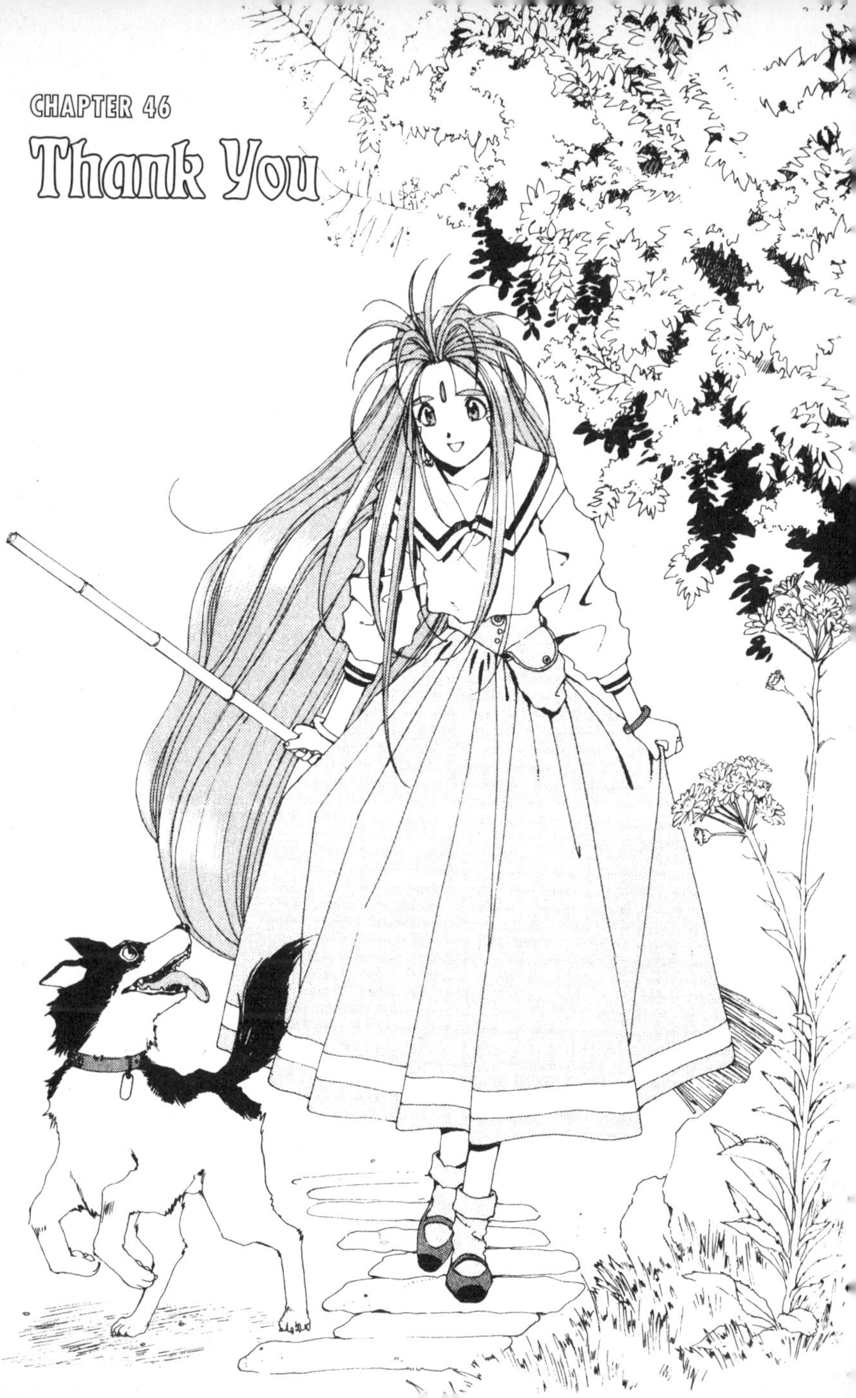

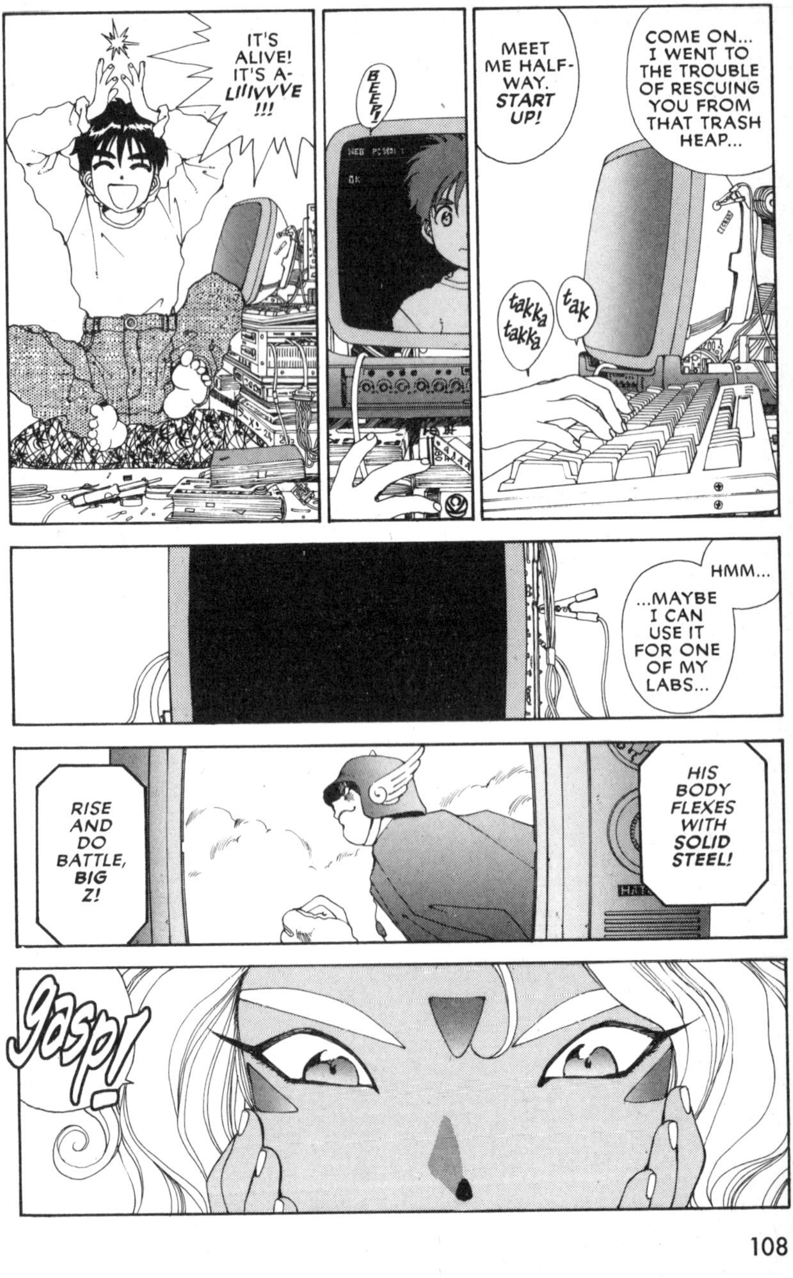
IT'S ALIVE! IT'S A-LIIIVVVE !!!
BEEP!
COME ON... I WENT TO THE TROUBLE OF RESCUING YOU FROM THAT TRASH HEAP...
MEET ME HALF-WAY. START UP!
takka takka
tak
HMM...
...MAYBE I CAN USE IT FOR ONE OF MY LABS...
RISE AND DO BATTLE, BIG Z!
HIS BODY FLEXES WITH SOLID STEEL!
gasp!

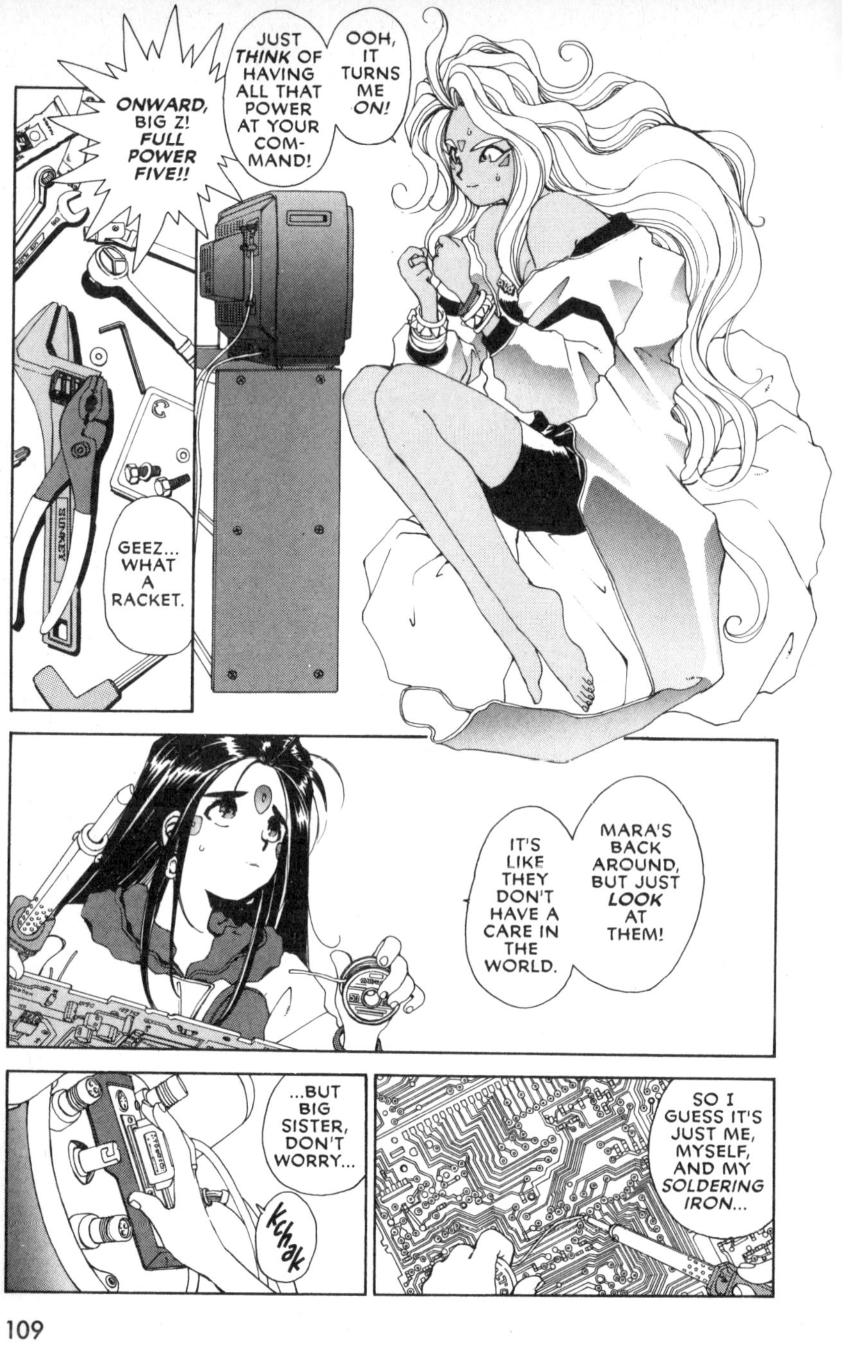
ONWARD, BIG Z! FULL POWER FIVE!!
JUST THINK OF HAVING ALL THAT POWER AT YOUR COMMAND!
OOH, IT TURNS ME ON!
GEEZ... WHAT A RACKET.
MARA'S BACK AROUND, BUT JUST LOOK AT THEM!
IT'S LIKE THEY DON'T HAVE A CARE IN THE WORLD.
...BUT BIG SISTER, DON'T WORRY...
Kchak
SO I GUESS IT'S JUST ME, MYSELF, AND MY SOLDERING IRON...

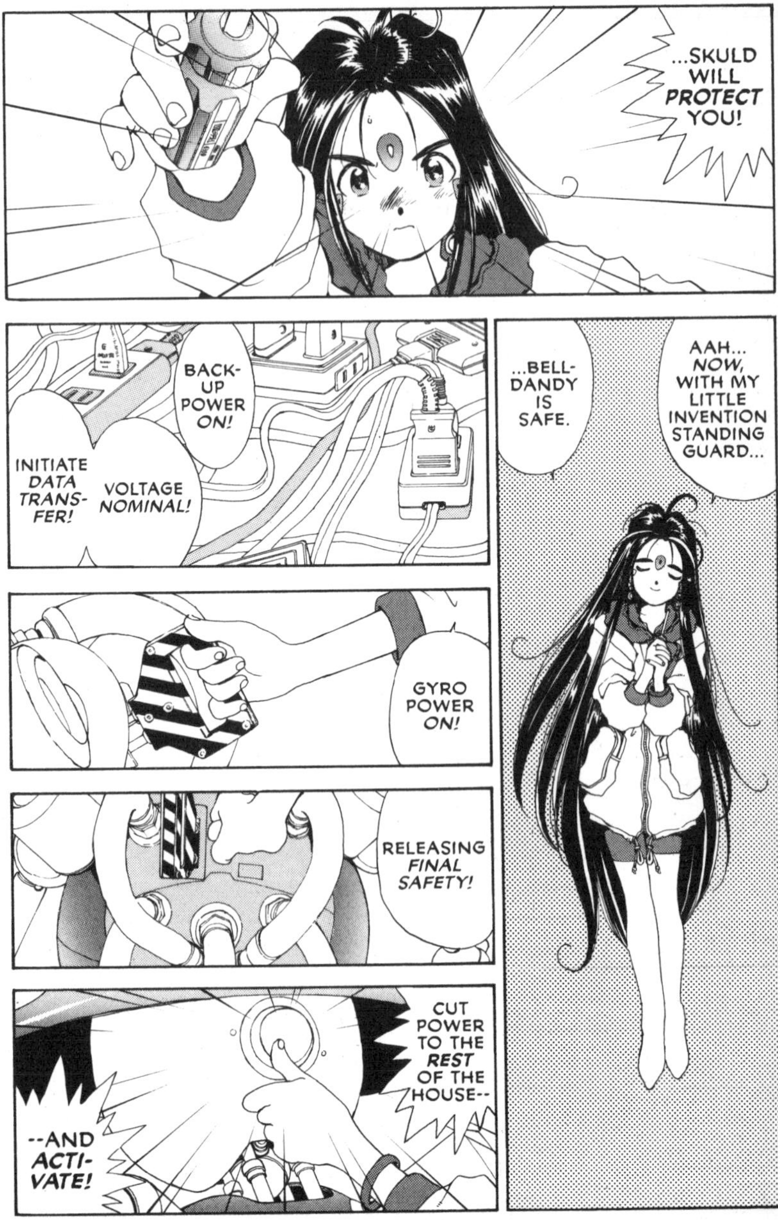
...SKULD WILL PROTECT YOU!
AAH... NOW, WITH MY LITTLE INVENTION STANDING GUARD...
...BELL-DANDY IS SAFE.
BACK-UP POWER ON!
VOLTAGE NOMINAL!
INITIATE DATA TRANS-FER!
GYRO POWER ON!
RELEASING FINAL SAFETY!
CUT POWER TO THE REST OF THE HOUSE--
--AND ACTI-VATE!

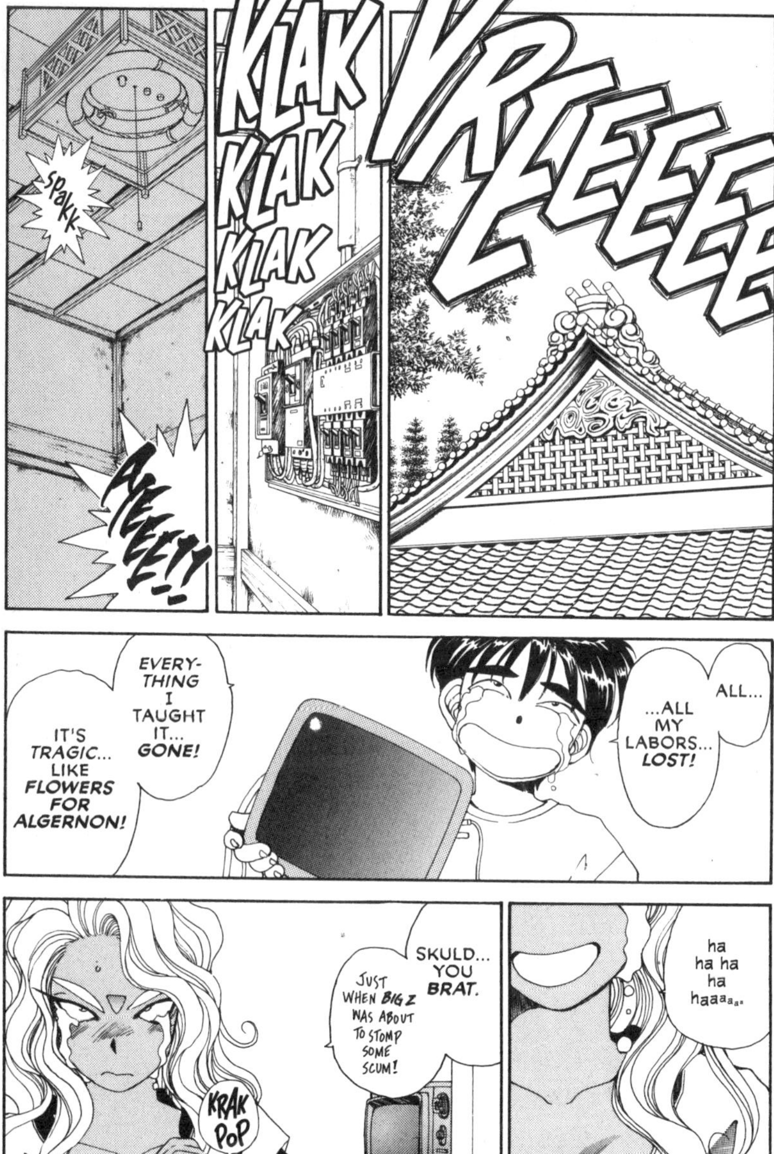
VRIEEEEEE
KLAK KLAK KLAK KLAK
SPAKK
AIEEEE!!
ALL... ...ALL MY LABORS... LOST!
EVERY-THING I TAUGHT IT... GONE!
IT'S TRAGIC... LIKE FLOWERS FOR ALGERNON!
ha ha ha ha haaaaaa
SKULD... YOU BRAT.
JUST WHEN BIG Z WAS ABOUT TO STOMP SOME SCUM!
KRAK POP

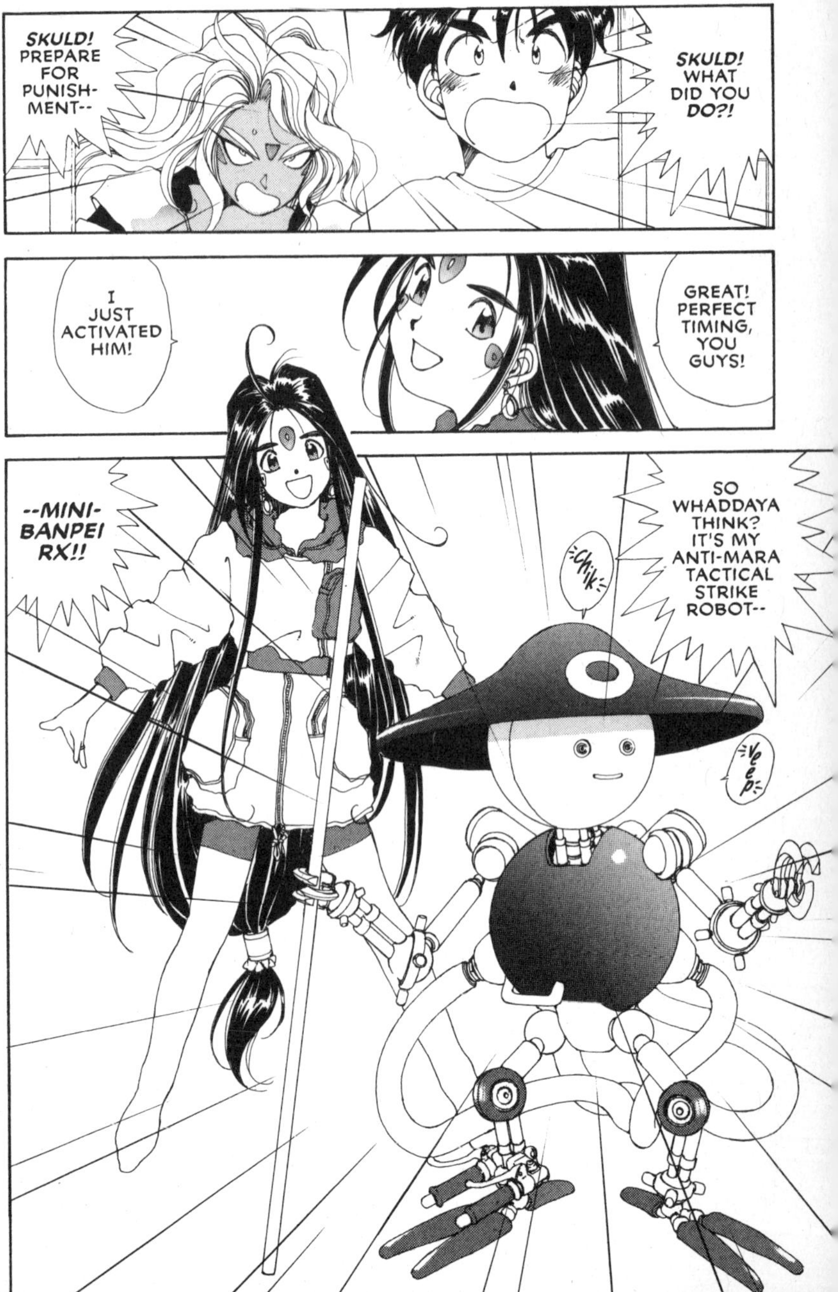
SKULD! WHAT DID YOU DO?!
SKULD! PREPARE FOR PUNISH-MENT--
GREAT! PERFECT TIMING, YOU GUYS!
I JUST ACTIVATED HIM!
SO WHADDAYA THINK? IT'S MY ANTI-MARA TACTICAL STRIKE ROBOT--
--MINI-BANPEI RX!!
Chik
Veep

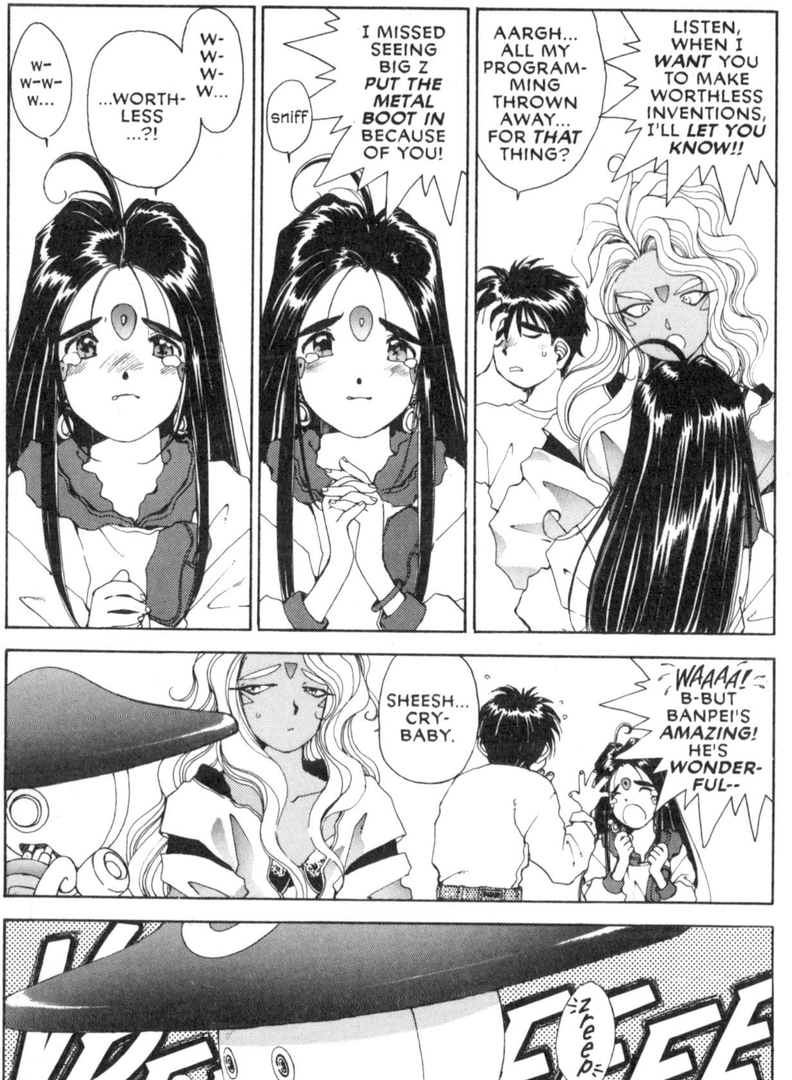
W-W-W-W...
...WORTH-LESS ...?!
W-W-W-W...
I MISSED SEEING BIG Z *PUT THE METAL BOOT IN* BECAUSE OF YOU!
sniff
AARGH... ALL MY PROGRAMMING THROWN AWAY... FOR *THAT* THING?
LISTEN, WHEN I *WANT* YOU TO MAKE WORTHLESS INVENTIONS, I'LL *LET YOU KNOW!!*
SHEESH... CRY-BABY.
WAAAA! B-BUT BANPEI'S *AMAZING!* HE'S *WONDERFUL--*
zreep
chik
!

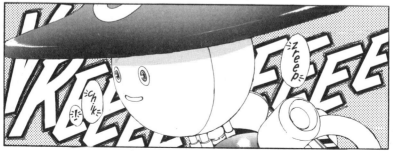

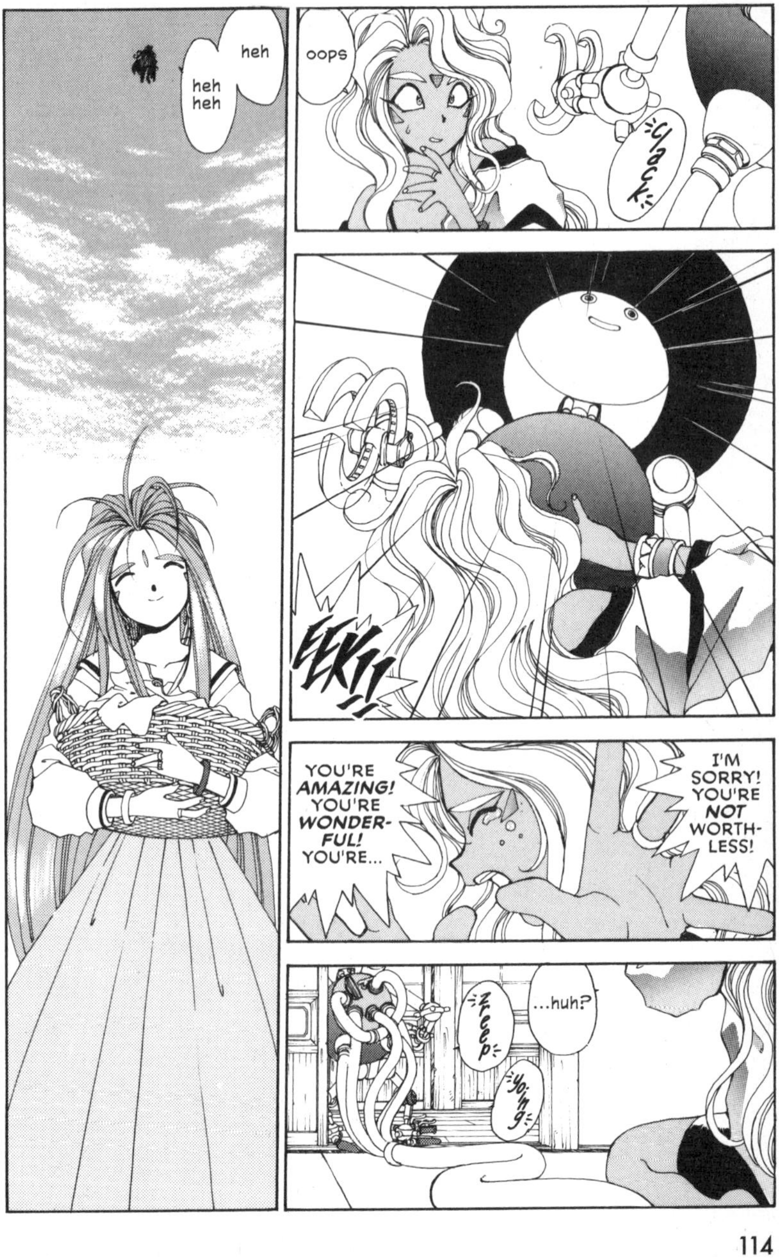
oops
clack
heh
heh heh
EEK!!
I'M SORRY! YOU'RE NOT WORTHLESS!
YOU'RE AMAZING! YOU'RE WONDERFUL! YOU'RE...
...huh?
zreeep
yoing

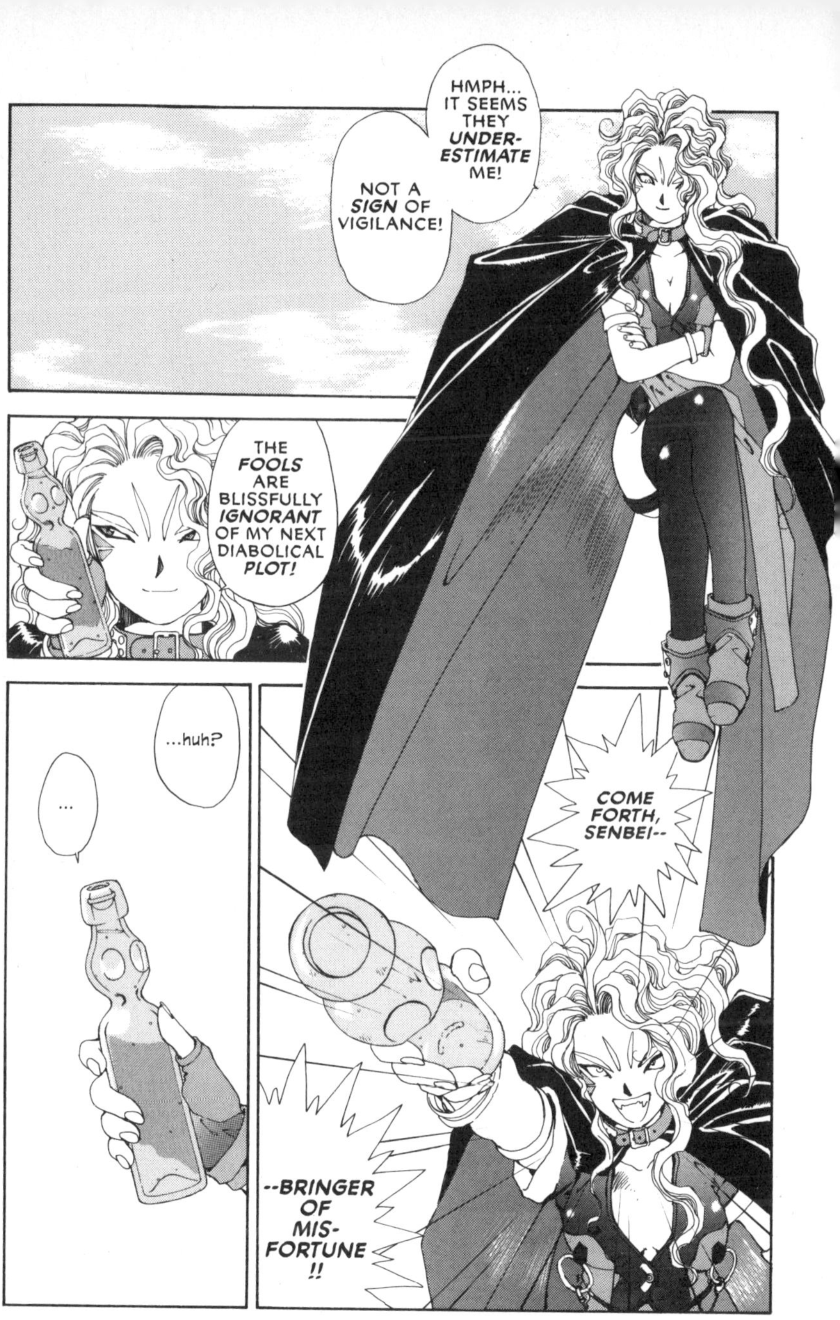
HMPH... IT SEEMS THEY UNDER-ESTIMATE ME!
NOT A SIGN OF VIGILANCE!
THE FOOLS ARE BLISSFULLY IGNORANT OF MY NEXT DIABOLICAL PLOT!
...huh?
...
COME FORTH, SENBEI--
--BRINGER OF MIS-FORTUNE !!

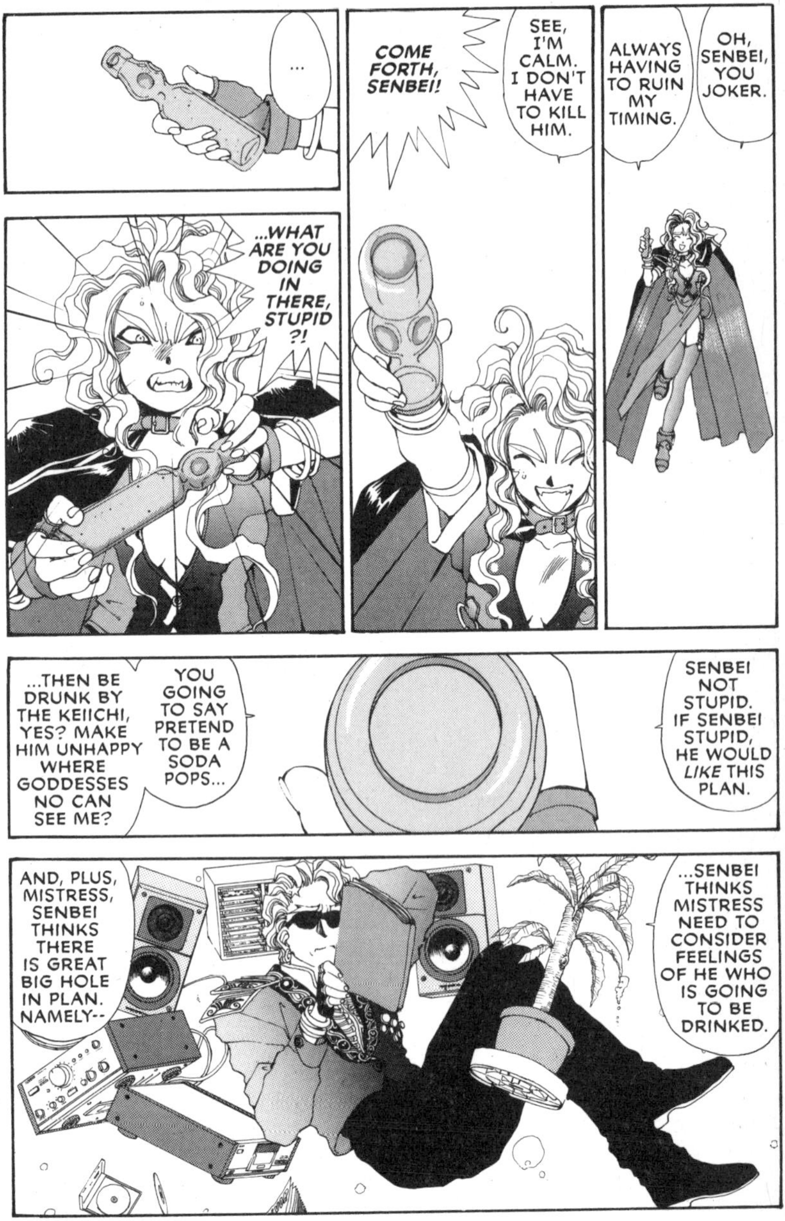
...
...WHAT ARE YOU DOING IN THERE, STUPID?!
SEE, I'M CALM. I DON'T HAVE TO KILL HIM.
COME FORTH, SENBEI!
OH, SENBEI, YOU JOKER.
ALWAYS HAVING TO RUIN MY TIMING.
SENBEI NOT STUPID. IF SENBEI STUPID, HE WOULD *LIKE* THIS PLAN.
YOU GOING TO SAY PRETEND TO BE A SODA POPS...
...THEN BE DRUNK BY THE KEIICHI, YES? MAKE HIM UNHAPPY WHERE GODDESSES NO CAN SEE ME?
AND, PLUS, MISTRESS, SENBEI THINKS THERE IS GREAT BIG HOLE IN PLAN. NAMELY--
...SENBEI THINKS MISTRESS NEED TO CONSIDER FEELINGS OF HE WHO IS GOING TO BE DRINKED.

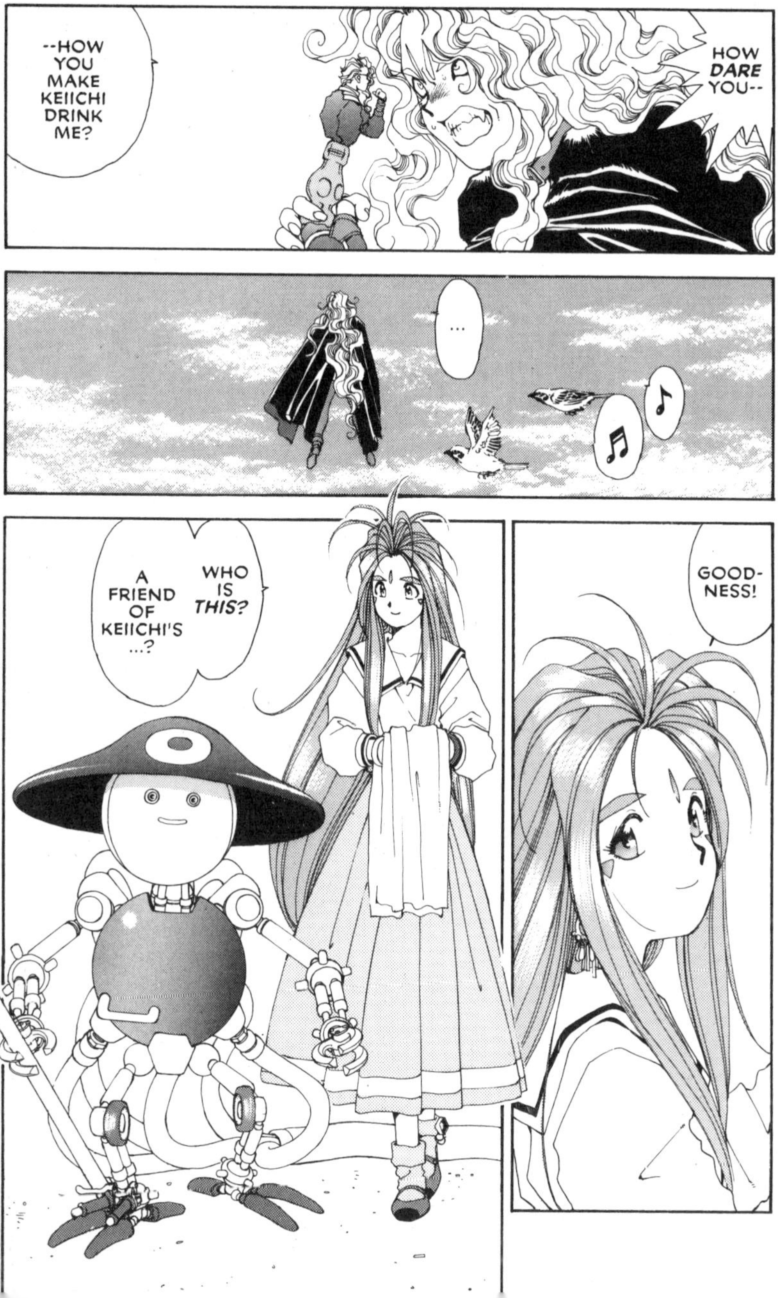
HOW DARE YOU--
--HOW YOU MAKE KEIICHI DRINK ME?
...
GOOD-NESS!
WHO IS THIS?
A FRIEND OF KEIICHI'S ...?

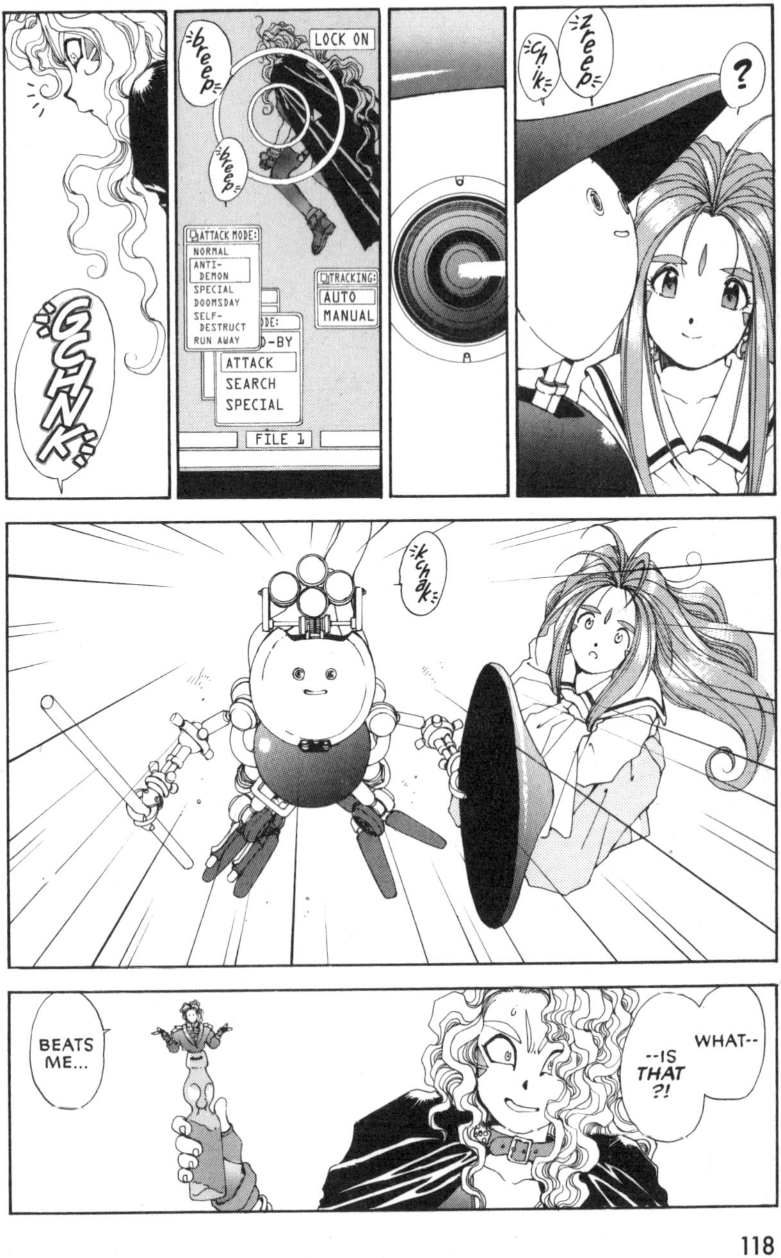
zreep
chik
?
LOCK ON
breep
breep
ATTACK MODE:
NORMAL
ANTI-DEMON
SPECIAL
DOOMSDAY
SELF-DESTRUCT
RUN AWAY
TRACKING:
AUTO
MANUAL
ATTACK
SEARCH
SPECIAL
FILE 1
GCHNK
kchak
WHAT--
--IS THAT?!
BEATS ME...

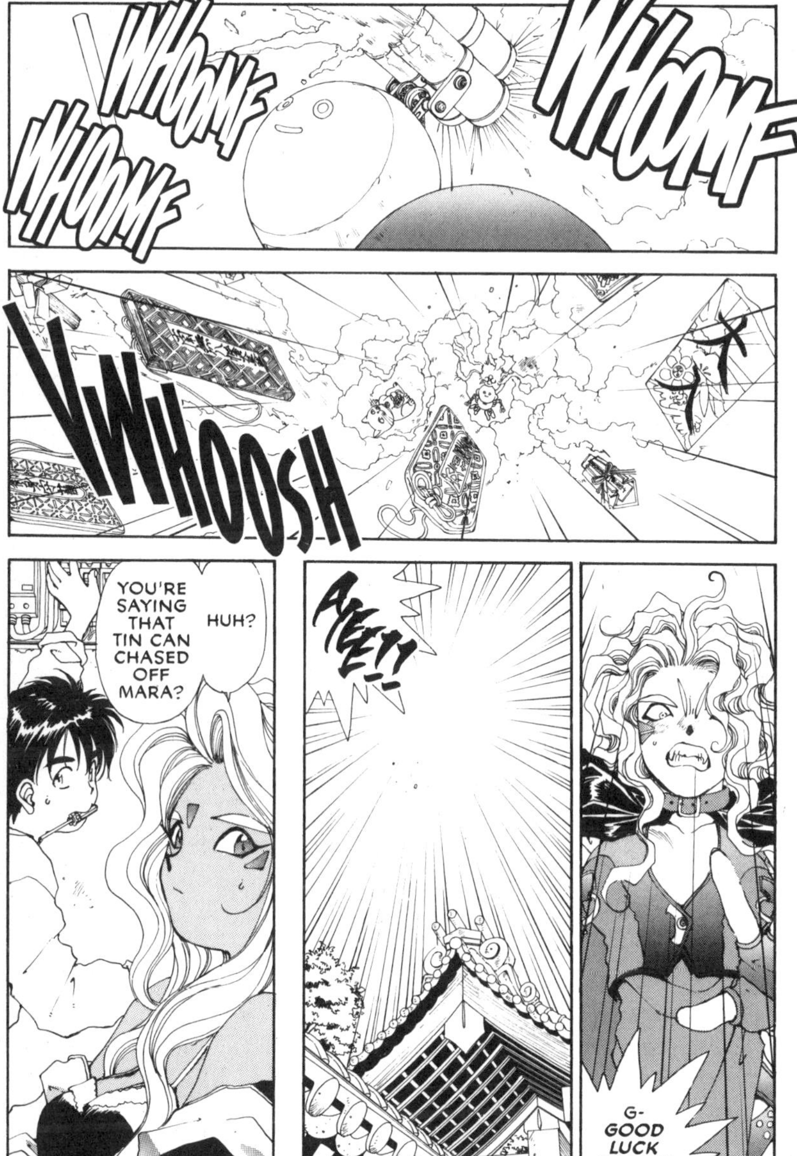
WHOOMF
WHOOMF
WHOOMF
VWHOOSH
YOU'RE SAYING THAT TIN CAN CHASED OFF MARA?
HUH?
AEE!!
G- GOOD LUCK CHARMS !!

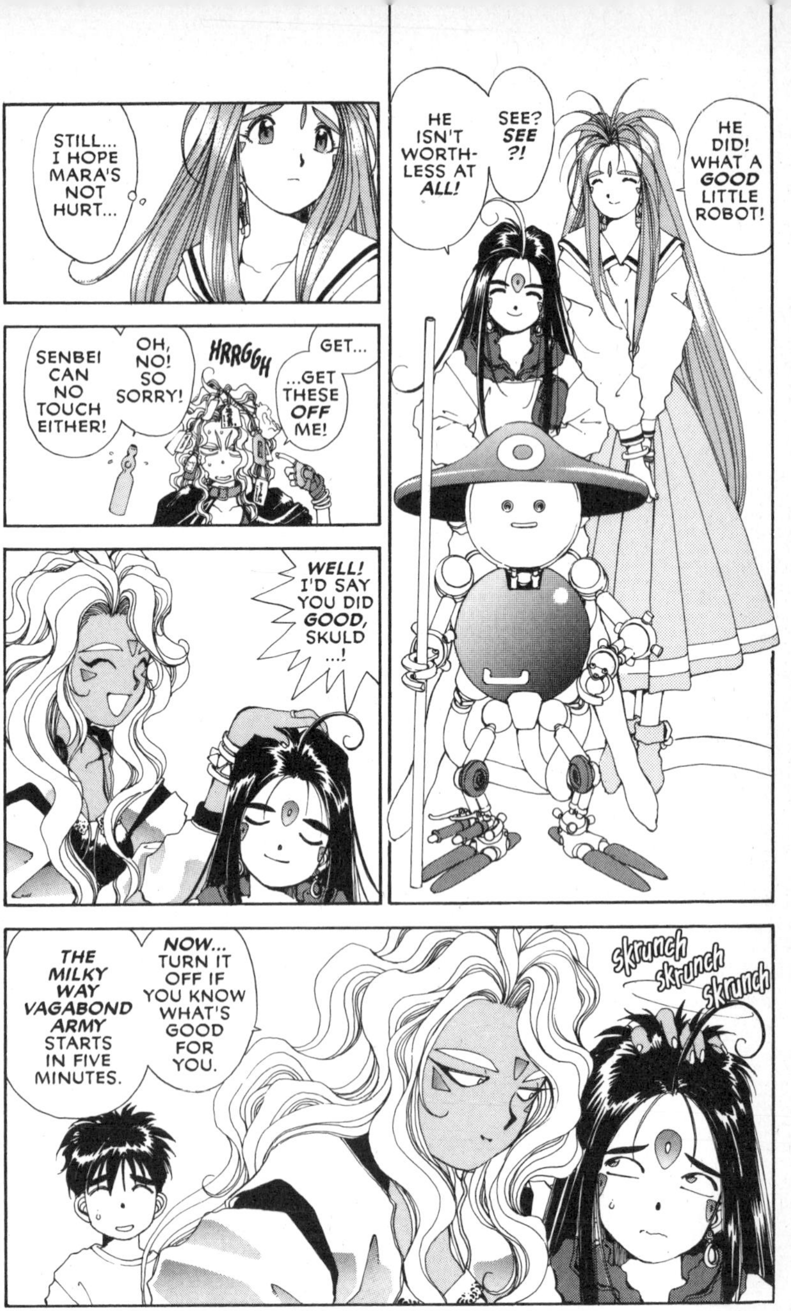
STILL... I HOPE MARA'S NOT HURT...
SENBEI CAN NO TOUCH EITHER!
OH, NO! SO SORRY!
HRRGGH
GET...
...GET THESE OFF ME!
WELL! I'D SAY YOU DID GOOD, SKULD ...!
HE ISN'T WORTH-LESS AT ALL!
SEE? SEE?!
HE DID! WHAT A GOOD LITTLE ROBOT!
THE MILKY WAY VAGABOND ARMY STARTS IN FIVE MINUTES.
NOW... TURN IT OFF IF YOU KNOW WHAT'S GOOD FOR YOU.
skrunch skrunch skrunch

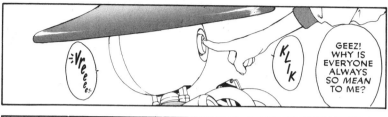

GEEZ! WHY IS EVERYONE ALWAYS SO *MEAN* TO ME?

AND AFTER I WENT TO ALL THAT TROUBLE MAKING HIM...

I GUESS I CAN AT LEAST LEAVE HIM ON STANDBY...

I WONDER IF HIS POWER'S ON?

OH, MY.

HE STOPPED RUN- NING ...?

MODE: STAND-BY

BACK-UP MEMORY GYRO ON

FILE 1

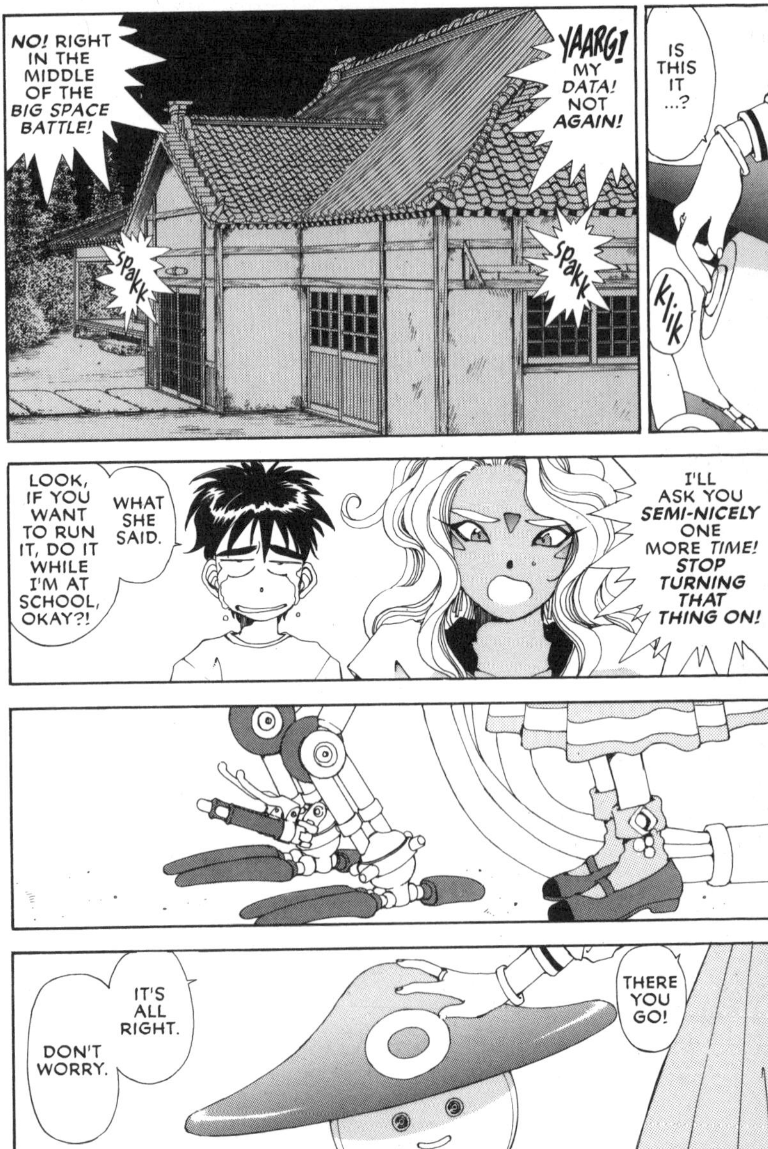
NO! RIGHT IN THE MIDDLE OF THE BIG SPACE BATTLE!
YAARG! MY DATA! NOT AGAIN!
spakk
spakk
IS THIS IT ...?
klik
LOOK, IF YOU WANT TO RUN IT, DO IT WHILE I'M AT SCHOOL, OKAY?!
WHAT SHE SAID.
I'LL ASK YOU SEMI-NICELY ONE MORE TIME! STOP TURNING THAT THING ON!
IT'S ALL RIGHT.
DON'T WORRY.
THERE YOU GO!

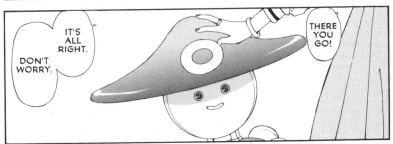

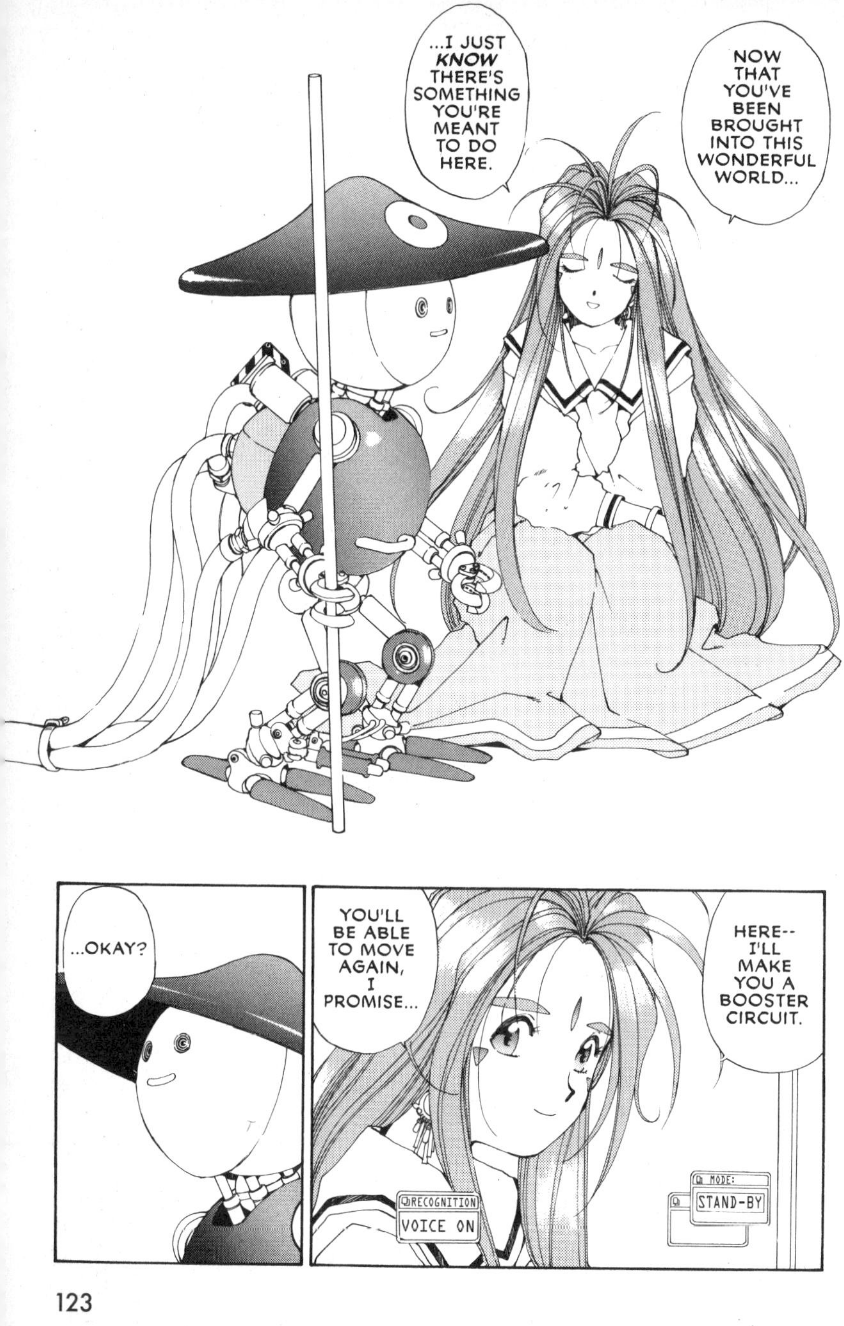
NOW THAT YOU'VE BEEN BROUGHT INTO THIS WONDERFUL WORLD...
...I JUST *KNOW* THERE'S SOMETHING YOU'RE MEANT TO DO HERE.
HERE-- I'LL MAKE YOU A BOOSTER CIRCUIT.
MODE:
STAND-BY
YOU'LL BE ABLE TO MOVE AGAIN, I PROMISE...
RECOGNITION
VOICE ON
...OKAY?

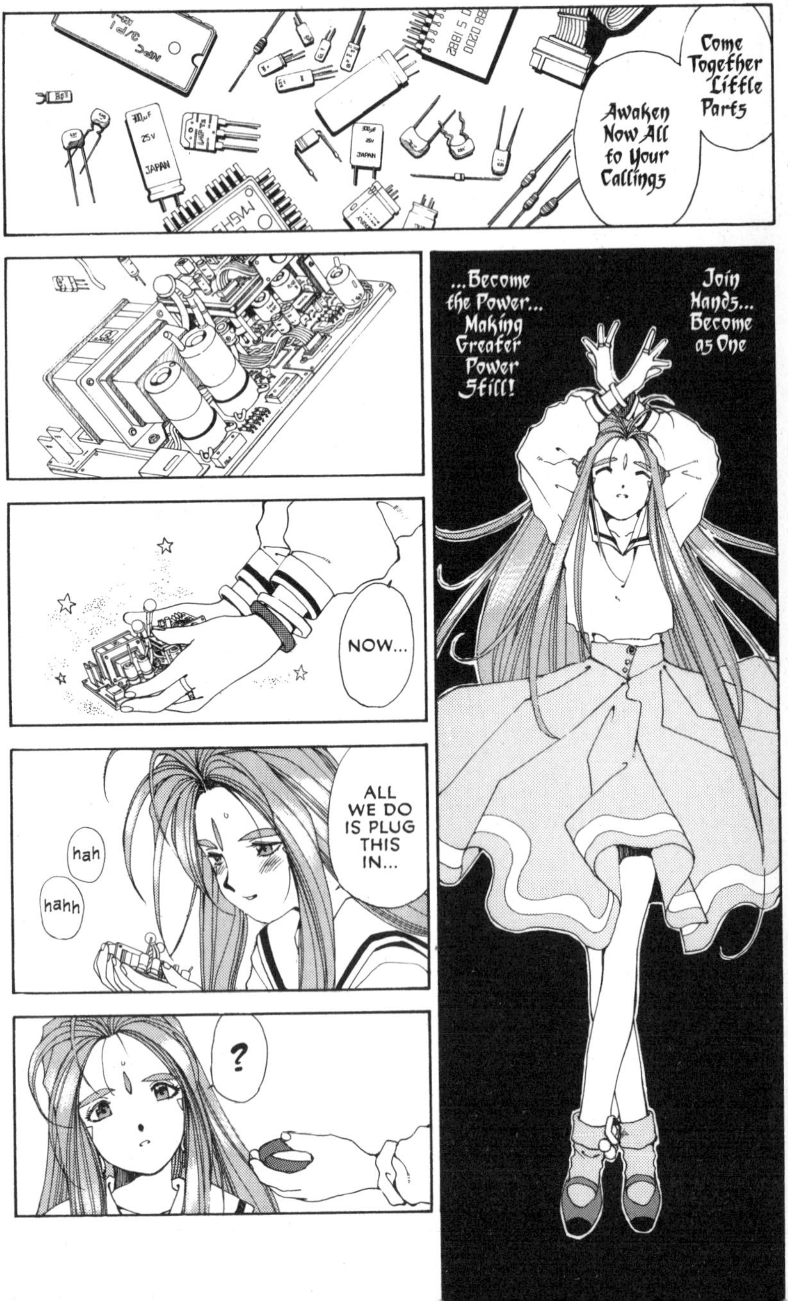
Come Together Little Parts
Awaken Now All to Your Callings
Join Hands... Become as One
...Become the Power... Making Greater Power Still!
NOW...
ALL WE DO IS PLUG THIS IN...
hah
hahh
?

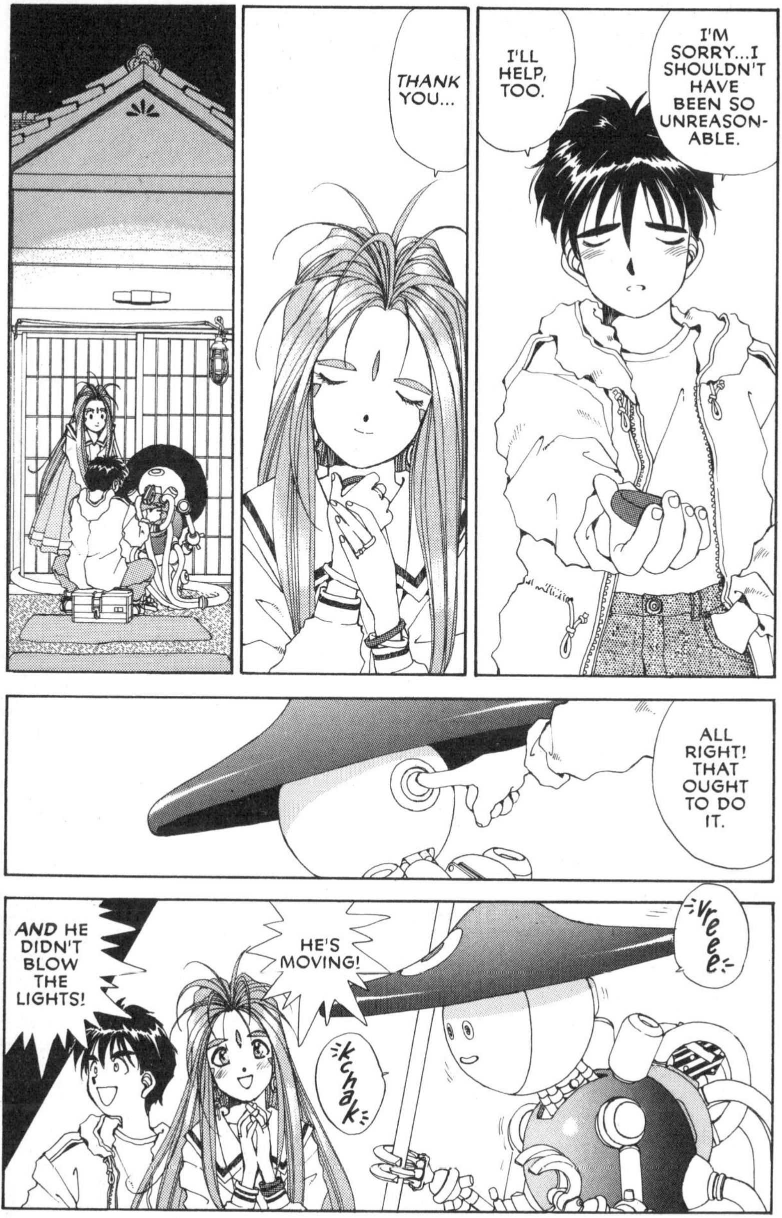
I'M SORRY...I SHOULDN'T HAVE BEEN SO UNREASON-ABLE.
I'LL HELP, TOO.
THANK YOU...
ALL RIGHT! THAT OUGHT TO DO IT.
vreee
HE'S MOVING!
kchak
AND HE DIDN'T BLOW THE LIGHTS!

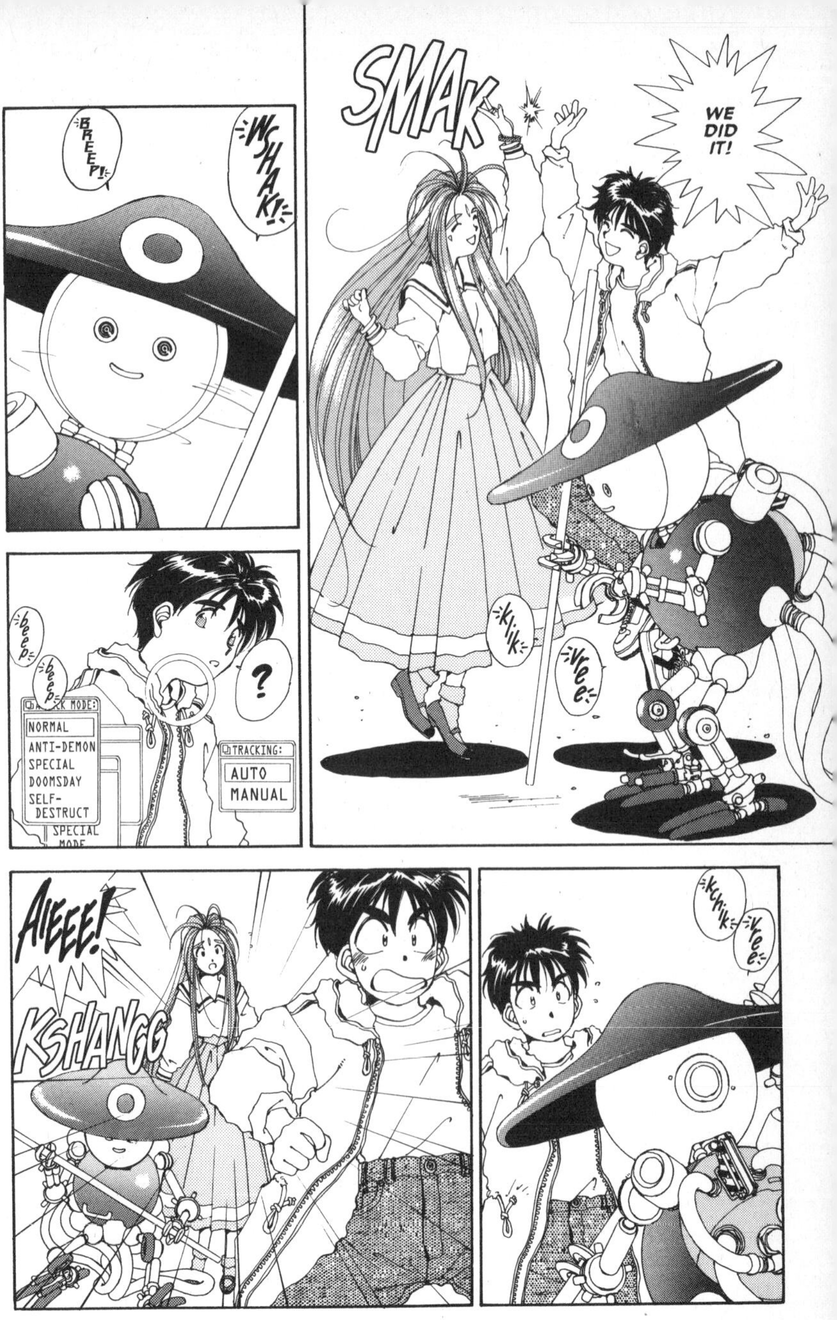
SMAK
WE DID IT!
KLIK
VREE
WSHAK!
BREEP!
beep
beep
?
CK MODE:
NORMAL
ANTI-DEMON
SPECIAL
DOOMSDAY
SELF-DESTRUCT
SPECIAL
TRACKING:
AUTO
MANUAL
AIEEE!
KSHANGG
KCHIK
VREE

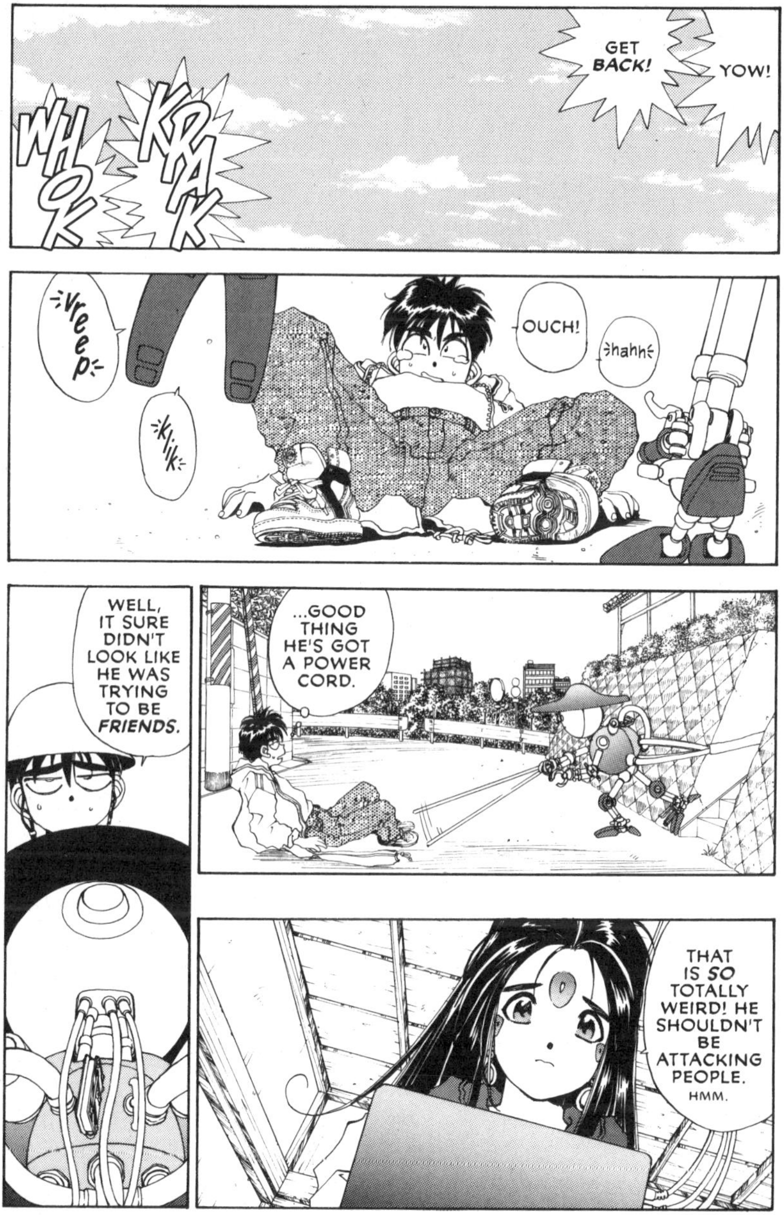
YOW!
GET BACK!
KRAKK
WHOKK
hahn
OUCH!
vreeep
klik
...GOOD THING HE'S GOT A POWER CORD.
WELL, IT SURE DIDN'T LOOK LIKE HE WAS TRYING TO BE FRIENDS.
THAT IS SO TOTALLY WEIRD! HE SHOULDN'T BE ATTACKING PEOPLE.
HMM.

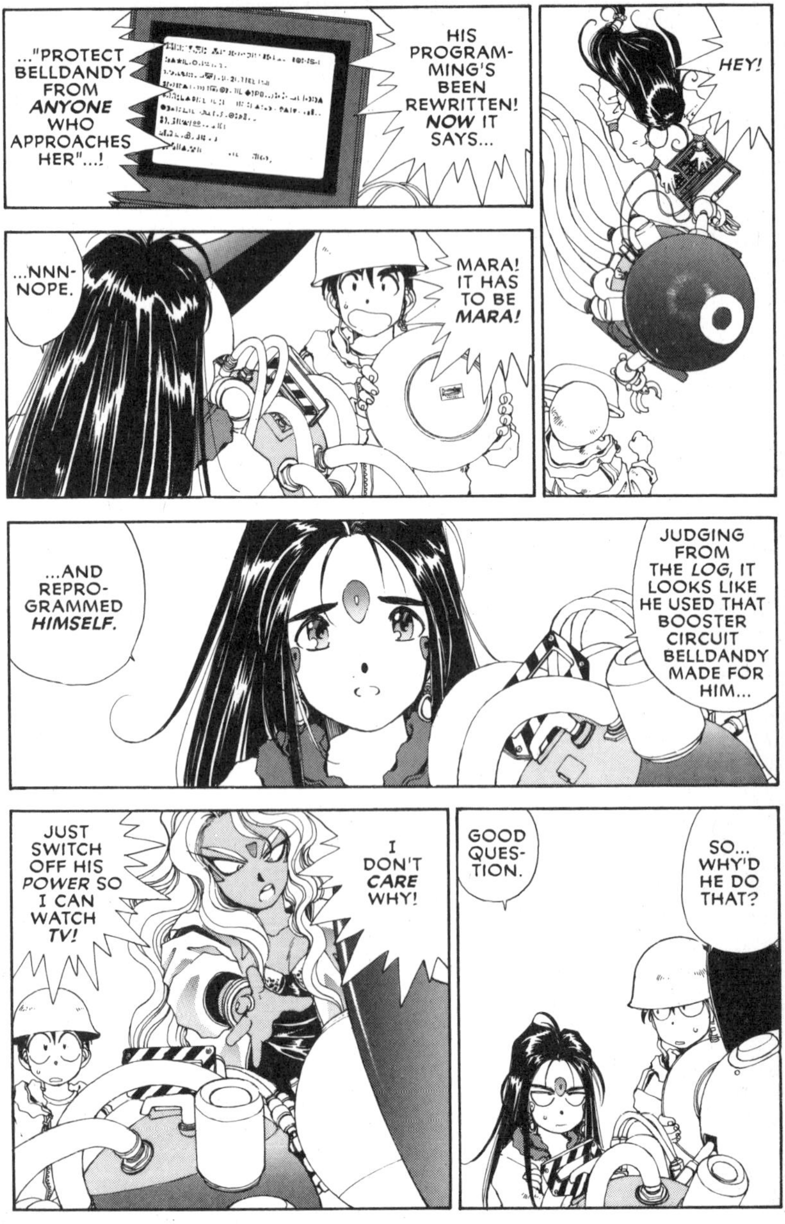
HEY!
HIS PROGRAMMING'S BEEN REWRITTEN! NOW IT SAYS...
..."PROTECT BELLDANDY FROM ANYONE WHO APPROACHES HER"...!
MARA! IT HAS TO BE MARA!
...NNN-NOPE.
JUDGING FROM THE LOG, IT LOOKS LIKE HE USED THAT BOOSTER CIRCUIT BELLDANDY MADE FOR HIM...
...AND REPROGRAMMED HIMSELF.
SO... WHY'D HE DO THAT?
GOOD QUESTION.
I DON'T CARE WHY!
JUST SWITCH OFF HIS POWER SO I CAN WATCH TV!

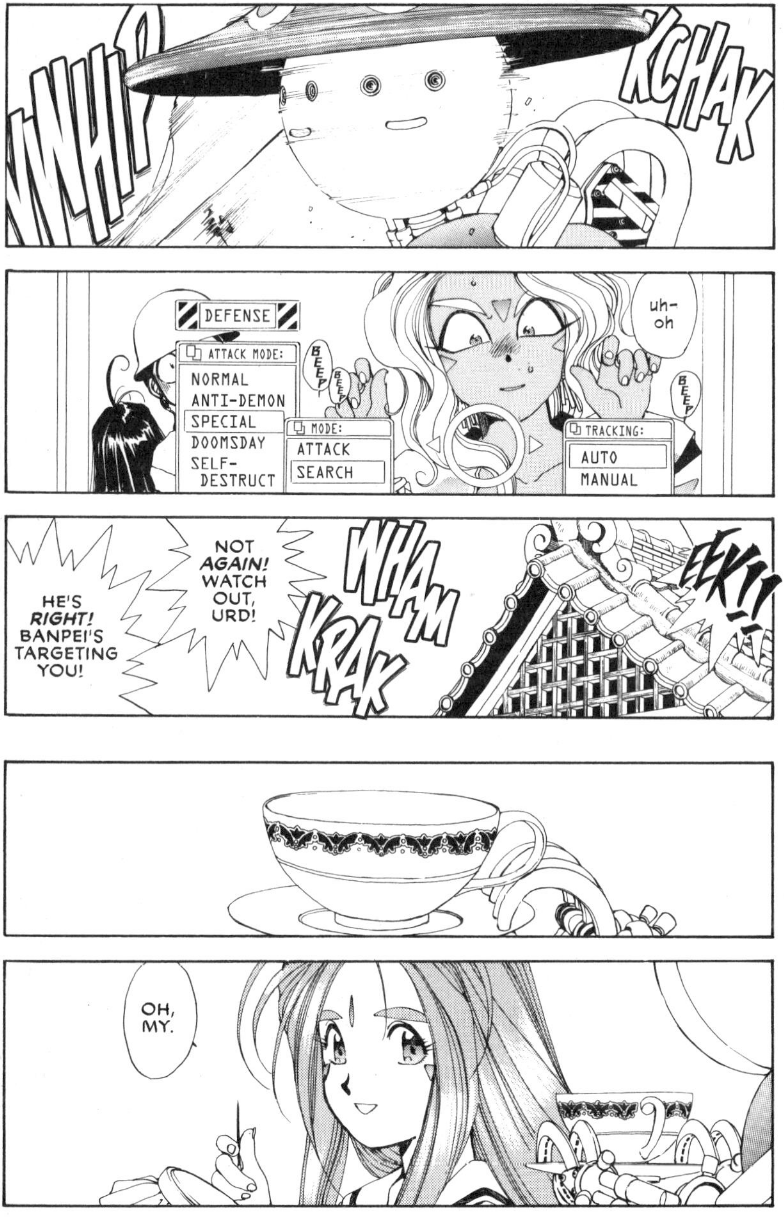
VWHIP
KCHAK
DEFENSE
ATTACK MODE:
NORMAL
ANTI-DEMON
SPECIAL
DOOMSDAY
SELF-DESTRUCT
BEEP
BEEP
MODE:
ATTACK
SEARCH
TRACKING:
AUTO
MANUAL
uh-oh
BEEP
EEK!!
WHAM
KRAK
NOT AGAIN! WATCH OUT, URD!
HE'S RIGHT! BANPEI'S TARGETING YOU!
OH, MY.

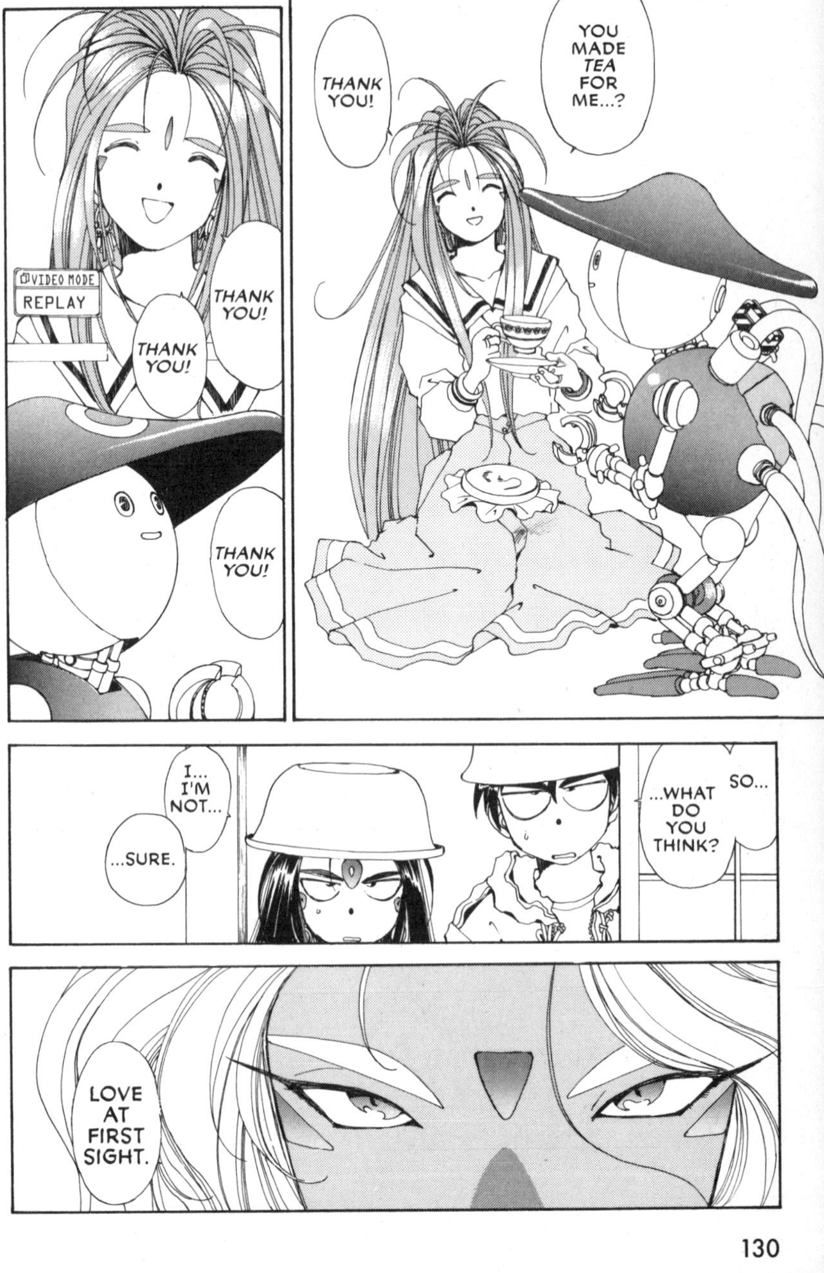
YOU MADE *TEA* FOR ME...?
THANK YOU!
THANK YOU!
THANK YOU!
VIDEO MODE
REPLAY
THANK YOU!
SO...
...WHAT DO YOU THINK?
I... I'M NOT...
...SURE.
LOVE AT FIRST SIGHT.

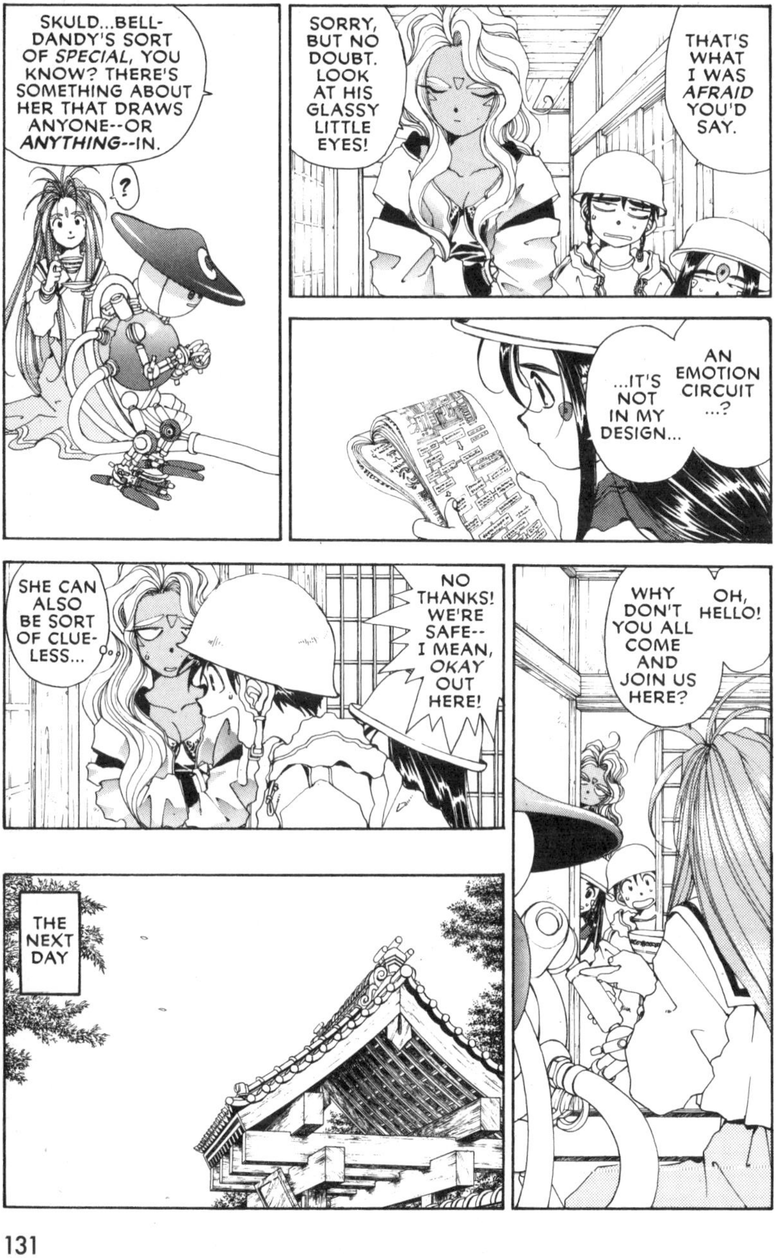
SKULD...BELL-DANDY'S SORT OF *SPECIAL*, YOU KNOW? THERE'S SOMETHING ABOUT HER THAT DRAWS ANYONE--OR ***ANYTHING***--IN.
?
SORRY, BUT NO DOUBT. LOOK AT HIS GLASSY LITTLE EYES!
THAT'S WHAT I WAS *AFRAID* YOU'D SAY.
AN EMOTION CIRCUIT ...?
...IT'S NOT IN MY DESIGN...
SHE CAN ALSO BE SORT OF CLUE-LESS...
NO THANKS! WE'RE SAFE-- I MEAN, *OKAY* OUT HERE!
OH, HELLO!
WHY DON'T YOU ALL COME AND JOIN US HERE?
THE NEXT DAY

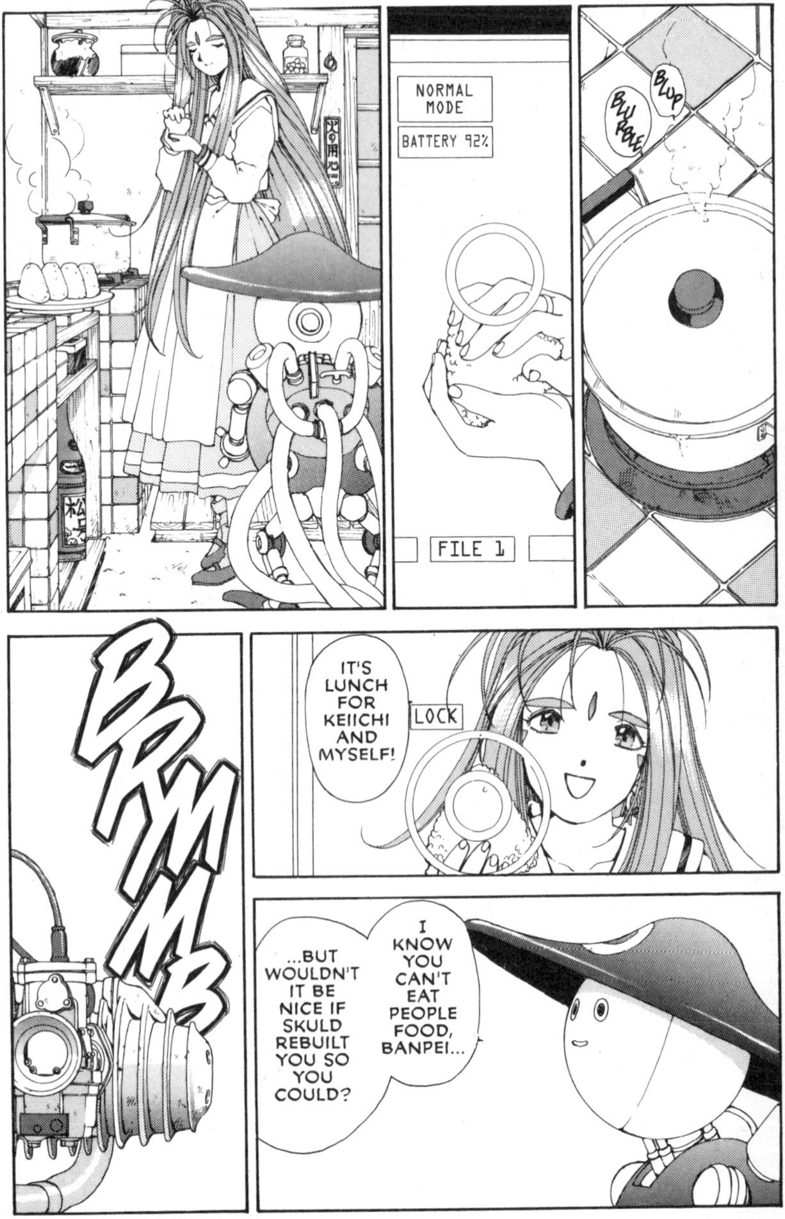
NORMAL MODE
BATTERY 92%
FILE 1
BLUP
BLUBBLE
IT'S LUNCH FOR KEIICHI AND MYSELF!
LOCK
BRMMB
I KNOW YOU CAN'T EAT PEOPLE FOOD, BANPEI...
...BUT WOULDN'T IT BE NICE IF SKULD REBUILT YOU SO YOU COULD?

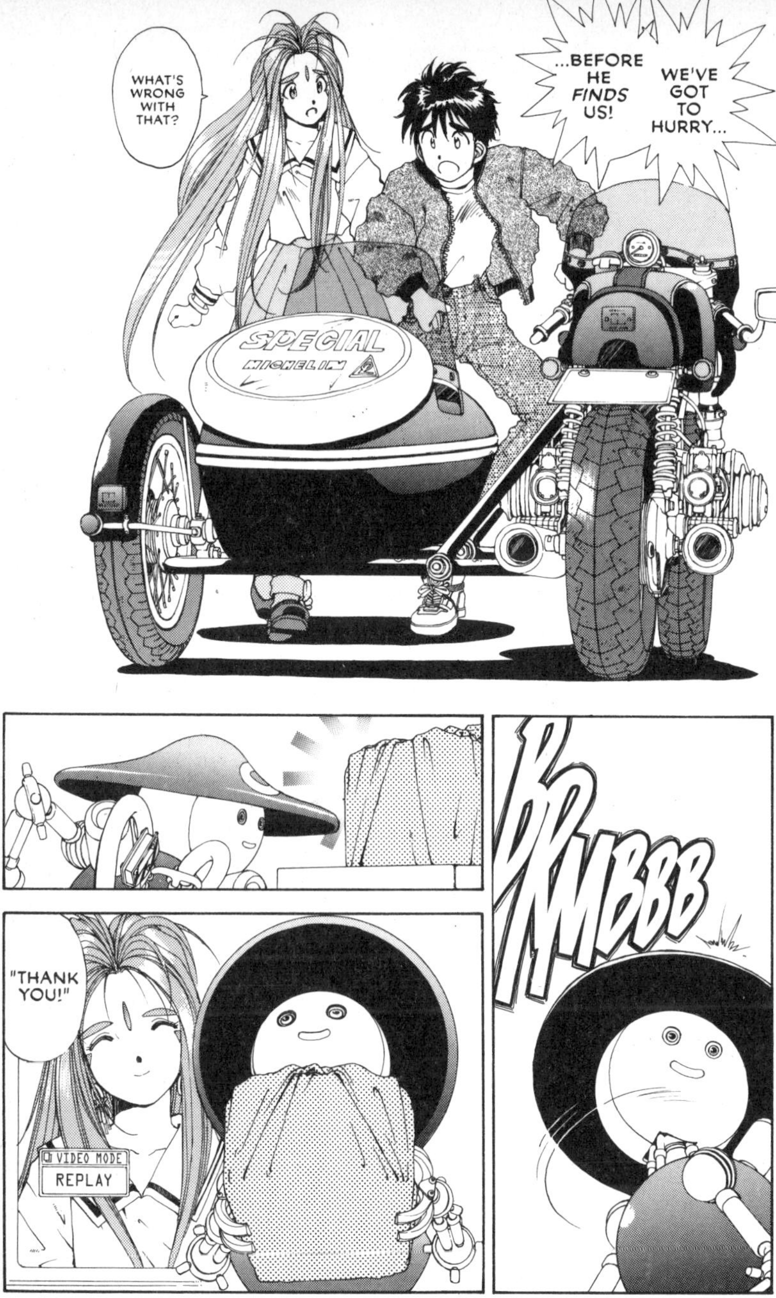

WHAT'S WRONG WITH THAT?
WE'VE GOT TO HURRY...
...BEFORE HE *FINDS* US!
"THANK YOU!"
VIDEO MODE
REPLAY

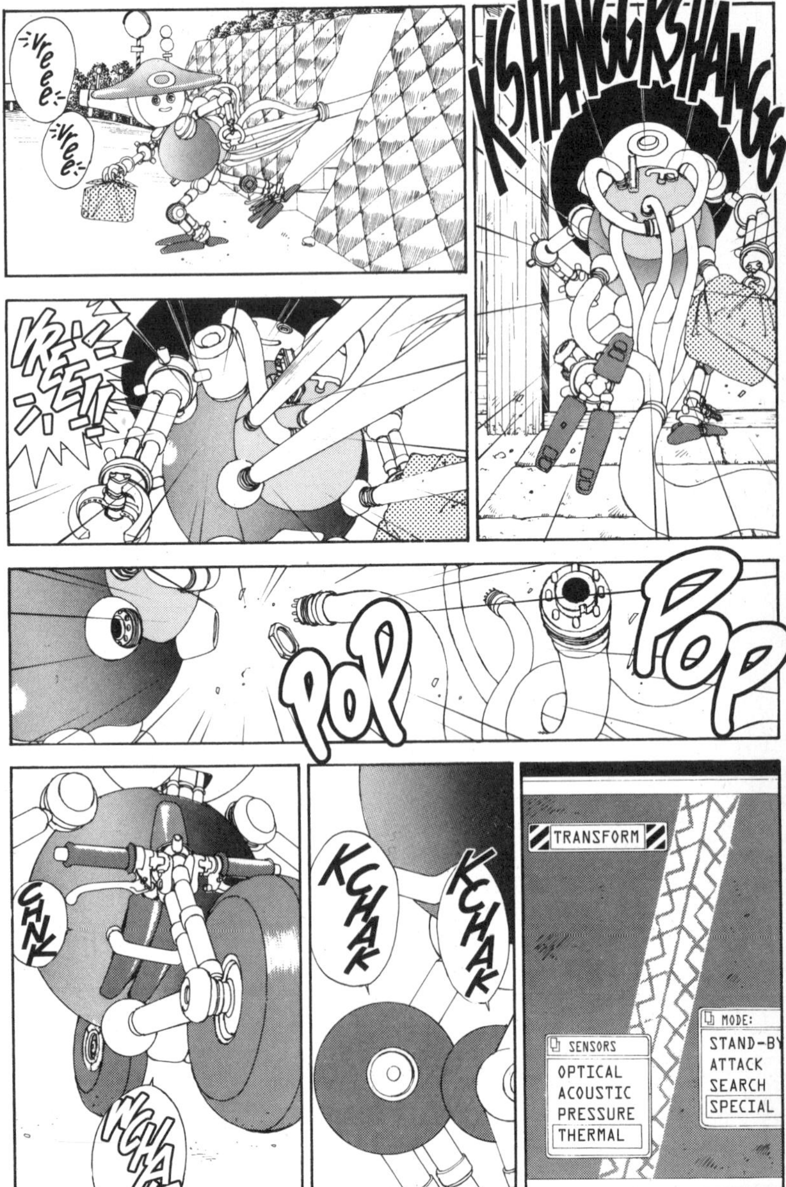
vreee
vreee
KSHANGG KSHANGG
VREEE!!
POP
POP
CANK
WCHAK
KCHAK
KCHAK
TRANSFORM
SENSORS
OPTICAL
ACOUSTIC
PRESSURE
THERMAL
MODE:
STAND-BY
ATTACK
SEARCH
SPECIAL

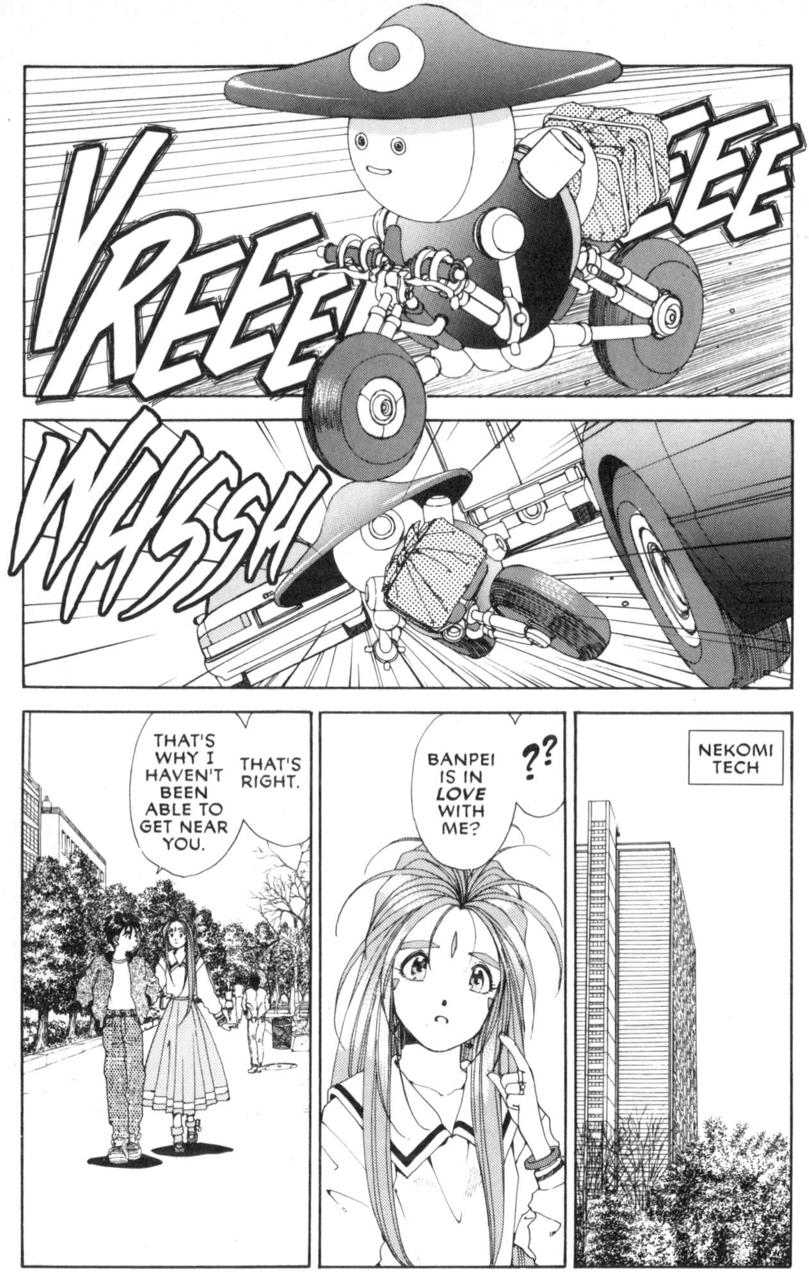

VREEEEEEEEE
WHASSH
NEKOMI TECH
BANPEI IS IN LOVE WITH ME?
??
THAT'S RIGHT.
THAT'S WHY I HAVEN'T BEEN ABLE TO GET NEAR YOU.

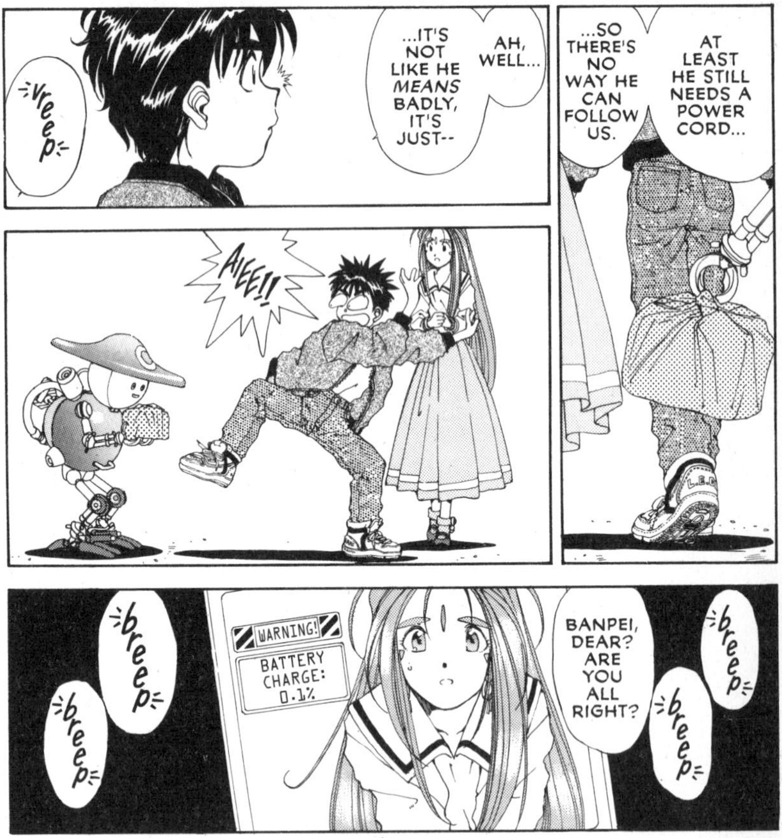
AT LEAST HE STILL NEEDS A POWER CORD...
...SO THERE'S NO WAY HE CAN FOLLOW US.
AH, WELL...
...IT'S NOT LIKE HE *MEANS* BADLY, IT'S JUST--
vreep
AIEE!!
breep
breep
BANPEI, DEAR? ARE YOU ALL RIGHT?
WARNING!
BATTERY CHARGE: 0.1%
breep
breep
BANPEI ?!
FWMP

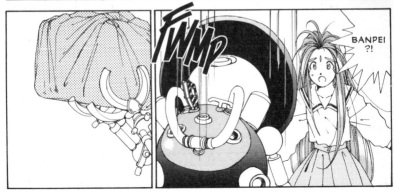

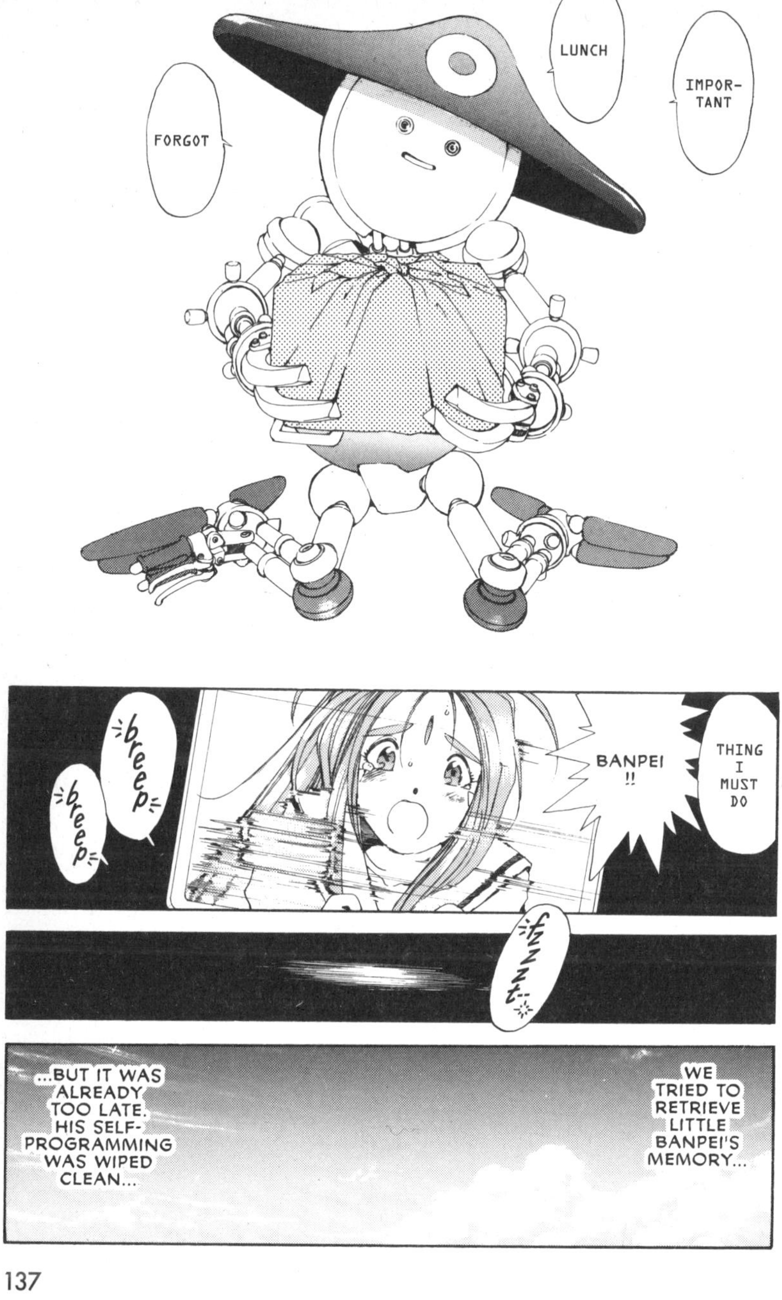
IMPOR-
TANT
LUNCH
FORGOT
THING
I
MUST
DO
BANPEI
!!
breep
breep
fzzzt
WE
TRIED TO
RETRIEVE
LITTLE
BANPEI'S
MEMORY...
...BUT IT WAS
ALREADY
TOO LATE.
HIS SELF-
PROGRAMMING
WAS WIPED
CLEAN...

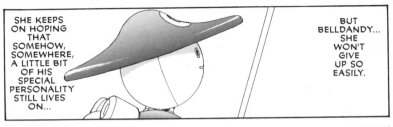

BUT BELLDANDY... SHE WON'T GIVE UP SO EASILY.
SHE KEEPS ON HOPING THAT SOMEHOW, SOMEWHERE, A LITTLE BIT OF HIS SPECIAL PERSONALITY STILL LIVES ON...
SEE YOU LATER, BANPEI!
Vreeee
COME BACK SOON.

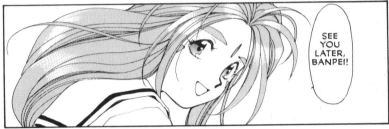

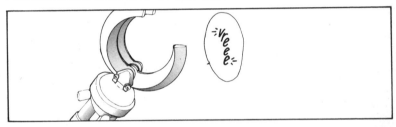

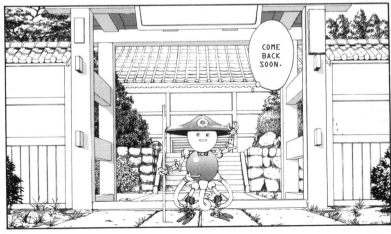

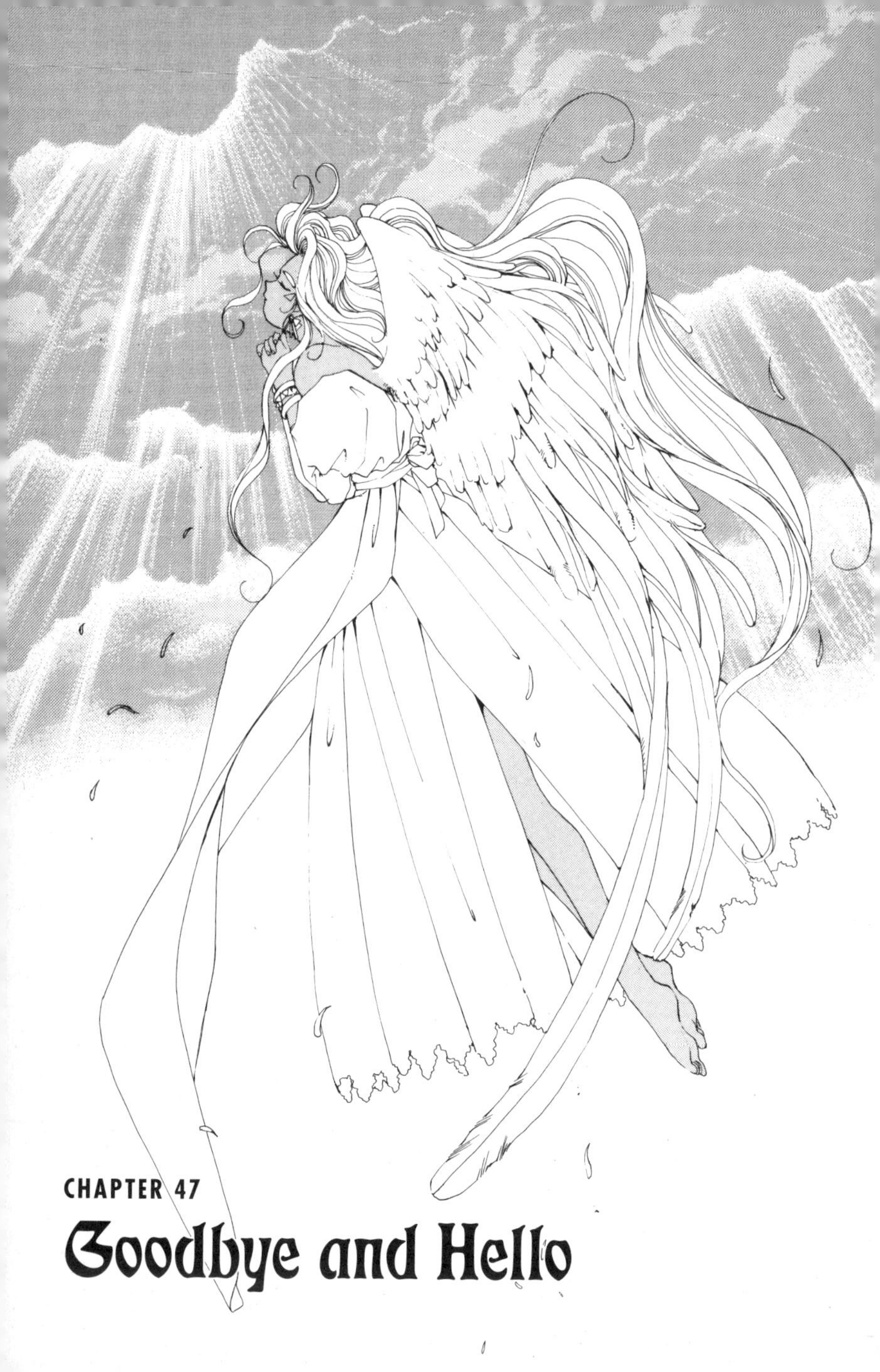

CHAPTER 47

Goodbye and Hello

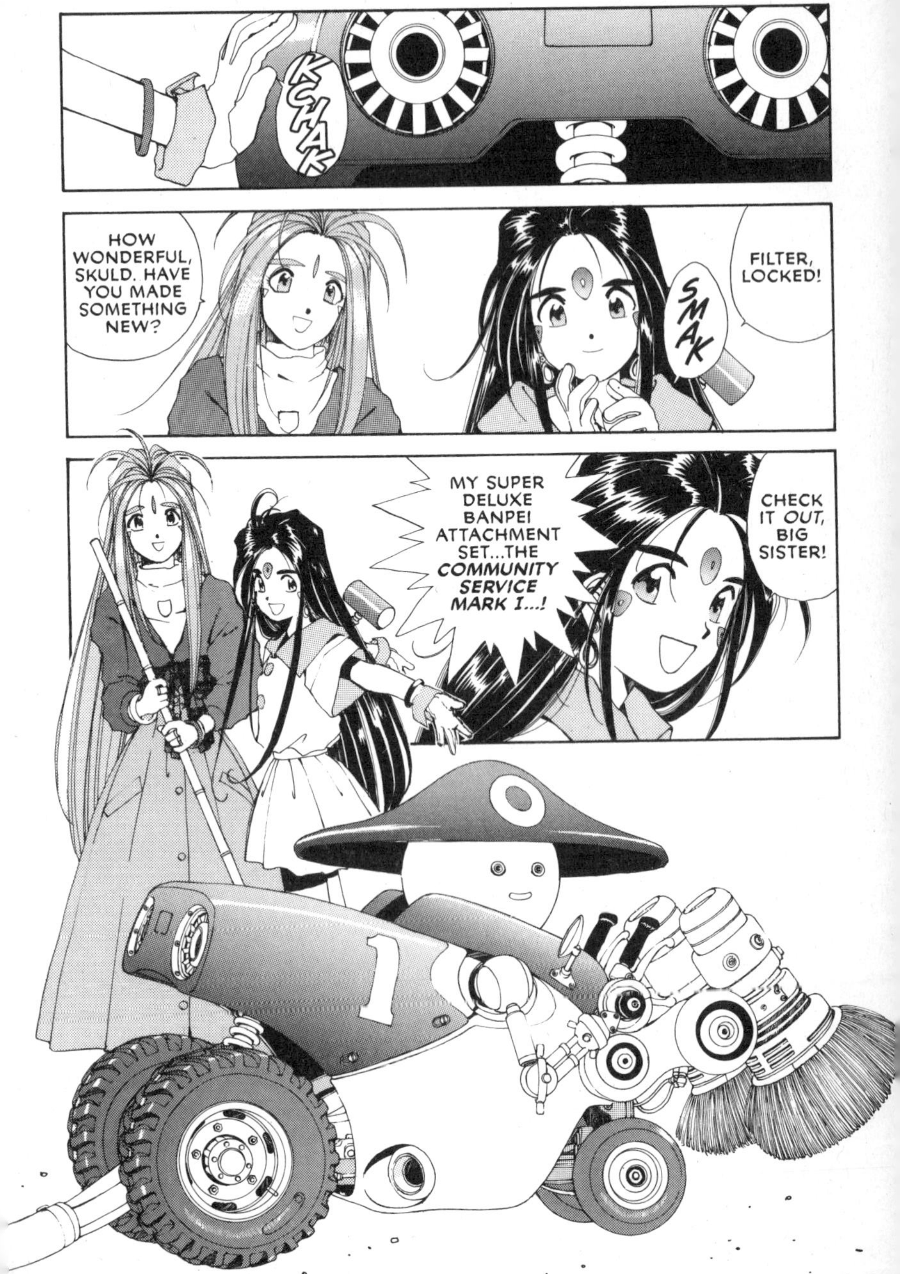
KCHAK
FILTER, LOCKED!
SMAK
HOW WONDERFUL, SKULD. HAVE YOU MADE SOMETHING NEW?
CHECK IT *OUT*, BIG SISTER!
MY SUPER DELUXE BANPEI ATTACHMENT SET...THE *COMMUNITY SERVICE MARK I...!*
1

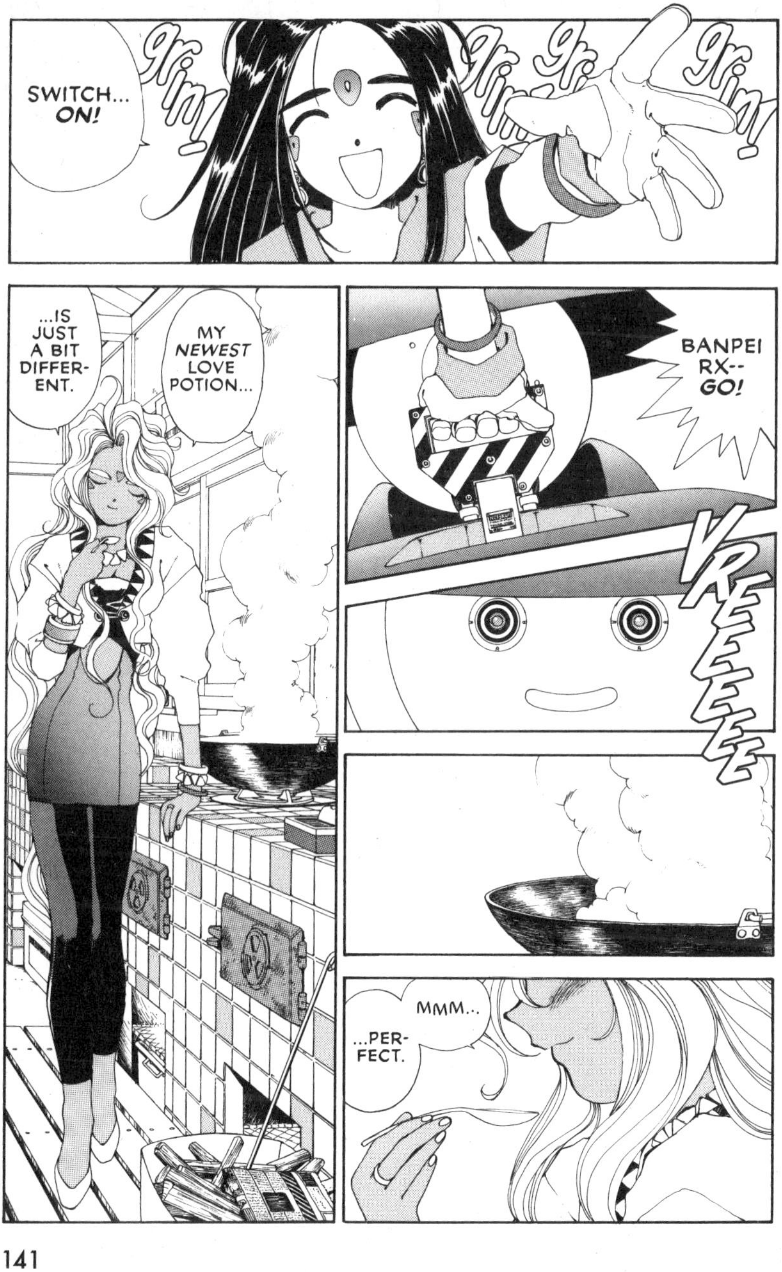
grin! grin! grin! grin!
SWITCH... ON!
MY NEWEST LOVE POTION...
...IS JUST A BIT DIFFER- ENT.
BANPEI RX-- GO!
VREEEEEE
MMM...
...PER- FECT.

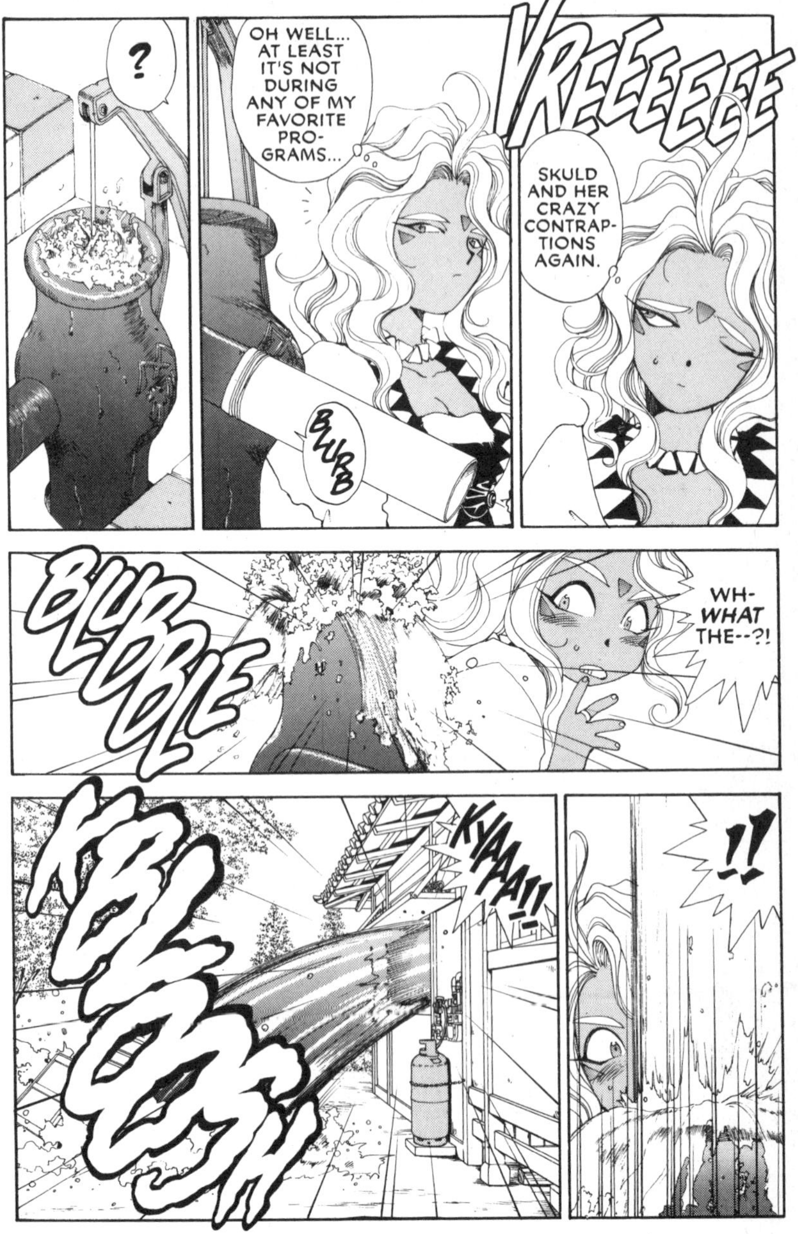
?
OH WELL... AT LEAST IT'S NOT DURING ANY OF MY FAVORITE PRO-GRAMS...
BLURB
VREEEEEEE
SKULD AND HER CRAZY CONTRAP-TIONS AGAIN.
BLUBBLE
WH- WHAT THE--?!
KYAAAA!!
!!

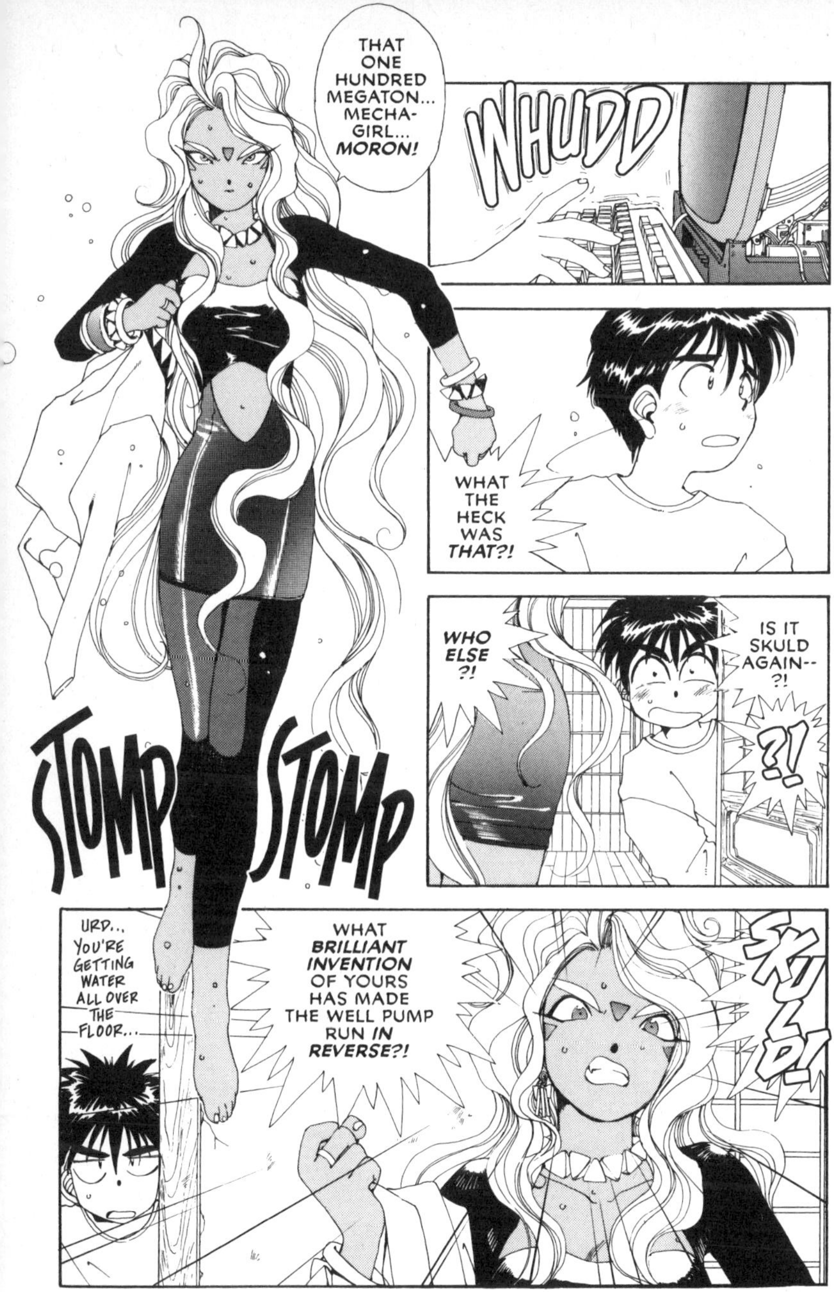
THAT ONE HUNDRED MEGATON... MECHA-GIRL... MORON!
WHUDD
WHAT THE HECK WAS THAT?!
IS IT SKULD AGAIN--?!
?!
WHO ELSE ?!
STOMP STOMP
WHAT BRILLIANT INVENTION OF YOURS HAS MADE THE WELL PUMP RUN IN REVERSE?!
SKULD!
URD... YOU'RE GETTING WATER ALL OVER THE FLOOR...

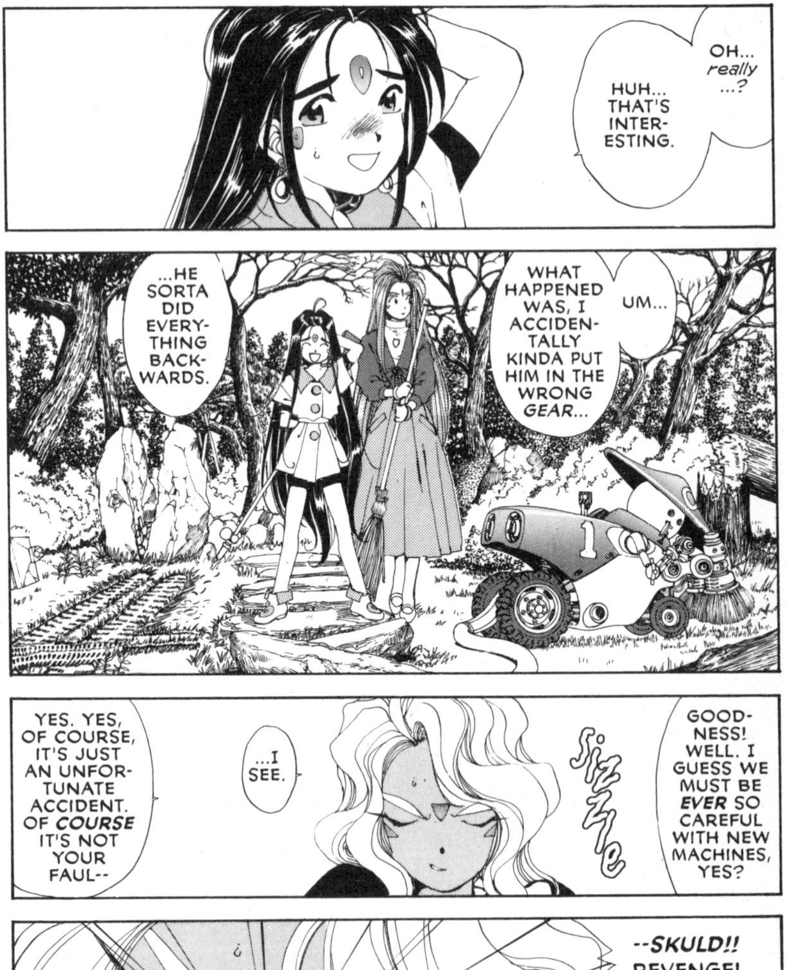
OH... *really* ...?
HUH... THAT'S INTER-ESTING.
UM...
WHAT HAPPENED WAS, I ACCIDEN-TALLY KINDA PUT HIM IN THE WRONG *GEAR*...
...HE SORTA DID EVERY-THING BACK-WARDS.
GOOD-NESS! WELL. I GUESS WE MUST BE ***EVER*** SO CAREFUL WITH NEW MACHINES, YES?
sizzle
...I SEE.
YES. YES, OF COURSE, IT'S JUST AN UNFOR-TUNATE ACCIDENT. OF ***COURSE*** IT'S NOT YOUR FAUL--
--***SKULD!!***
REVENGE!
REVENGE !!

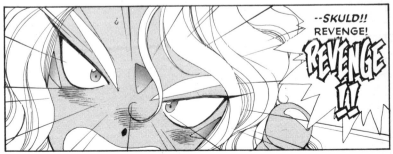

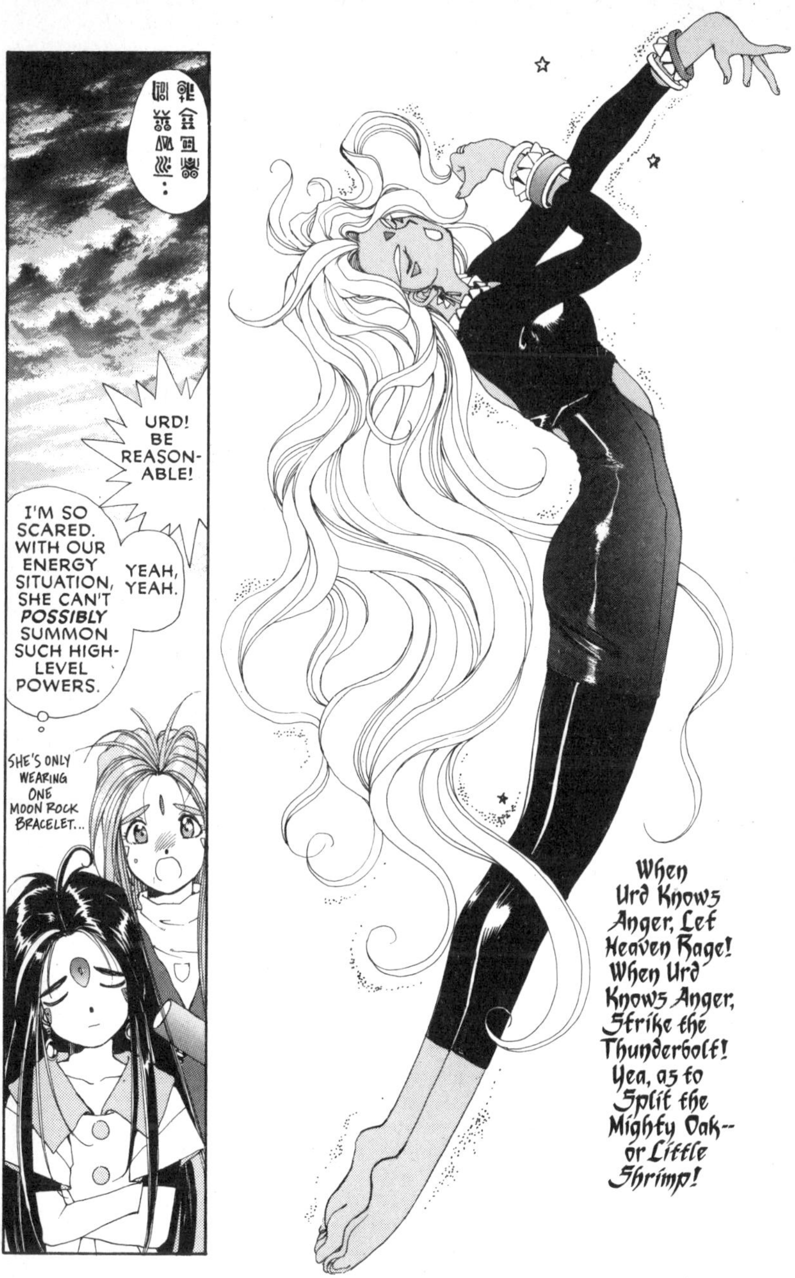
URD! BE REASONABLE!
YEAH, YEAH.
I'M SO SCARED. WITH OUR ENERGY SITUATION, SHE CAN'T *POSSIBLY* SUMMON SUCH HIGH-LEVEL POWERS.
SHE'S ONLY WEARING ONE MOON ROCK BRACELET...
When Urd Knows Anger, Let Heaven Rage! When Urd Knows Anger, Strike the Thunderbolt! Yea, as to Split the Mighty Oak--or Little Shrimp!

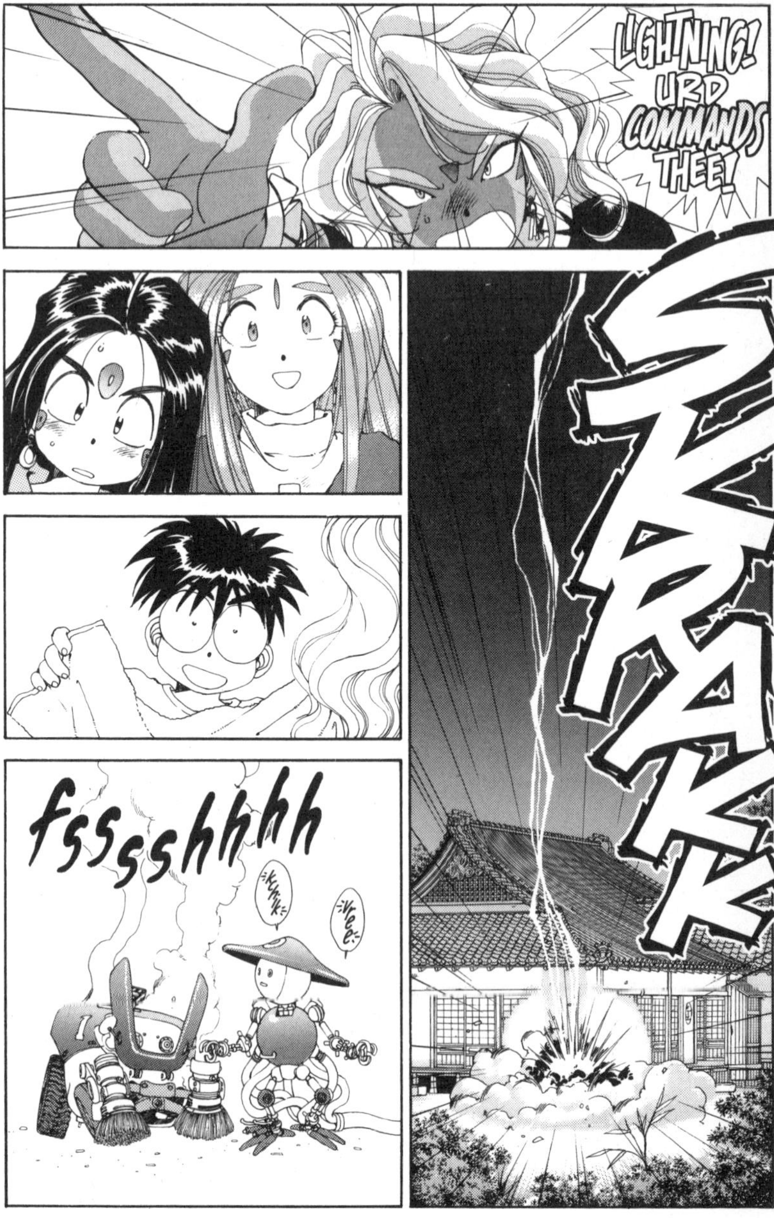
LIGHTNING! URD COMMANDS THEE!
KRAAKK
fsssshhhhh
kchik
vree

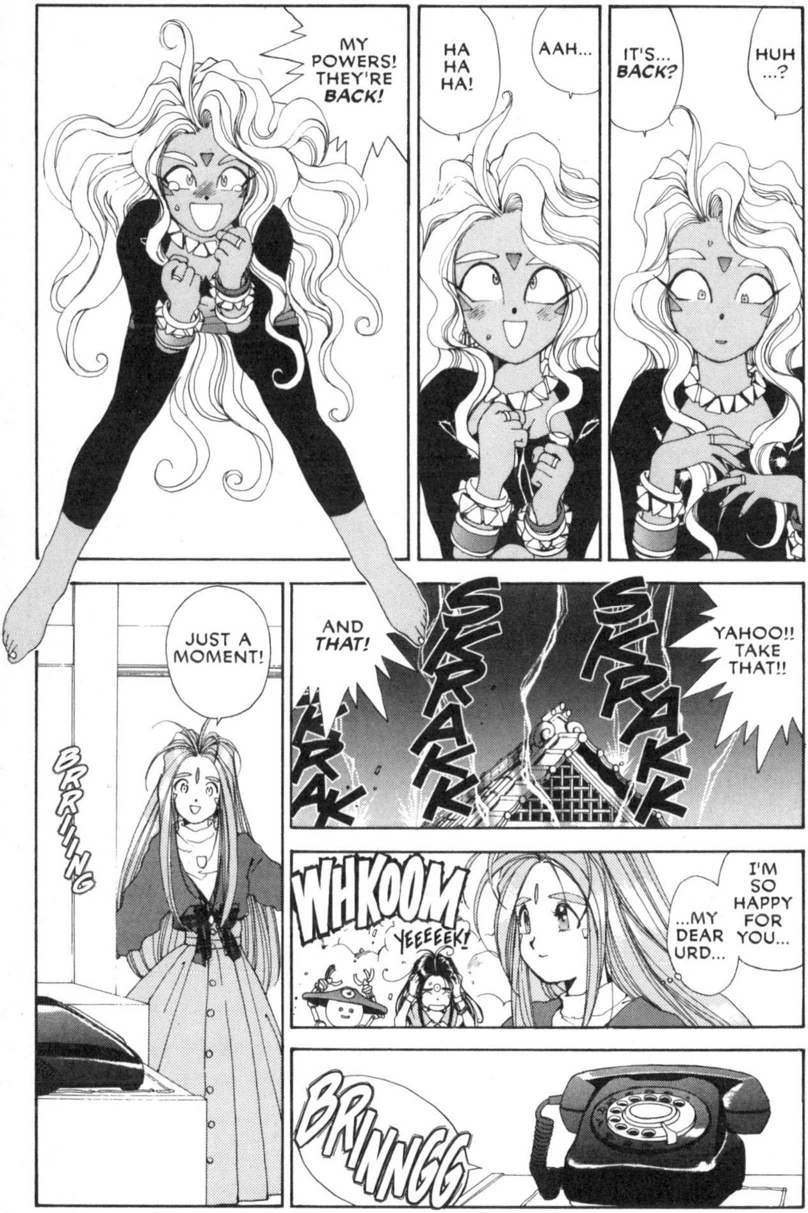
MY POWERS! THEY'RE BACK!
HA HA HA!
AAH...
IT'S... BACK?
HUH ...?
JUST A MOMENT!
BRRIIIING
AND THAT!
SKRAKK
SKRAKK
YAHOO!! TAKE THAT!!
WHKOOM
YEEEEEK!
...MY DEAR URD...
I'M SO HAPPY FOR YOU...
BRINNGG

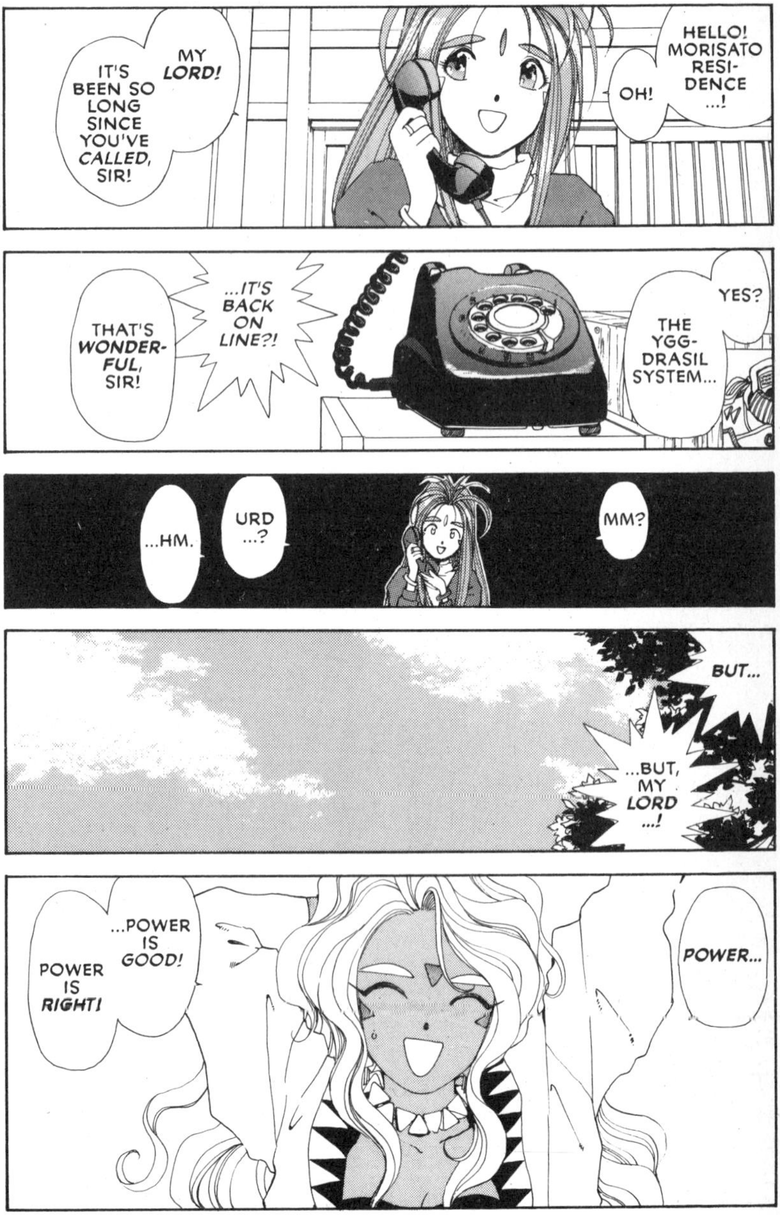
HELLO! MORISATO RESI-DENCE ...!
OH!
MY *LORD!*
IT'S BEEN SO LONG SINCE YOU'VE *CALLED,* SIR!
YES?
THE YGG-DRASIL SYSTEM...
...*IT'S BACK ON LINE?!*
THAT'S *WONDER-FUL,* SIR!
MM?
URD ...?
...HM.
BUT...
...BUT, MY *LORD* ...!
POWER...
...POWER IS *GOOD!*
POWER IS *RIGHT!*

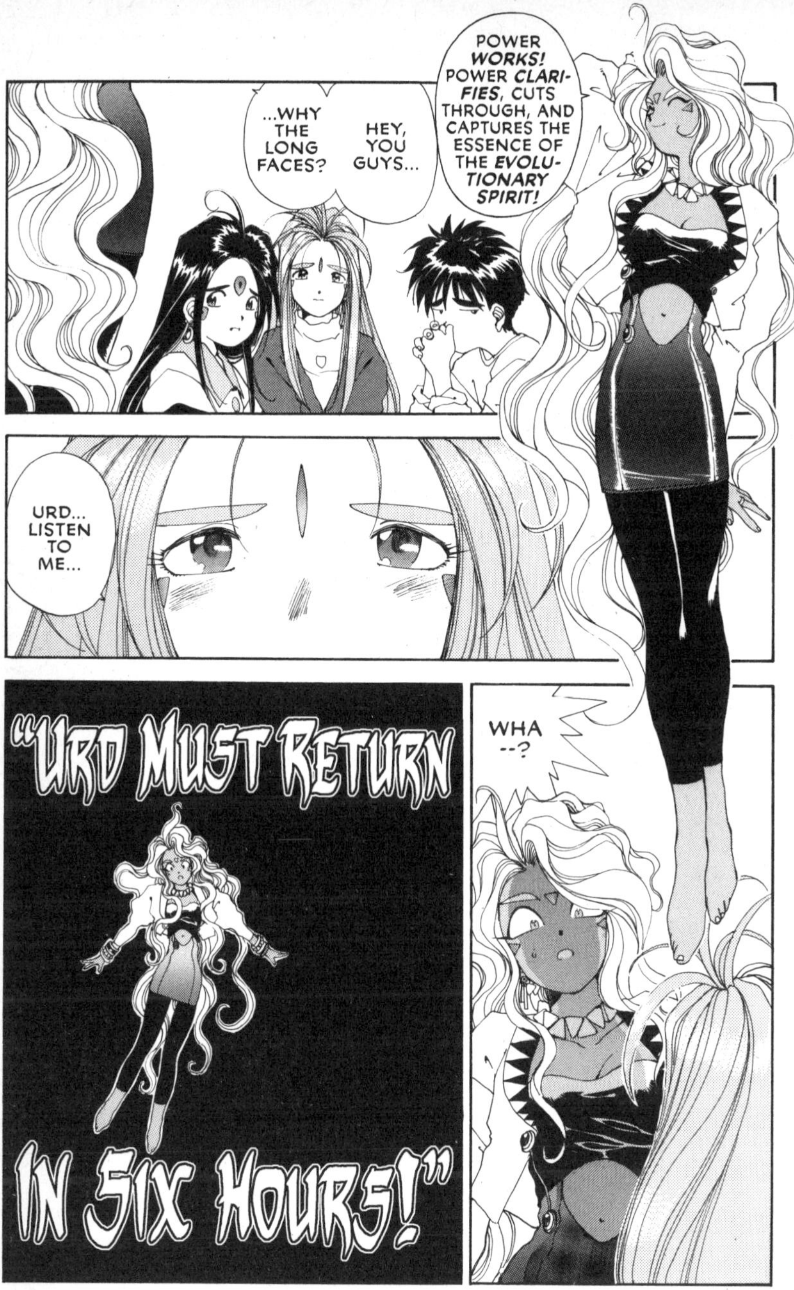
POWER WORKS! POWER CLARIFIES, CUTS THROUGH, AND CAPTURES THE ESSENCE OF THE EVOLUTIONARY SPIRIT!
HEY, YOU GUYS...
...WHY THE LONG FACES?
URD... LISTEN TO ME...
WHA --?
"URD MUST RETURN IN SIX HOURS!"

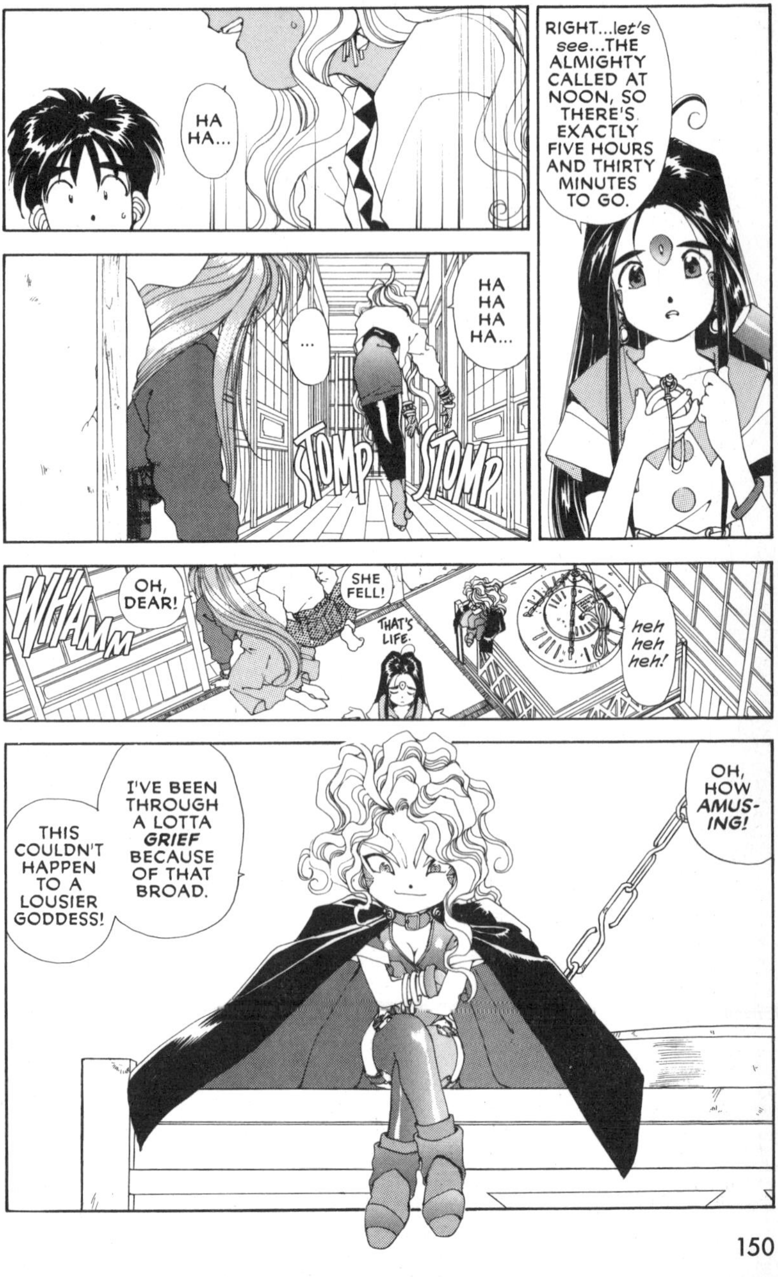

RIGHT...*let's see*...THE ALMIGHTY CALLED AT NOON, SO THERE'S EXACTLY FIVE HOURS AND THIRTY MINUTES TO GO.
HA HA...
HA HA HA HA...
...
STOMP STOMP
heh heh heh!
SHE FELL!
OH, DEAR!
WHAMM
THAT'S LIFE.
OH, HOW *AMUSING!*
I'VE BEEN THROUGH A LOTTA *GRIEF* BECAUSE OF THAT BROAD.
THIS COULDN'T HAPPEN TO A LOUSIER GODDESS!

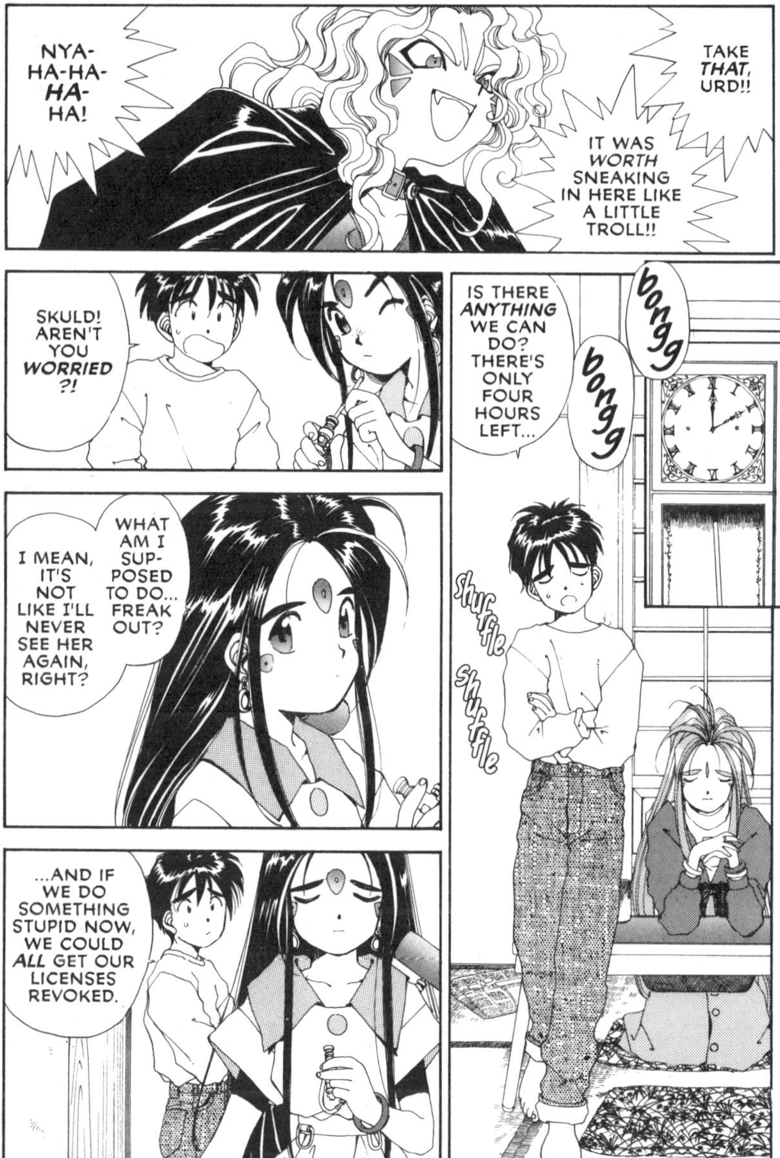
NYA-HA-HA-HA-HA!
TAKE THAT, URD!!
IT WAS WORTH SNEAKING IN HERE LIKE A LITTLE TROLL!!
SKULD! AREN'T YOU WORRIED?!
WHAT AM I SUPPOSED TO DO... FREAK OUT?
I MEAN, IT'S NOT LIKE I'LL NEVER SEE HER AGAIN, RIGHT?
...AND IF WE DO SOMETHING STUPID NOW, WE COULD ALL GET OUR LICENSES REVOKED.
IS THERE ANYTHING WE CAN DO? THERE'S ONLY FOUR HOURS LEFT...
bongg
bongg
shuffle
shuffle

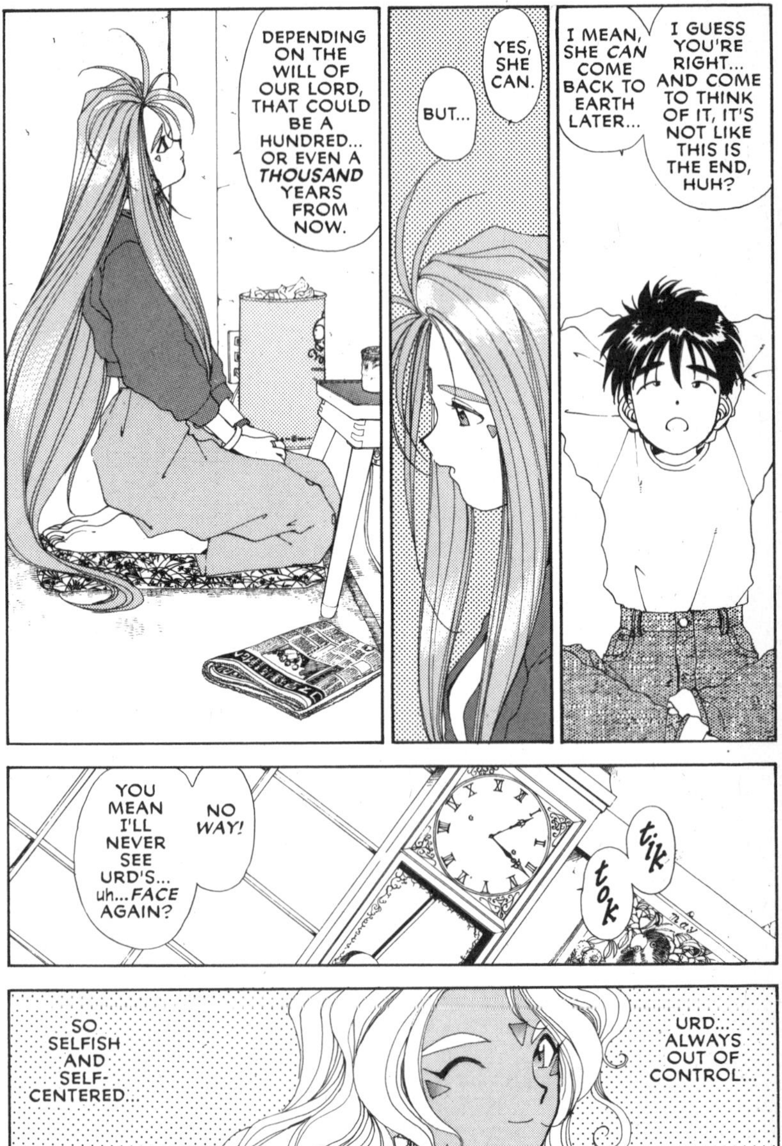

I GUESS YOU'RE RIGHT... AND COME TO THINK OF IT, IT'S NOT LIKE THIS IS THE END, HUH?
I MEAN, SHE *CAN* COME BACK TO EARTH LATER...
YES, SHE CAN.
BUT...
DEPENDING ON THE WILL OF OUR LORD, THAT COULD BE A HUNDRED... OR EVEN A ***THOUSAND*** YEARS FROM NOW.
NO *WAY!*
YOU MEAN I'LL NEVER SEE URD'S... uh...*FACE* AGAIN?
tik
tok
URD... ALWAYS OUT OF CONTROL...
SO SELFISH AND SELF-CENTERED...

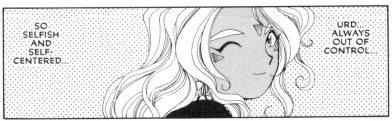

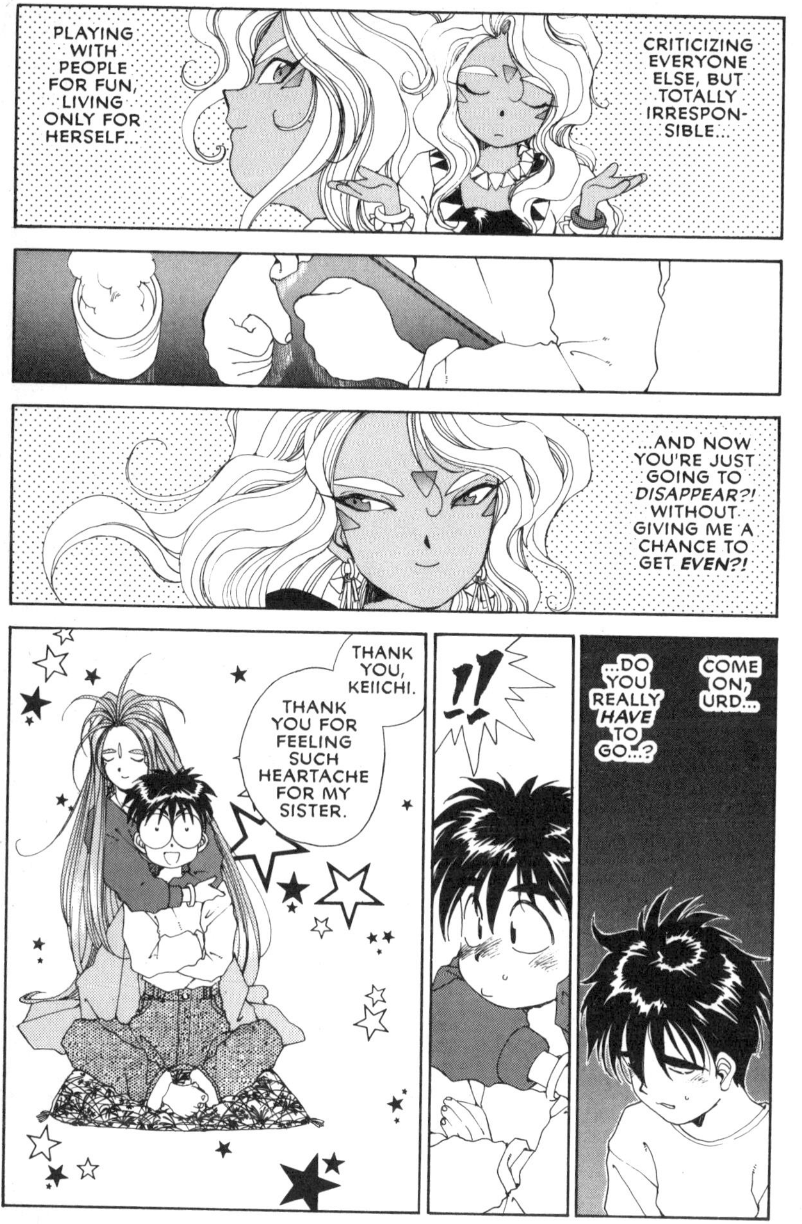
CRITICIZING EVERYONE ELSE, BUT TOTALLY IRRESPON-SIBLE...
PLAYING WITH PEOPLE FOR FUN, LIVING ONLY FOR HERSELF...
...AND NOW YOU'RE JUST GOING TO DISAPPEAR?! WITHOUT GIVING ME A CHANCE TO GET EVEN?!
COME ON, URD...
...DO YOU REALLY HAVE TO GO...?
!!
THANK YOU, KEIICHI.
THANK YOU FOR FEELING SUCH HEARTACHE FOR MY SISTER.

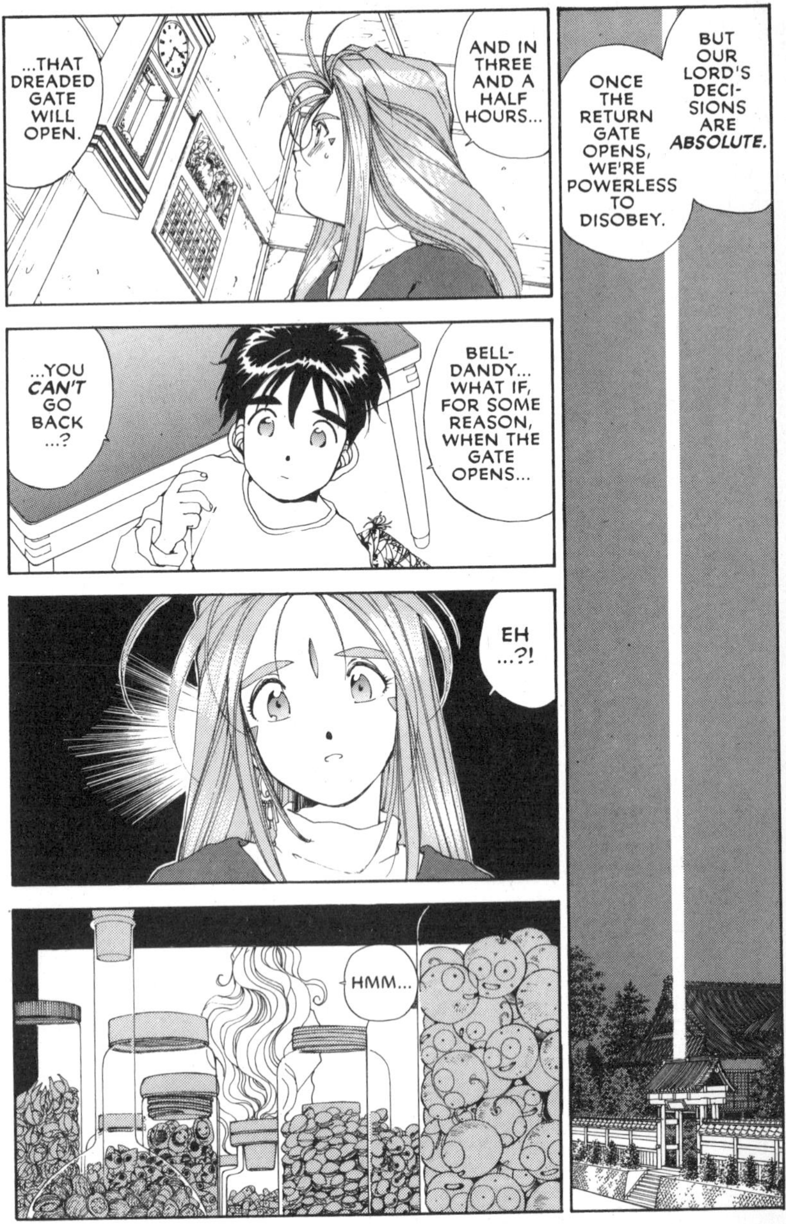
AND IN THREE AND A HALF HOURS...
...THAT DREADED GATE WILL OPEN.
ONCE THE RETURN GATE OPENS, WE'RE POWERLESS TO DISOBEY.
BUT OUR LORD'S DECISIONS ARE *ABSOLUTE.*
BELL-DANDY... WHAT IF, FOR SOME REASON, WHEN THE GATE OPENS...
...YOU *CAN'T* GO BACK ...?
EH ...?!
HMM...

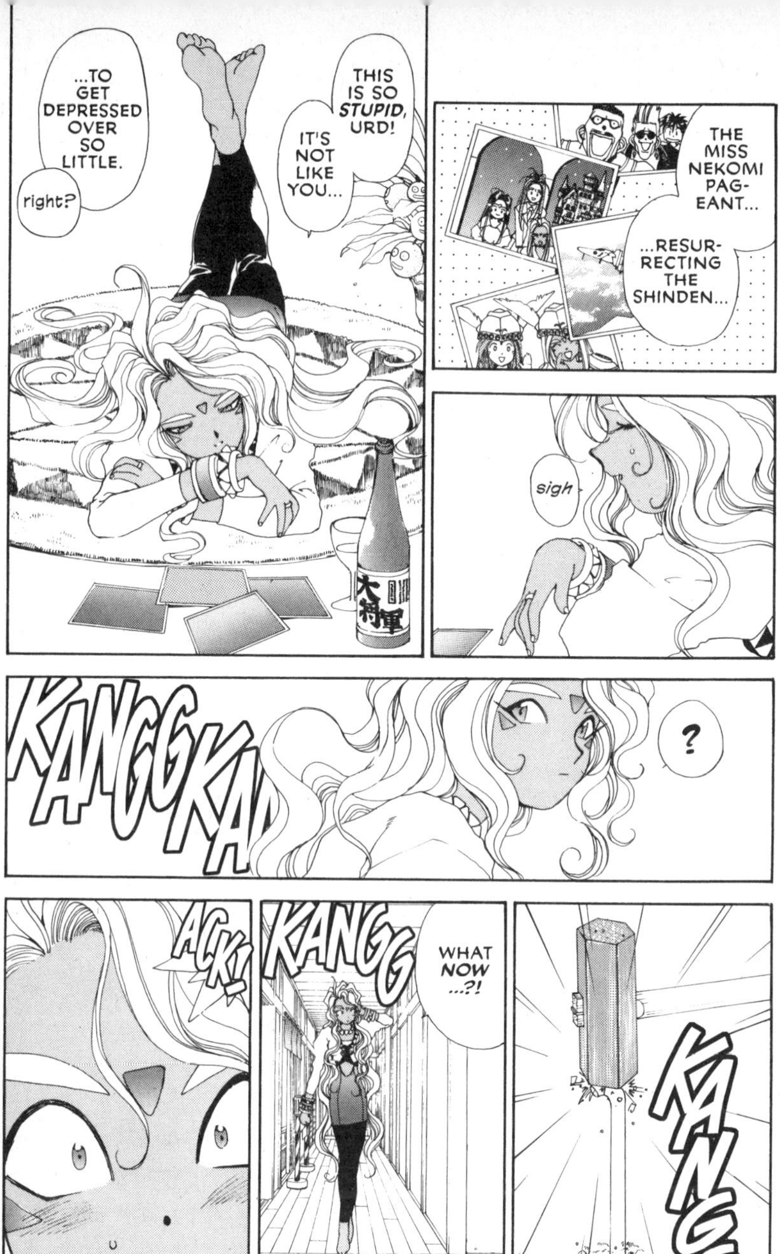
THIS IS SO STUPID, URD!
IT'S NOT LIKE YOU...
...TO GET DEPRESSED OVER SO LITTLE.
right?
THE MISS NEKOMI PAGEANT...
...RESURRECTING THE SHINDEN...
sigh
KANGG KA
?
ACK!
KANGG
WHAT NOW ...?!
KANNGG

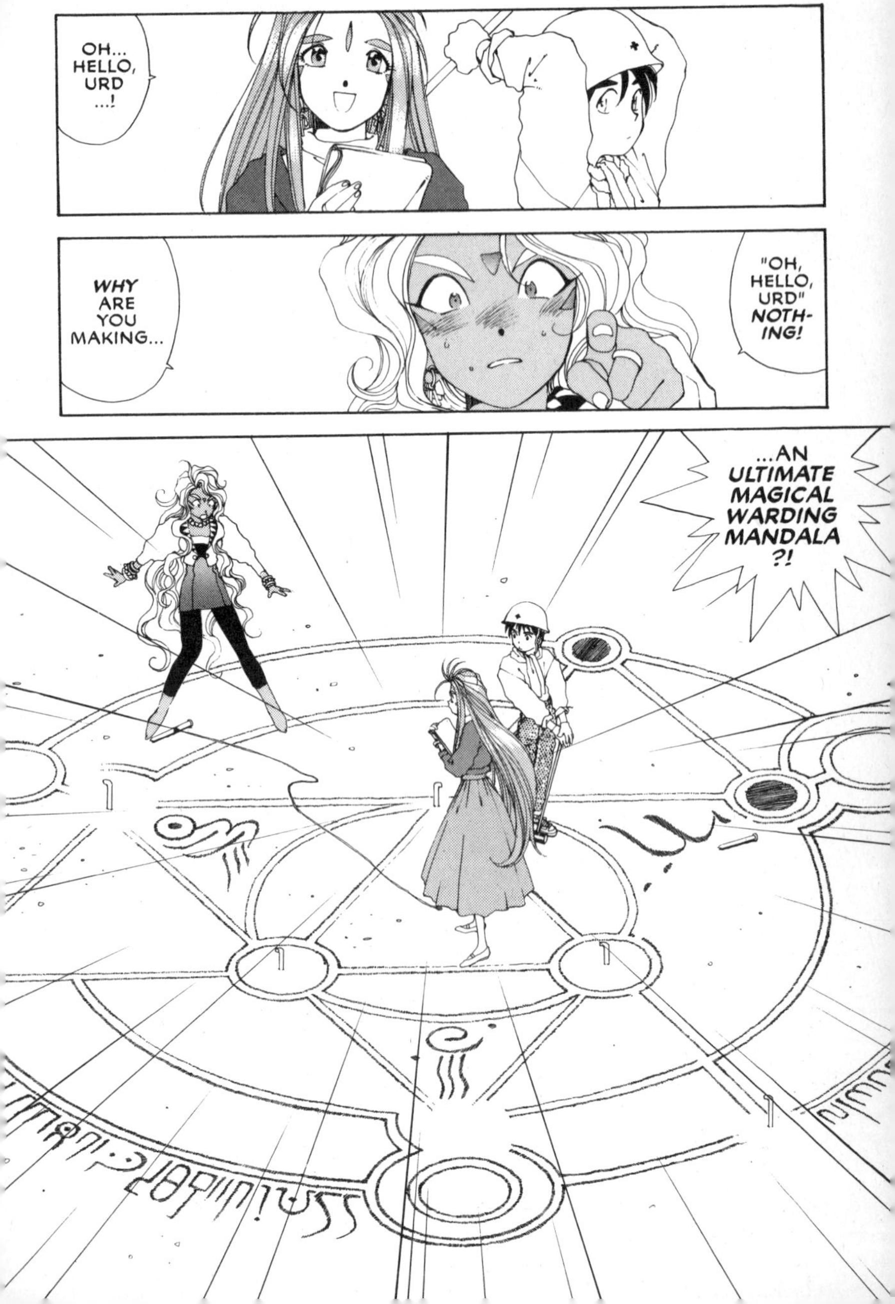
OH... HELLO, URD ...!
"OH, HELLO, URD" *NOTHING!*
WHY ARE YOU MAKING...
...AN *ULTIMATE MAGICAL WARDING MANDALA* ?!

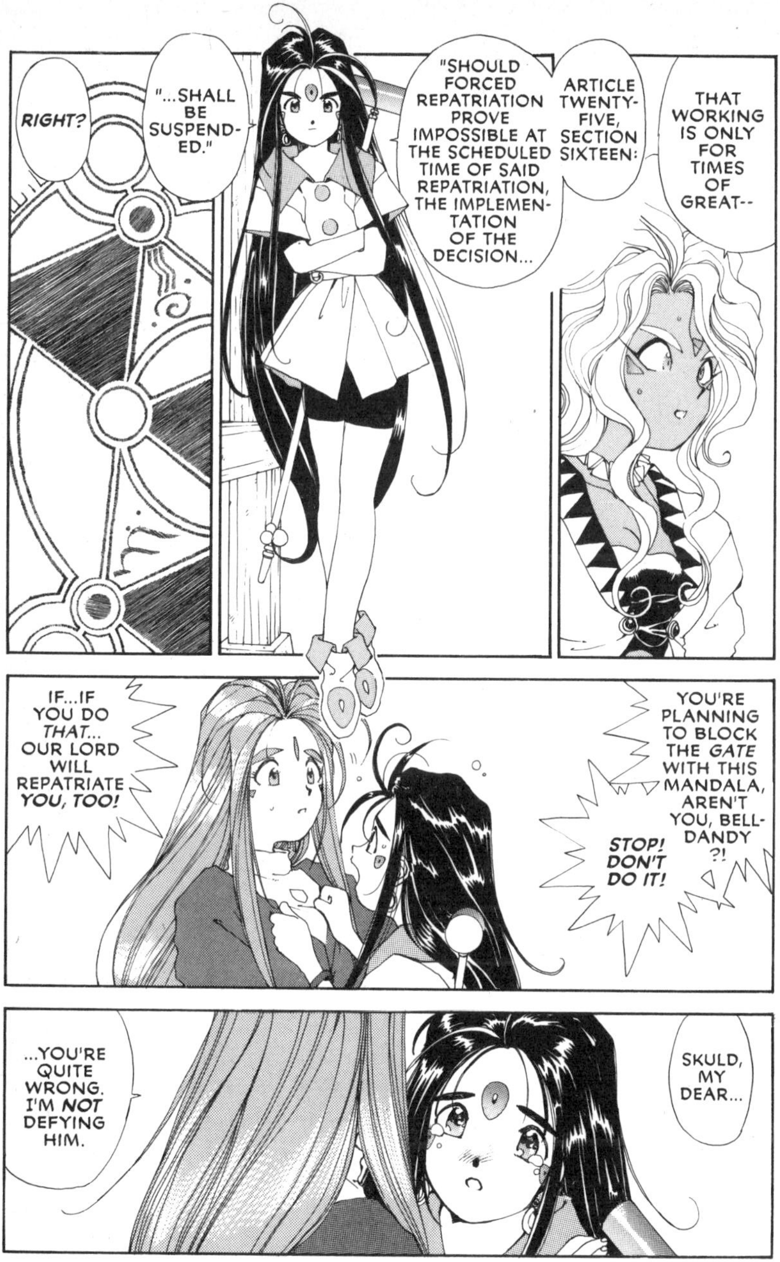
THAT WORKING IS ONLY FOR TIMES OF GREAT--
ARTICLE TWENTY-FIVE, SECTION SIXTEEN:
"SHOULD FORCED REPATRIATION PROVE IMPOSSIBLE AT THE SCHEDULED TIME OF SAID REPATRIATION, THE IMPLEMENTATION OF THE DECISION...
"...SHALL BE SUSPENDED."
RIGHT?
YOU'RE PLANNING TO BLOCK THE *GATE* WITH THIS MANDALA, AREN'T YOU, BELLDANDY ?!
STOP! DON'T DO IT!
IF...IF YOU DO *THAT*... OUR LORD WILL REPATRIATE *YOU, TOO!*
SKULD, MY DEAR...
...YOU'RE QUITE WRONG. I'M *NOT* DEFYING HIM.

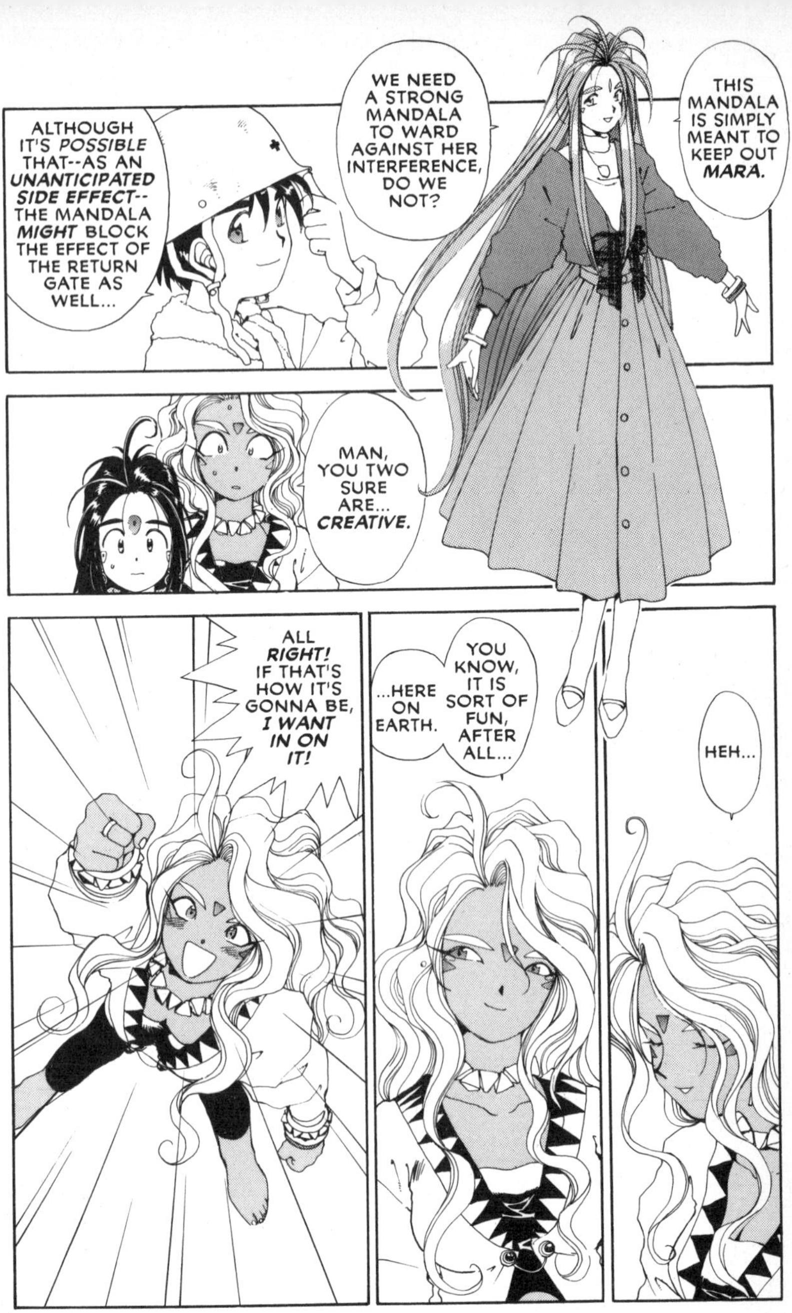
ALTHOUGH IT'S *POSSIBLE* THAT--AS AN *UNANTICIPATED SIDE EFFECT*--THE MANDALA *MIGHT* BLOCK THE EFFECT OF THE RETURN GATE AS WELL...
WE NEED A STRONG MANDALA TO WARD AGAINST HER INTERFERENCE, DO WE NOT?
THIS MANDALA IS SIMPLY MEANT TO KEEP OUT *MARA.*
MAN, YOU TWO SURE ARE... *CREATIVE.*
ALL *RIGHT!* IF THAT'S HOW IT'S GONNA BE, *I WANT IN ON IT!*
YOU KNOW, IT IS SORT OF FUN, AFTER ALL...
...HERE ON EARTH.
HEH...

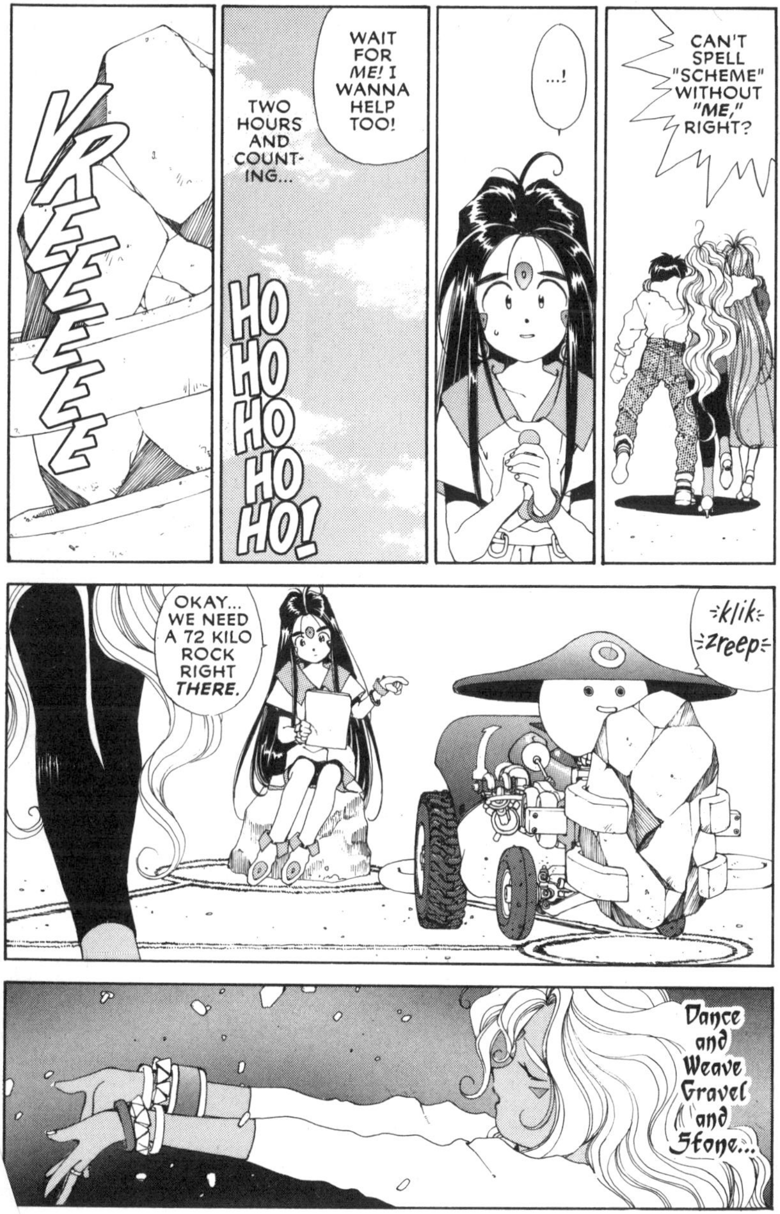
CAN'T SPELL "SCHEME" WITHOUT "ME," RIGHT?
...!
WAIT FOR ME! I WANNA HELP TOO!
TWO HOURS AND COUNTING...
HO HO HO HO HO HO!
VREEEEEEE
-klik- zreep-
OKAY... WE NEED A 72 KILO ROCK RIGHT THERE.
Dance and Weave Gravel and Stone...

Obey We
Goddesses
Three
Past,
Present,
and
Future...

...Hark
to the
Covenant
of Urd,
Belldandy,
and
Skuld...

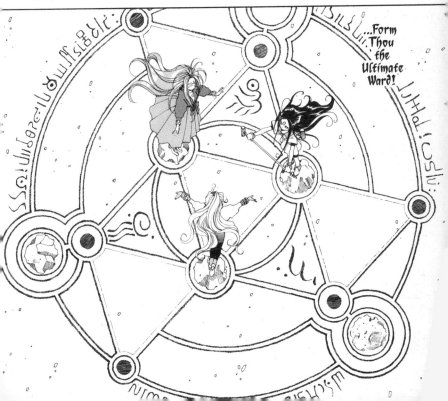

...Form
Thou
the
Ultimate
Ward!

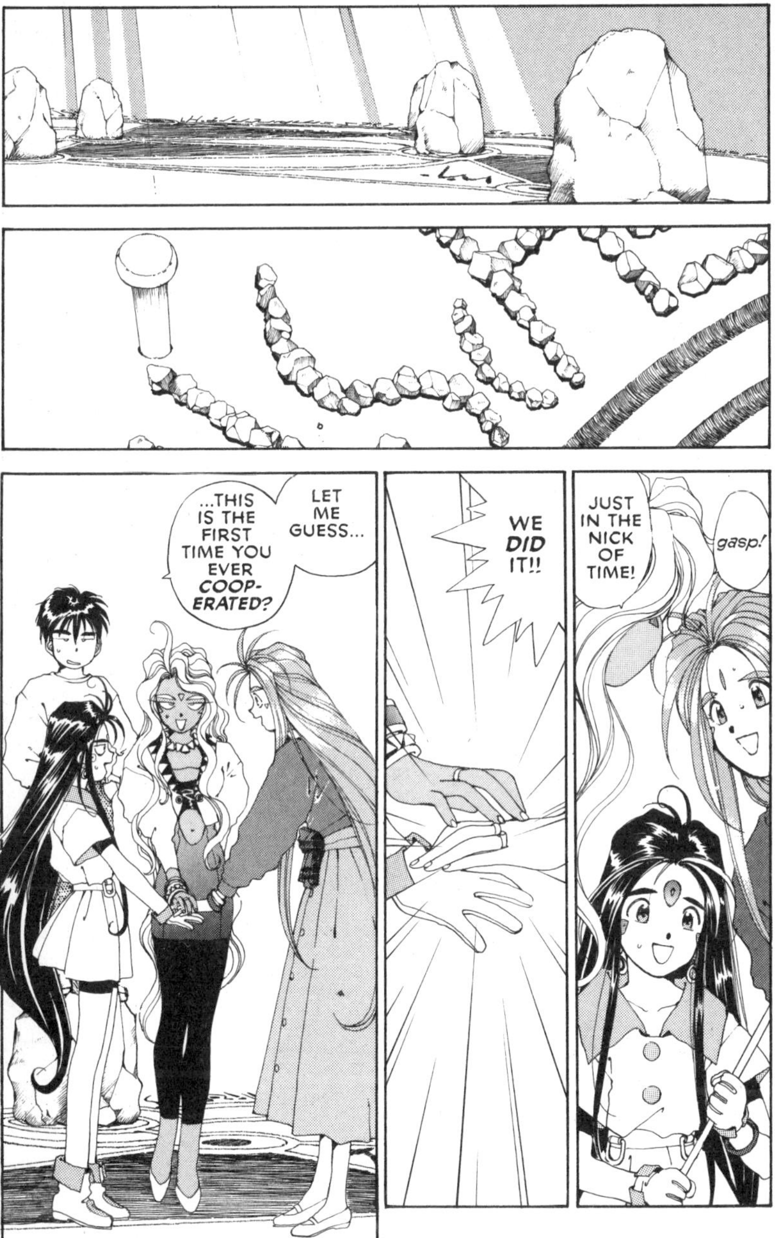

gasp!
JUST IN THE NICK OF TIME!
WE *DID* IT!!
LET ME GUESS...
...THIS IS THE FIRST TIME YOU EVER *COOPERATED?*

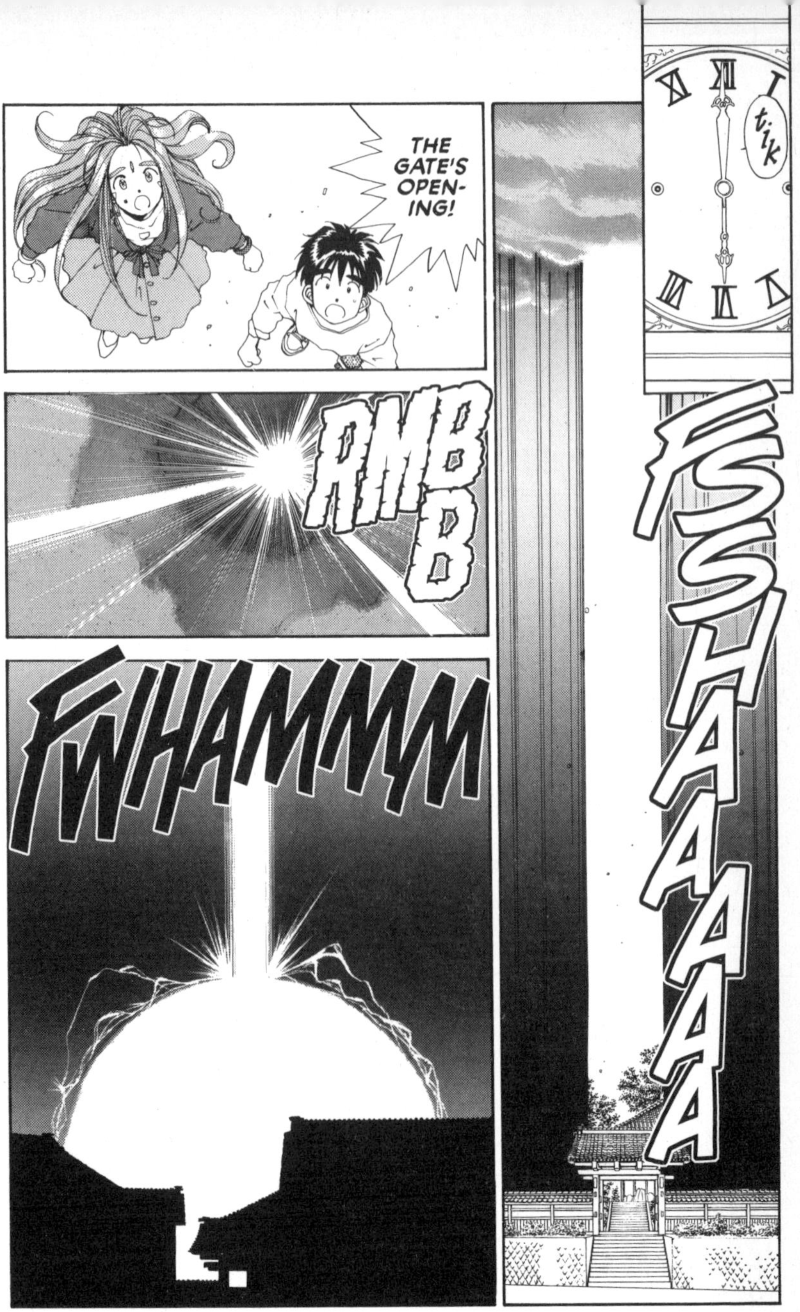
tik
FSSHAAAAAA
THE GATE'S OPEN- ING!
RMB B
FWHAMMMM

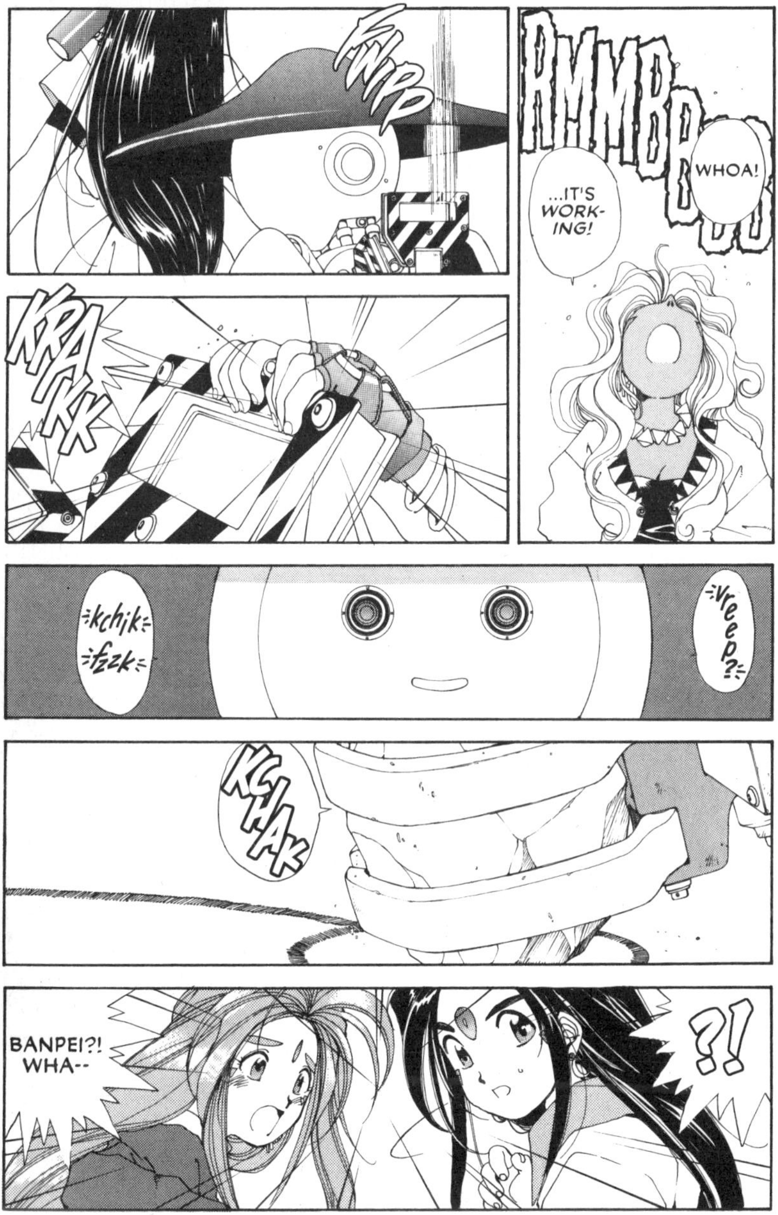
RMMBBBOO
WHOA!
...IT'S WORKING!
KWIPP
KRAKK
vreeep?
kchik fzzk
KCHAK
?!
BANPEI?! WHA--

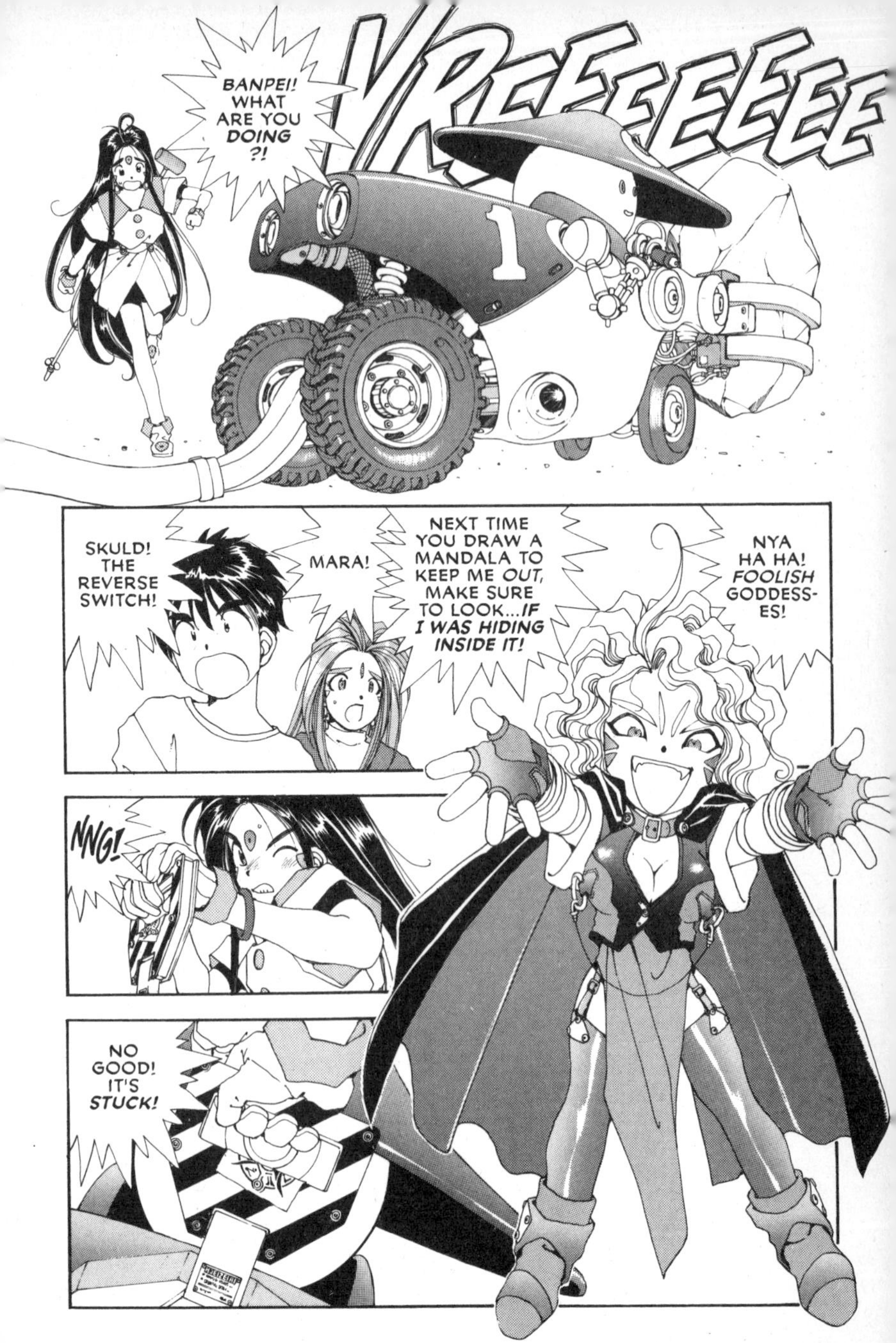
BANPEI! WHAT ARE YOU DOING ?!
VREEEEEEE
SKULD! THE REVERSE SWITCH!
MARA!
NEXT TIME YOU DRAW A MANDALA TO KEEP ME OUT, MAKE SURE TO LOOK...IF I WAS HIDING INSIDE IT!
NYA HA HA! FOOLISH GODDESS-ES!
NNG!
NO GOOD! IT'S STUCK!

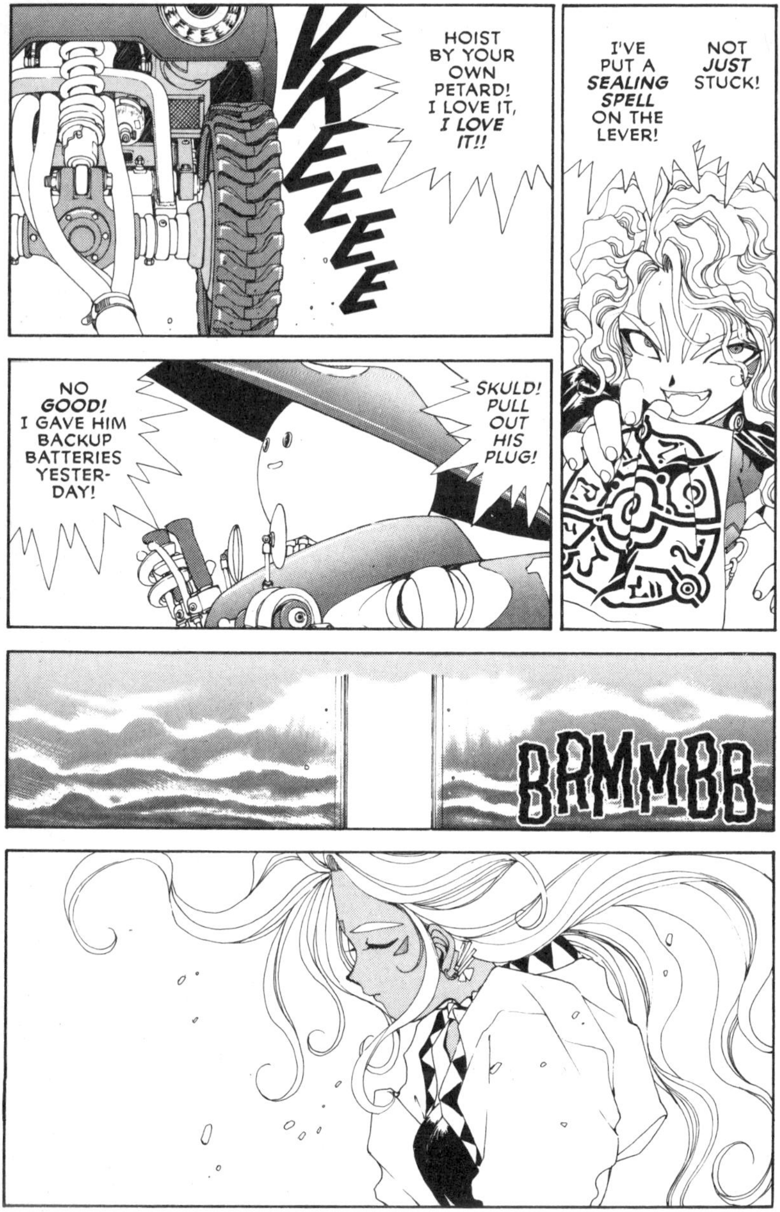
VKEEEEE
HOIST BY YOUR OWN PETARD! I LOVE IT, *I LOVE IT!!*
NOT *JUST* STUCK!
I'VE PUT A *SEALING SPELL* ON THE LEVER!
SKULD! PULL OUT HIS PLUG!
NO *GOOD!* I GAVE HIM BACKUP BATTERIES YESTER-DAY!
BRMMBB

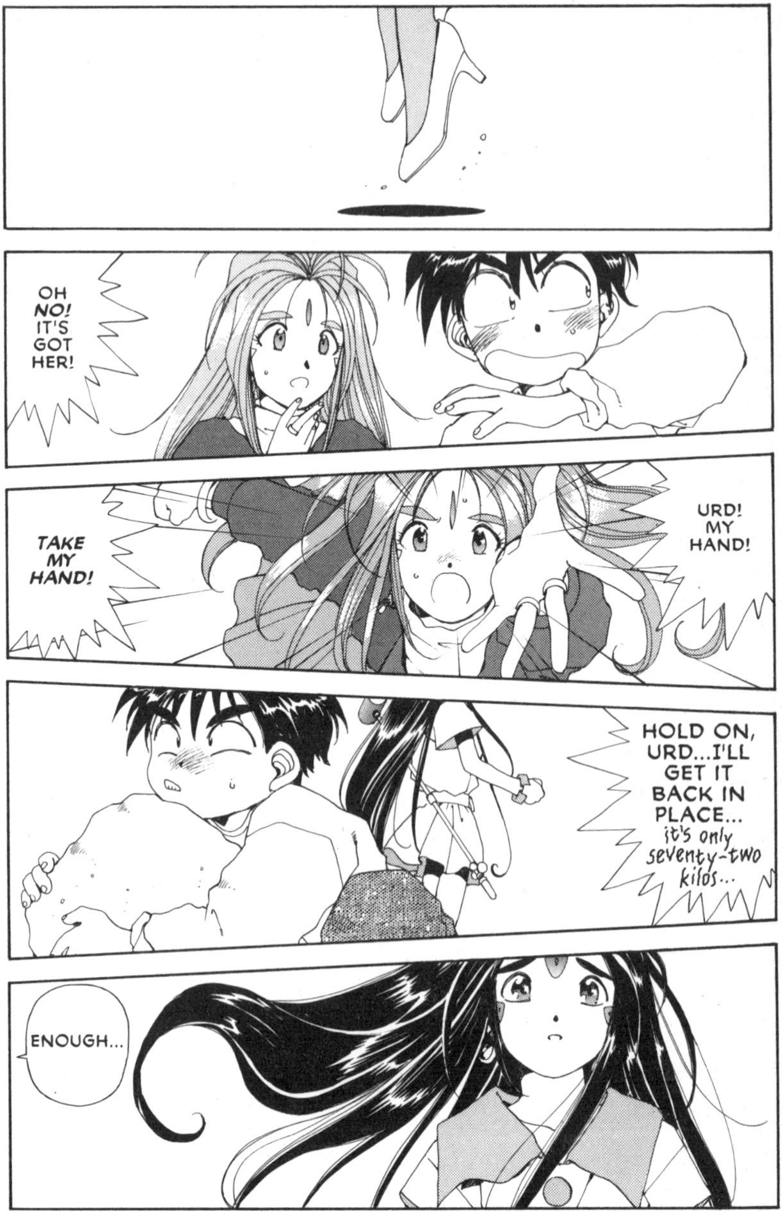
OH NO! IT'S GOT HER!
TAKE MY HAND!
URD! MY HAND!
HOLD ON, URD...I'LL GET IT BACK IN PLACE...
it's only seventy-two kilos...
ENOUGH...

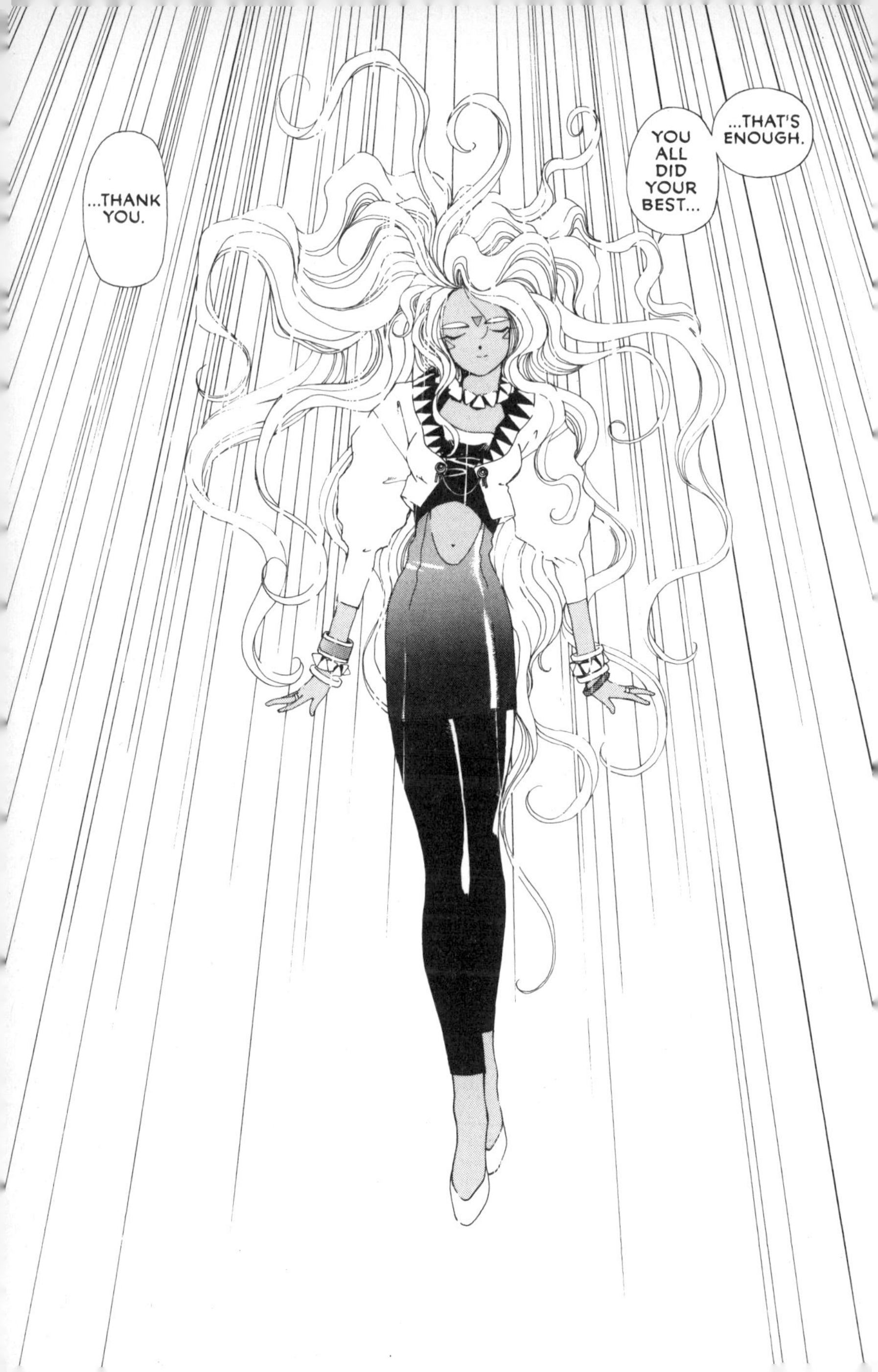
...THAT'S ENOUGH.
YOU ALL DID YOUR BEST...
...THANK YOU.

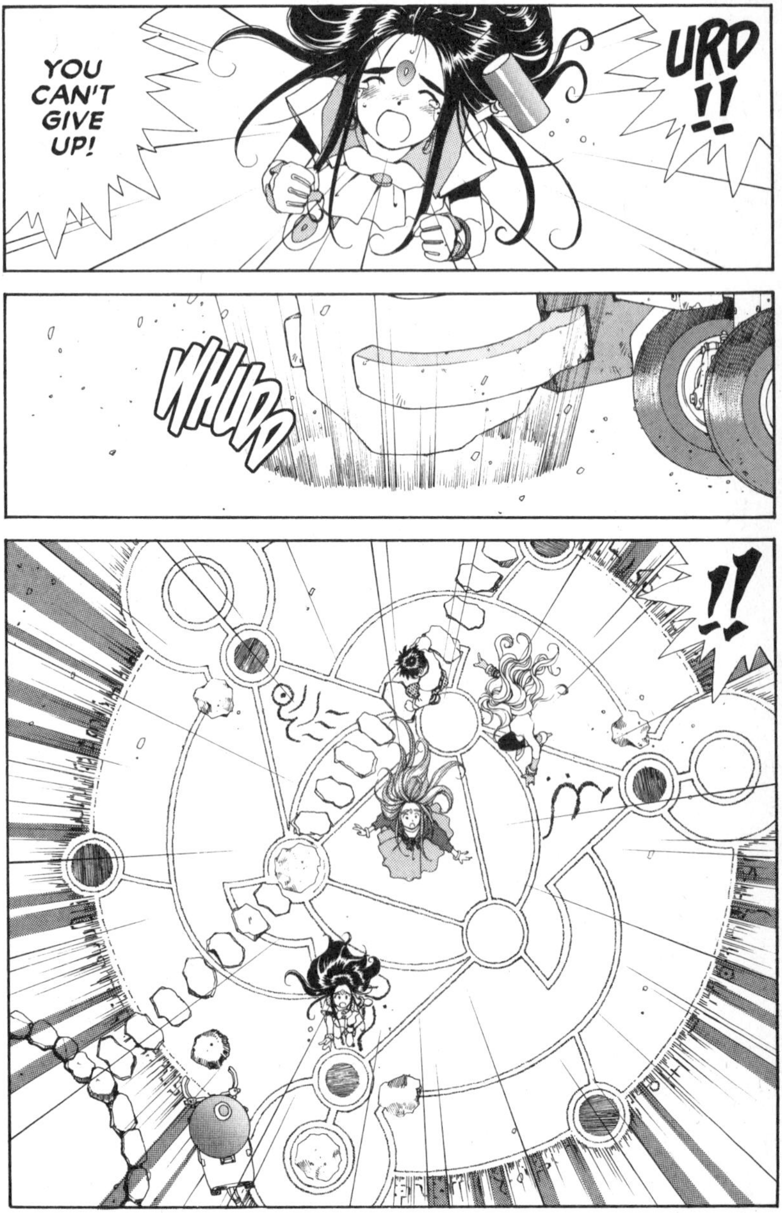
YOU CAN'T GIVE UP!
URD !!
WHUDD
!!

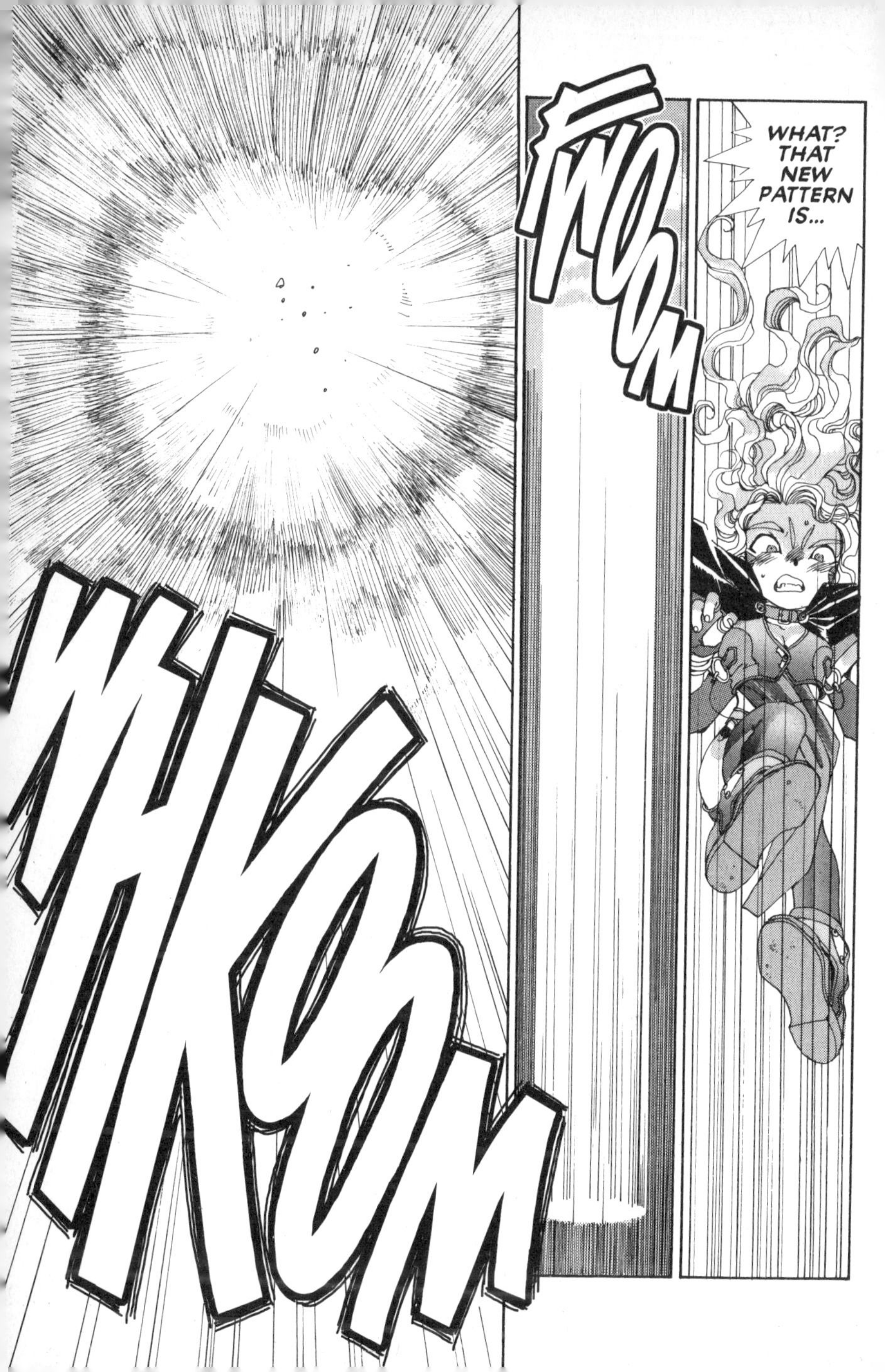
WHAT? THAT NEW PATTERN IS...
FWOOM
WHOOM

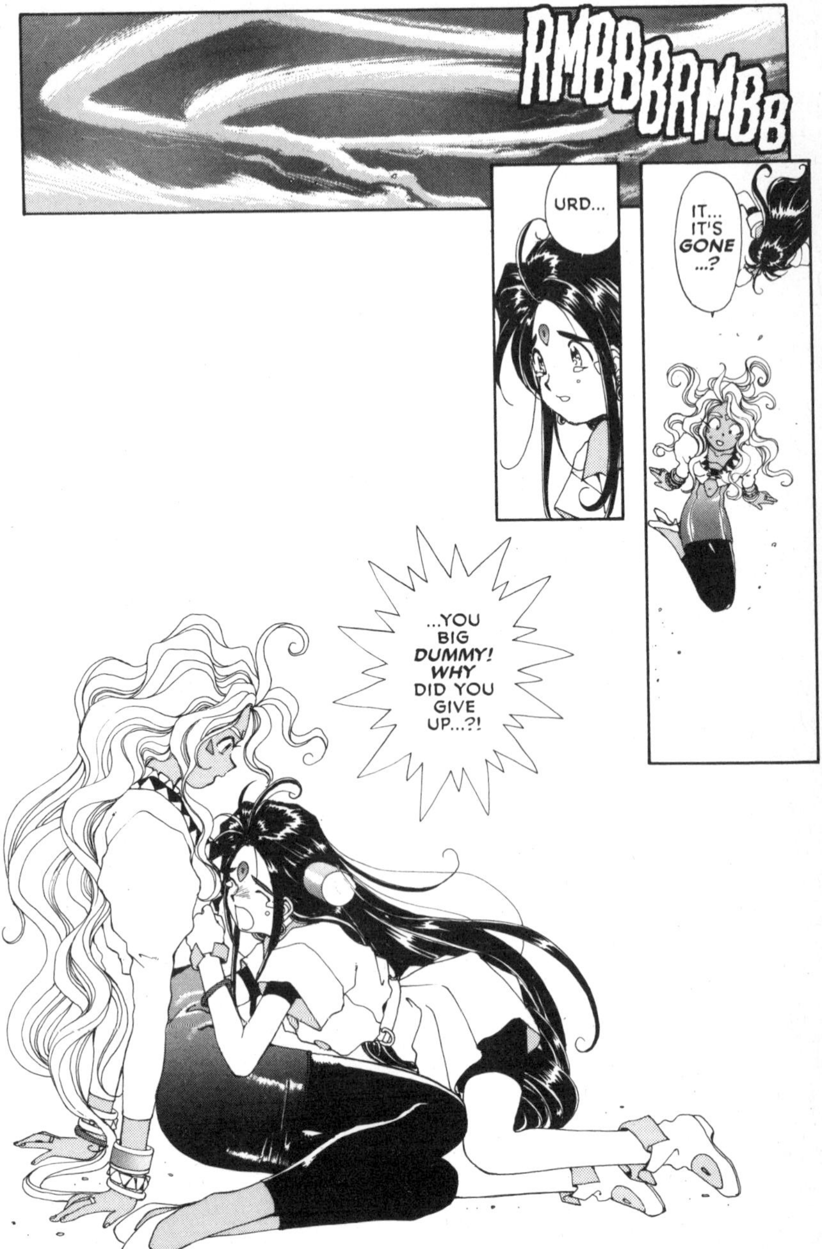
RMBBBRMBB
IT... IT'S GONE ...?
URD...
...YOU BIG DUMMY! WHY DID YOU GIVE UP...?!

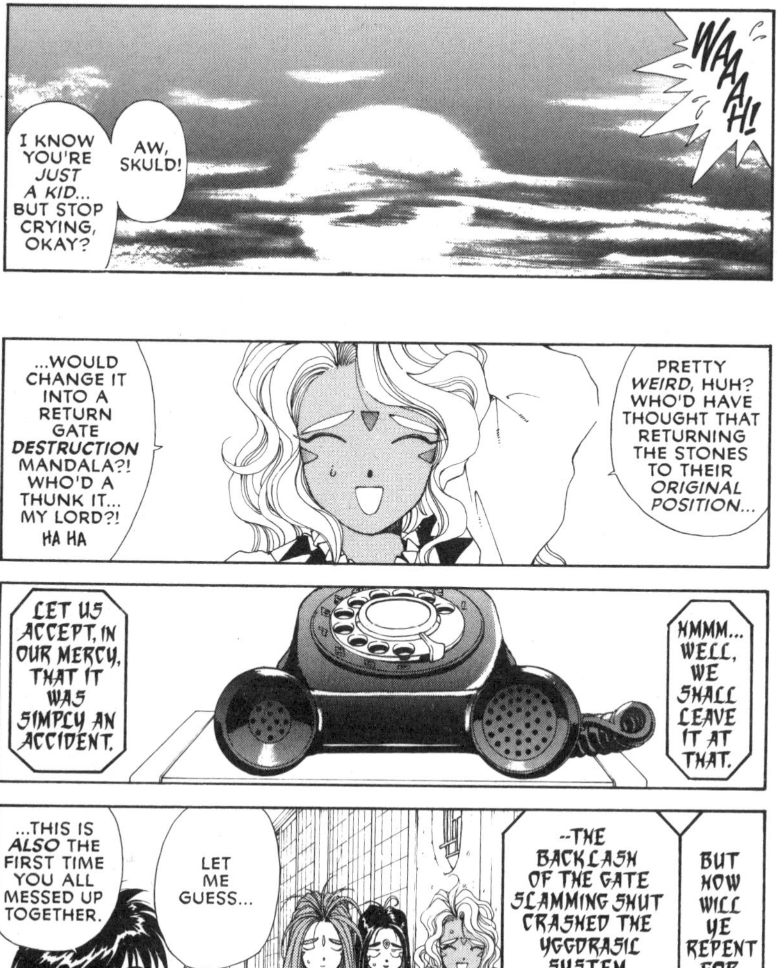

WAAAH!
AW, SKULD!
I KNOW YOU'RE JUST A KID... BUT STOP CRYING, OKAY?
PRETTY WEIRD, HUH? WHO'D HAVE THOUGHT THAT RETURNING THE STONES TO THEIR ORIGINAL POSITION...
...WOULD CHANGE IT INTO A RETURN GATE DESTRUCTION MANDALA?! WHO'D A THUNK IT... MY LORD?!
HA HA
HMMM... WELL, WE SHALL LEAVE IT AT THAT.
LET US ACCEPT, IN OUR MERCY, THAT IT WAS SIMPLY AN ACCIDENT.
--THE BACKLASH OF THE GATE SLAMMING SHUT CRASHED THE YGGDRASIL SYSTEM AGAIN!
BUT HOW WILL YE REPENT FOR THIS--
LET ME GUESS...
...THIS IS ALSO THE FIRST TIME YOU ALL MESSED UP TOGETHER.
I CAN'T UNDERSTAND THAT DIVINE SPEECH, BUT THE TONE'S PRETTY CLEAR...

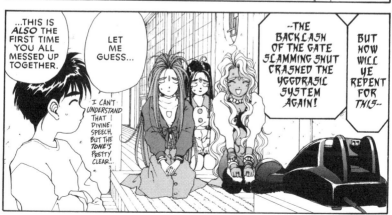

THE ADVENTURES OF MINI-URD

With the Miracle Ingredient: MINI-SKULD!

◆ BLOOMERS OF DOOM ◆

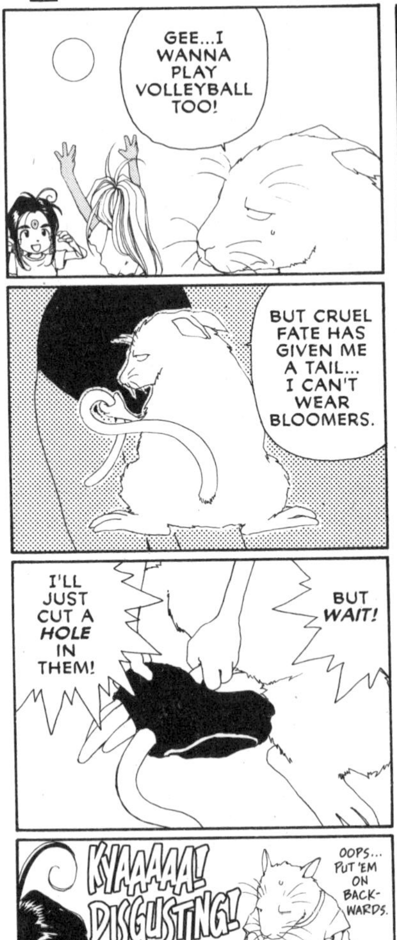

GEE...I WANNA PLAY VOLLEYBALL TOO!
BUT CRUEL FATE HAS GIVEN ME A TAIL... I CAN'T WEAR BLOOMERS.
I'LL JUST CUT A HOLE IN THEM!
BUT WAIT!
KYAAAAA! DISGUSTING!
OOPS... PUT 'EM ON BACKWARDS.

◆ FORWARD TO THE FUTURE! ◆

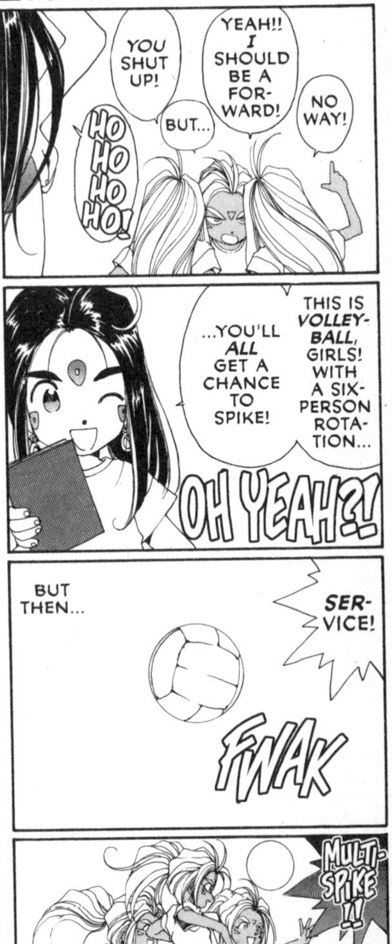

HO HO HO HO!
YOU SHUT UP!
BUT...
YEAH!! I SHOULD BE A FORWARD!
NO WAY!
THIS IS VOLLEYBALL, GIRLS! WITH A SIX-PERSON ROTATION...
...YOU'LL ALL GET A CHANCE TO SPIKE!
OH YEAH?!
BUT THEN...
SERVICE!
FWAK
MULTI-SPIKE!!
WILL YOU GUYS JUST LISTEN FOR ONCE?!

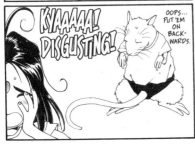

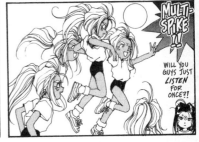

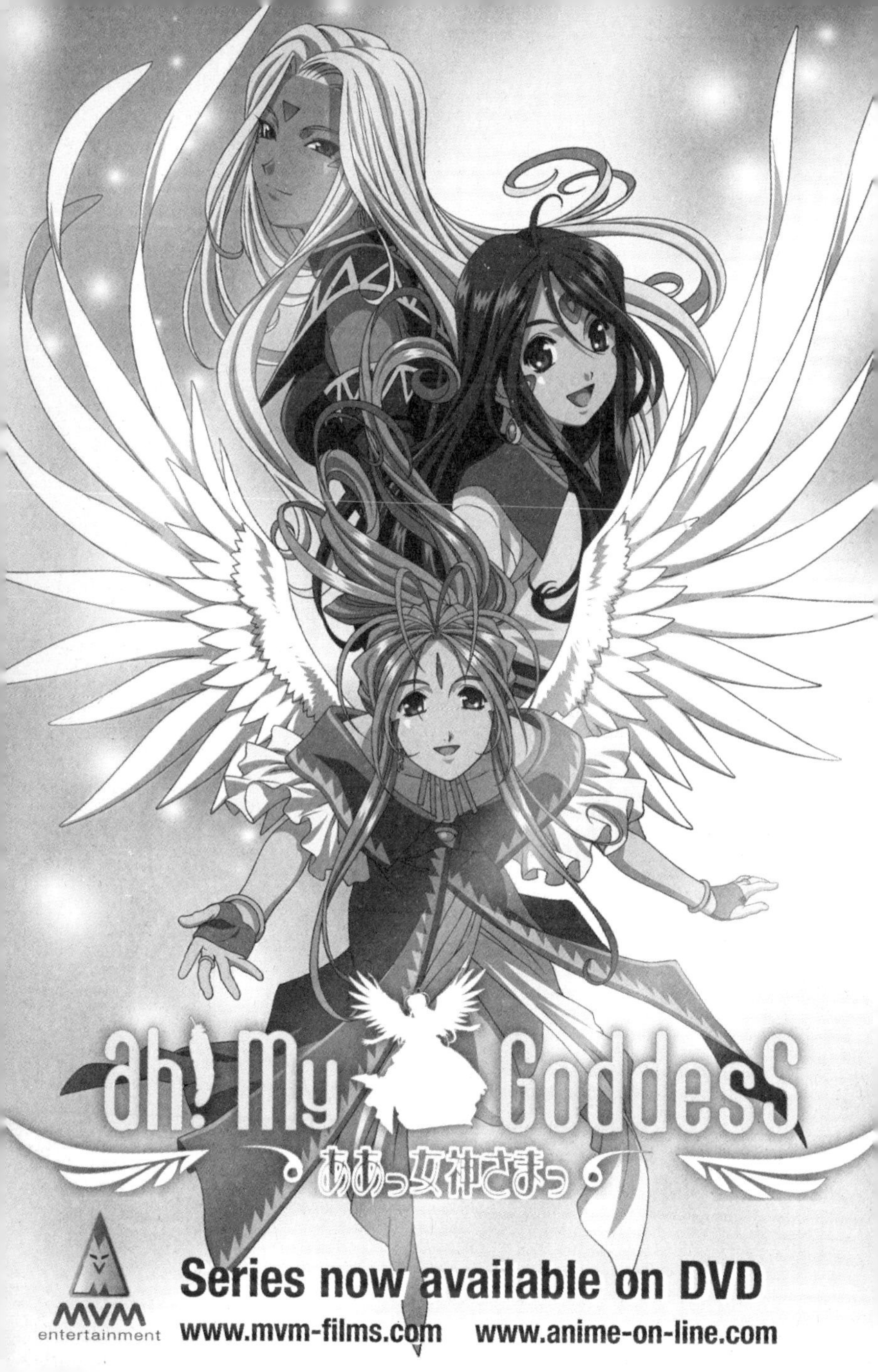
ah! My GoddesS
ああっ女神さまっ
MVM
entertainment
Series now available on DVD
www.mvm-films.com
www.anime-on-line.com

Creator Kosuke Fujishima in 1992!

His message to fans in the original Japanese *Oh My Goddess!* Vol. 7:

"Yes, yes y'all—check it out, my new machine: the Panda Bamboo 250!! Employing the latest in design, it completely annihilates any need for older models! We're pushin' it to the limit here! No one can touch this! Me and this thing are one and the same!! Anyone up for a challenge?!

"P.S.: Besides this, I am also riding my Elephant AAARR-RUNNNGHHH!* 600 and the Dance Rabbit 125 daily."

**The sound of an elephant's trumpet ^_^ —ed.*